Fair-Weather Flying

FAIR- WEATHER FLYING

SECOND EDITION

RICHARD L. TAYLOR

MACMILLAN PUBLISHING CO., INC.
New York

COLLIER MACMILLAN PUBLISHERS
London

Illustrations by Terry Campbell.

Macmillan Publishing Co., Inc.
866 Third Avenue, New York, N.Y. 10022
Collier Macmillan Canada, Inc.

Library of Congress Cataloging in Publication Data

Taylor, Richard L.
  Fair-weather flying.

  1. Airplanes—Piloting. I. Title.
TL710.T36 1981   629.132′52   81-12328
ISBN 0-02-616730-1

---

10   9   8   7   6   5   4   3   2   1

Printed in the United States of America

629.13252
T

Contents

Contents

Preface

WHEN I ASSEMBLED THE WORDS that became the first edition of
Fair-Weather Flying, I had taken aim at a particular segment
of the general aviation population. The intended audience
was those pilots who were not qualified for instrument flying,
and who might never try to jump through the hoops that
stood between them and the IFR rating. I reasoned this was a
rather special group, one that might benefit from some tips
on better ways to handle simple aircraft in non-IFR weather,
and one that was probably not associated to a great extent
with complex airplanes—those with retractable landing gear,
high-powered and turbo-charged engines, airplanes with more
than one powerplant, and so on.

I will stand by my reasoning with regard to the unique-
ness of this group of pilots, but, boy, was I wrong on the
noncomplex issue! General aviation in America has taken a
decided turn toward flying machines that carry their occupants faster, higher, and farther than ever before. Systems
that were not too many years ago the exclusive domain of
the corporate flying set are now found as standard equipment on a host of production-line "everyday" aircraft. The
picture has definitely changed.

There was really no intent ever to revise *Fair-Weather Flying,* no need perceived to add to or expand the techniques and procedures it discussed. But piloting *has* changed, if only because of the increased aviation consciousness in this country—more people are doing routinely what was supposed to be Superman's task a short while ago. As I travel around the country observing other pilots at their work and/or play, and in my work as chief flight instructor for a large university, I am convinced that in order for pilots to get the most out of themselves and their machines, more general information must be made available.

And so this is the second time around for *Fair-Weather Flying.* You'll find most of the first edition here, updated where necessary in the light of changing rules and procedures, plus a considerable amount of new material—most of it intended to provide at least a conversational knowledge of aircraft systems, procedures, and techniques applicable to some of those complex "everyday" airplanes appearing in the general-aviation fleet. *Fair-Weather Flying* is a collection of one pilot's ideas and theories and practices, which have been discovered, learned, and nurtured by the experiences and observations of more than twenty-six years of flying, both in uniform and out. If you seem to detect a strong flavor of military aviation training in these chapters, you're right on target; those channels are very deeply grooved in this pilot's gray matter, and I still consider it the finest flight training available.

I know better, after all these years of teaching and writing about flying, than to think for one minute that there won't be some disagreement with some of the things you read here (there *are* a few controversial matters between here and the last page), but if your disagreements make you stop and *think* about something you've always taken for granted, I'll be happy. Who knows . . . there may be better ways, more efficient and faster ways, perhaps even *safer* ways to get a particular flying task accomplished. Too many pilots, concerned that they might do something *wrong* (heaven forbid!), never venture outside the narrow channels of their training days, plodding through their aeronautical lives never know-

ing what they or their airplanes can really do. As an old
friend and former Air Force classmate used to say, "Fortune
favors the bold." He was, it *did,* and he's now wearing stars
on his shoulders.

You'll likely have to break with routine to go along with
some of the techniques I've suggested here. You'll have to be
a bit bold now and then. Skills, like muscles, won't develop
unless they're exercised. BUT HEED THIS WARNING:
SOME OF THE OPERATIONS IN FAIR-WEATHER FLYING
MAY WELL BE MORE THAN YOUR TRAINING AND
EXPERIENCE HAVE PREPARED YOU TO HANDLE. CON-
SULT WITH A GOOD INSTRUCTOR BEFORE YOU PUT
YOURSELF OR YOUR AIRPLANE IN AN UNFAMILIAR
SITUATION.

You might consider this book a series of short courses in
a wide variety of aviation subjects . . . which means that
there must be a lot more information out there somewhere,
and I hope that you'll be inspired to seek out that additional
knowledge in the areas that concern you. *Fair-Weather Flying*
should stretch your mind a little.

When you stop improving, you might as well stop flying.

Enjoy, enjoy.

February 1981   R . L . T A Y L O R

Fair-Weather Flying

1

Fuel Conservation Techniques

"IT SEEMS TO ME I've heard that song before. . . ." You sure did, back in '73 and '74 when OPEC turned the tap on the oil supply, and we all got very concerned about stretching each gallon of avgas. The aviation press was full of ways to make the supply go farther; the FAA came up with profile descents, Fuel Advisory Departures (ATC procedures to minimize engine running time for aircraft destined for an airport experiencing prolonged delays), and so on. The campaign to conserve fuel was as much moral and patriotic as economic then, because the problem was shortage, not price. For whatever reasons, more fuel appeared, and the emphasis on making each gallon go farther softened somewhat; but the fat's in the fire for good now, and they—whoever "they" are—are really hitting us below the belt . . . right in the old wallet.

While there are no hard figures to back it up, it's a pretty good bet that most of us are in the habit of letting out the reins on our airplanes, using all that power we paid for to get us from here to there in the least time possible; and with good reason, because up until now, saving time *has* been more economically sound than saving gasoline. Whether you're a renter or an owner, chances are that the proportion of total

cost represented by fuel has increased nearly 100 percent in
the past several years. And if you intend to contain the expense of flying within reasonable bounds, it makes sense to
start whittling away at the highest-cost portion of the bill.
There *are* ways to get the job done with considerable fuel
savings and only a slight time penalty; there are also fuel-
conservation techniques which look good on the surface, but
which make hardly any difference when you're operating a
light, reciprocating-engine airplane.

A STRAIGHT LINE IS *STILL*
THE SHORTEST DISTANCE

Fuel conservation should begin when you spread out the
charts to plan a trip. Inclement weather, restricted airspace,
and reluctance to fly over water are common obstacles to
emulating the crows, but the pilot who draws a straight line
from here to there and stays on it religiously is the pilot who
will use the smallest amount of fuel, all other conditions being the same. There are at least two ways to handle the problem of restricted airspace; get a clearance to go on through
(if appropriate), or plan the flight to avoid the area with the
least possible course deviation. It's the zigs and zags that add
to the mileage. If you've become accustomed to flying from
one VOR to the next, give some consideration to dead reckoning when the radio stations aren't located in a straight line;
the VORs can serve as checks along the way, but by ironing
out the wrinkles in a long trip, you'll save some additional
fuel. (Weather avoidance and overwater flights will have to
be handled on a case-by-case basis.)

Instrument pilots run up against more formidable obstacles
when they elect to go direct, because the interests and safety
of a lot of other folks have to be accommodated. For the most
part, the published preferred routes are as "direct" as you're
likely to get, especially in heavy-traffic parts of the airspace
. . . otherwise, why would there be preferred routes? But
when published airways take on the appearance of a dog's
hind leg, and the choice of routing is up to you, lay out your
course in a straight line, bend it where necessary to cross

convenient VORs, file direct, and hope for the best. Even when ATC turns down your request and clears you via airways, there's nothing wrong with asking again when you're airborne; on many occasions, a controller can let you go direct after you're in the system, when he can see that there's no conflict. Save a mile here, a couple of minutes there; every little bit adds up.

The pilot flying an RNAV-equipped airplane has a built-in fuel saver, one that gets more significant with airplane size and higher fuel consumption. With a few exceptions, and those mostly in congested areas where such random navigation apparently can't be handled by the ATC system, controllers will honor requests to go "RNAV direct." Properly used, area navigation always results in straight-line navigation, and the corners you don't have to turn become fuel you don't burn. How much? Well, it depends a great deal on a pilot's pre-RNAV techniques, but there are operators who are realizing five- to seven-percent time and fuel reductions by using RNAV whenever possible. It's not a staggering amount, but sometimes enough to pay for the RNAV equipment in a relatively short period of time, and from there on out, it's all money in the bank . . . or fuel in the tank. Generalization Number One: Flying in straight lines saves fuel.

The straight-line technique is not a mind-blowing revelation, it produces generally small-scale results, and adherence to a policy of direct flights is often beyond your control; so what else is available to make your fuel-conservation efforts worthwhile? The operational areas that must be considered are airspeed, altitude, weight, winds aloft, mixture management, and power setting. Some of these are very important, some are nearly negligible in their effects on fuel economy. One at a time then, airspeed first.

The fuel-conservation qualities of slow flight were not divined yesterday. In a 1906 letter to Octave Chanute, Wilbur Wright described some of the general features of the flying machines he and his brother had invented: ". . . the weights of the various power machines ranged from 750 to 925 pounds, and the horsepower from 12 to 20. *The speed of minimum power consumption is below that at which the machine usually flies* [my italics]." The Wrights, homegrown, self-taught aeronautical engineers that they were, had become very aware of lift-drag relationships. Unfortunately, their machines were so festooned with drag-producing wires and wood struts that they had to fly at full power just to stay in the air. Today's airplanes are aerodynamically cleaner than Wilbur or Orville would have dreamed, and given the option of flying at any one of a rather wide range of speeds, the effect of *reducing* airspeed is a dramatic one in terms of fuel consumption.

Figure 1–1 is a plot of airspeed versus fuel flow (or power required—for a recip-propeller combination, there's no difference), which shows that in general, power requirements

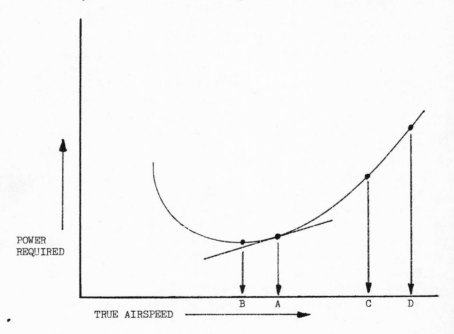

Figure 1–1. True airspeed vs. fuel flow.

increase with airspeed. If a line is drawn from the origin of the graph tangent to the curve, the intersection (Point A) represents the airspeed at which the lift-drag ratio is greatest . . . it's known as L/D_{max}, it's the most efficient airspeed in terms of fuel usage, and it's also the airspeed for maximum range. You won't be able to plot this curve for your airplane, at least not from the *Pilot's Operating Handbook,* because Points A and B (which is the airspeed for maximum *endurance*) are far below the "normal" cruise airspeeds.

However, move up to the higher speeds at which you most likely operate, and note that those speeds are on a more lineal part of the curve. When airspeed is changed in this range, power requirements change in the same direction, and at nearly the same rate (i.e., slowing from airspeed *D* to airspeed *C,* there's a corresponding decrease in fuel flow). For example, consulting the cruise performance charts for a Cessna Turbo 210, a reduction in true airspeed from 193 mph to 140 mph (the range of speeds shown on the 10,000-foot chart) cuts down fuel consumption by 39.8 percent. Now, that's fuel conservation in spades . . . but of course it takes longer to get where you're going. (By the way, if you'd like to know what the L/D_{max} airspeed is for your airplane, look up the best power-off glide speed; it's the speed at which the wing is doing its best work in order to let you glide the farthest distance if the engine quits. Can you imagine routinely flying a Turbo 210 at somewhere around 90 mph indicated? You'd be saving lots of fuel, but that's hardly a tolerable speed in light of the investment in the airplane.)

The production-line, Ford-and-Chevy airplanes most of us fly were not designed for assaults on world records in either speed or range, and as such represent a compromise of those two qualities. These airplanes are relatively efficient within the range of speeds found in the cruise-performance charts, and considering fuel consumption *only,* there's a lot to be said for flying slowly. One way to express the low-speed benefits is in miles per gallon. Here are the figures extracted from the 5000-foot cruise-performance chart for a normally aspirated Cessna 210:

TRUE AIRSPEED	MILES PER GALLON
186	11.8
182	12.8
177	12.8
171	13.4
165	14.0
155	13.9
147	15.0
140	15.0
131	15.0

That's a 21.3 percent reduction in fuel consumption from top to bottom, and nothing to sneeze at as long as nothing but fuel consumption is considered . . . the *bad* news is the attendant speed reduction of 29.5 percent. So, the second generalization: You can *indeed* save fuel by slowing down.

NEXT QUESTION: HOW HIGH TO FLY?

A pilot's selection of altitude for a particular flight is perhaps subject to more variables than any of the operational considerations involved. Personal preference, weather, terrain, winds aloft, turbulence, and distance to go will affect the altitude decision. But once again considering fuel consumption *only*, there's an interesting relationship between airspeed and power required as altitude is changed.

You've no doubt used the rule of thumb which says that true airspeed increases approximately two percent for each thousand feet above sea level; and it's a good rule. But what you must also realize is that the increase in airspeed, an apparent freebie, is achieved only with a higher power setting, and therefore higher fuel flow. The two percent increase only applies if the same *calibrated* airspeed can be maintained at altitude. And, of course, it takes more horses to do that. Figure 1–2 shows the same plots of airspeed versus power required, this time at two different altitudes; the tangent point again serves as a reference, and you can see that the airspeed that produces L/D_{max} (or any other airspeed, for that matter), requires a corresponding increase in power as altitude increases. The upshot of this illustration is that there's no such thing as a free lunch; fly a reciprocating-engine aircraft at higher altitudes to get the higher true air-

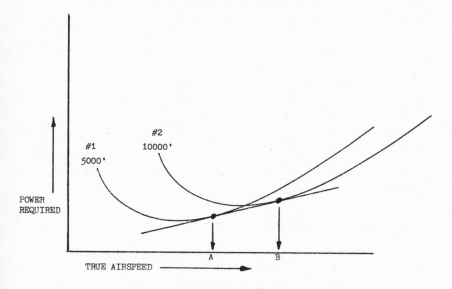

Figure 1–2. True airspeed vs. power required at different altitudes.

speed, and it's gonna cost you some gasoline—at altitude and all the way up. Unless you climb at a cruise-power setting (which will take more time), it's probably best to reserve high-altitude operations for the long flights with strong tailwinds.

For example, using the normally aspirated 210, a calibrated airspeed of 155 mph at 10,000 feet generates 7.77 percent more true airspeed than at 5000; and the corresponding fuel-flow jump is 6.38 percent—a slight victory for the airspeed interests, due to an efficient engine-propeller combination. For the turbocharged 210, a CAS of 151 mph at both 5000 and 20,000 feet (the higher altitude chosen to show the walloping increase in TAS because of the turbo's ability to operate up there at relatively high power settings) produces

162 and 206 mph TAS, respectively. That's a 27.16 percent bonus, but the piper must be paid, and the power required increases by 21.6 percent. (As an aside, the ratio of TAS increase to fuel-flow increase is nearly identical for the turbo and the normally aspirated engines.) Therefore, for all practical purposes, the payoff at higher altitudes in *fuel savings alone* is not very significant. (Turboprops and pure jets enjoy a unique benefit of high-altitude flight in that they thrive on the colder air aloft, and the miles-per-pound figure shows remarkable increases with altitude, accounting for the extreme unhappiness whenever a big jet has to execute a missed-approach on a hot day.) Therefore, the third generalization: The higher true airspeeds at altitude are gained at the expense of an almost equal increase in power required, and do not *by themselves* represent a significant saving in total fuel consumed.

WHAT ABOUT WEIGHT?

One of the most important flight-crew jobs on a large airplane, particularly a large *jet* aircraft, is cruise control; the process of figuring out the airspeed-power combinations that will provide optimum cruise conditions, and management of power controls in accordance with those calculations. Cruise-control techniques become an indispensable part of flight management because such a large part of the aircraft weight is in fuel, and because of the very high rates of fuel consumption. In other words, the weight of a large airplane changes much more rapidly and significantly than that of a small one, and the large-aircraft crew will need to reduce power at regular intervals to keep the airspeed at the optimum; with a small machine, the fuel burn—even on a long flight—doesn't represent enough weight reduction to require changes in airspeed or power settings.

Figure 1–3 is a plot of true airspeed and fuel flow on three curves: a basic weight (curve 1), a higher weight (2), and a lighter weight (3). Indeed, this chart demonstrates the basic truth that a lighter airplane can maintain level flight at a lower airspeed (and therefore lower fuel consumption) than

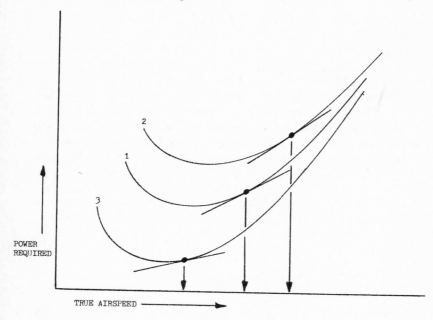

Figure 1–3. True airspeed vs. fuel flow at three different aircraft weights.

a heavier one; check any point on the three curves, and you'll find that the lower weight always wins the fuel-burn contest. But move the curves closer together, as would be the case with a typical light, propeller-driven aircraft (in other words, not much difference in weight as fuel is burned), and it becomes apparent that the airspeed/fuel-flow requirements don't change much with weight. Also note that the curves are closer together at higher airspeeds—in the normal cruise range—which makes weight change even less significant. The fact that cruise performance charts for light aircraft are almost invariably based on maximum allowable gross weight gives you a clue as to the relative unimportance of this factor.

It would be folly to completely ignore the effect of reduced weight. While the differences in light airplanes are not terribly significant (there's the fourth generalization in this treatise), you should always attempt to fly at the lightest weight consistent with required load, distance to go, and a safe reserve. The days of "top 'em off" as a standard fueling order should be considered gone forever. You *can* show some fuel savings by flying your airplane at the lowest weight possible *consistent with safety.* (Given the notorious inaccuracy of the fuel gauges in light aircraft, a pilot who intends to fly with less-than-full tanks should consider installing one of the fuel-computing systems now available. Combining contemporary computer technology and accuracy with electronic reliability and instant readout, these computer systems make fuel-state monitoring much easier and safer. There are five suppliers in the business, with prices ranging from $800 to $2500.)

WINDS ALOFT: BLESSING
AND CURSE COMBINED

Taylor's Law of Wind Direction states that "If the headwind which made today's trip an hour longer than normal can turn around and blow in your face on the way home, it will." And it would seem at first glance that if you fly at the same speed out and back under the influence of the same wind, the two conditions should average out. Such is not the case, since you are exposed to the disadvantage of the headwind for a longer period of time. Is there a way to beat the winds-aloft rap? Yes, you can apply the technique of speeding up in a headwind and slowing down in a tailwind . . . but unfortunately for the recip crowd, the net effect is not very significant unless you're being hassled by really strong winds.

For example, a Turbo 210 cruising at 10,000 feet at a true airspeed of 173 mph requires 78 pounds of fuel per hour; if a 20-mph headwind is encountered and the pilot speeds up to counter the effect of the wind, the fuel flow increases to 98 pph, a jump of 25 percent. Turn the airplane around, reduce power so as to match the effect of the 20-mph tailwind, and fuel flow drops to 65 pounds per hour, or a savings of nearly 16 percent. (Keep in mind that these figures represent what's necessary to exactly offset the effect of the wind, and would produce the same elapsed time over a given distance.) What happens if you elect to leave the power handles right where they are, and accept whatever the wind dishes out? Using a 200-mile leg as an illustration, you'd burn 101 pounds of fuel flying into the wind (same power setting, but lower groundspeed and, therefore, more elapsed time to cover the distance), and only 68 pounds with the wind at your back.

Increase the wind speed remarkably and these figures really begin to grow apart; with a 50-mph wind blowing, you'd use *73 percent* more fuel if you didn't increase power on the upwind leg, and would reach the end of 200-mile downwind segment in so much less time that only 53 pounds of gasoline would be required. That's a fuel saving of 41 percent!

This matter of whether to power up or power down according to the wind velocity you're experiencing cannot be resolved reasonably without taking *time* into consideration. Unless the winds are blowing more than 25 percent of your cruise speed, there's little to be gained by changing airspeed to minimize the effect of a headwind or maximize the effect of a tailwind. But since we're talking right now about fuel versus wind *only*, remember that an altitude change has little effect on fuel flow, so a general rule can be established: When flying a recip-powered airplane, select the altitude with the most favorable (or least unfavorable) winds, use a power setting that is an acceptable compromise of fuel burn and elapsed time—and take your lumps in headwinds.

CONTROLLING THE FIRE YOU'VE LIGHTED

All of the cruise-performance charts in your airplane's handbook are based on something called "Normal Lean Mixture," or "Recommended Mixture Setting," or something very similar. Whatever the wording, range and endurance figures in the charts are based on a fuel-air ratio that provides "best economy"—a term implying that the engine is using as much of the fuel energy as possible for propulsion.

(In this condition, a small part of the fuel is used for internal cooling.) There's a companion term, "best *power*," which is a slightly richer mixture, and which provides additional fuel for propulsion—it's a compromise of speed and range.

Since a reciprocating engine runs best when the fuel-air ratio is adjusted properly (either BEST ECONOMY or BEST POWER, depending on the situation), and since a considerable amount of fuel is available for engine cooling whenever the mixture control is set at full rich, it is imperative that proper mixture-management techniques be used for even rough-cut fuel conservation. In general (certain high-power engine installations are exceptional, and you *must* refer to the *Pilot's Operating Handbook* for the powerplant in your airplane), the mixture should be leaned at any time the engine is delivering 75 percent power or less . . . altitude is irrelevant, it's power output that counts. Suffice it to say that a pilot who always flies his airplane with the mixture control knob snuggled up against the instrument panel is not only wasting gasoline, he's probably doing at least some harm to his engine. (See Chapter 5, "Leaning Techniques," for more detail on this procedure.)

Is proper leaning worthwhile in a fuel-conscious situation? The Turbo 210 handbook indicates that the use of Best Power instead of Best Economy generates an additional one or two mph of true airspeed, but costs eight percent in range. When the figures are run out on the Turbo 210 at 10,000 feet and 75 percent power with the mixture set at BEST POWER and using the maximum two mph speed increase, you'd be the winner in a 500-mile race, but only by about two-and-a-half minutes. The "tortoise" would arrive at the same point having used 3.66 fewer gallons of gas. At today's prices, that's about seven bucks for two and a half minutes—you decide.

Generalization Number Four: Proper leaning is a *must*, and is very definitely enhanced by some sort of exhaust-gas-temperature-sensing system.

Climbing and descending at speed and power settings that optimize the performance of a light, recip-powered airplane gets very complicated; there are a number of factors at work, and only very general conclusions as to the proper technique can be drawn. If for no other reason than the restrictions placed on climb or descent by terrain and/or Air Traffic Control, the problem is a knotty one. Based on the generalizations mentioned earlier, it seems sensible to climb and descend at a higher airspeed when going against the wind, and the opposite when the wind is behind you. Aircraft weight makes a significant contribution to climb performance, and for the larger airplanes, you'll likely find the cruise-climb charts are set up for a range of likely climb weights; the Beechcraft Duke, for example, shows a 50 percent improvement in time-to-climb at one of the lighter weights on the chart.

When booming along with a healthy tailwind at altitude, you naturally hate to leave all that happiness any sooner than necessary, but the longer you wait to start down, the faster you must move vertically. The resultant high-rate descent may bend either your ears or the engine—one because of the pressure changes, the other because of the rapid cooling due to a prolonged low-power setting in the descent. There's a compromise that seems to work out well most of the time, and which satisfies the needs of the engine (enough power to keep it warm and prevent the prop from driving the powerplant) as well as your eardrums. Make an estimate of the increase in groundspeed in a 500-feet-per-minute descent at cruise power (most light airplanes pick up anywhere from 20 to 30 knots—some more, few less), convert that to miles per minute, calculate how long it will take you to descend to pattern altitude, and, finally, figure how many miles from the airport you should start the descent. Winds change on the way down, but this Kentucky-windage procedure gives you something to start with, and the variables tend to average out and make it work satisfactorily most of the time. It's a matter of using the potential energy of altitude which was stored during the climb. Of course, the same thing happens when you wait a little longer, then reduce power and descend at cruise airspeed; the decision is very much a matter of personal preference.

THERE'S GOTTA BE A BOTTOM LINE SOMEWHERE

You can see that a problem as complex as this—taking into account the variables of weight, winds, how to climb, how to descend, what altitude is best—require the mental agility of a computer. And indeed, that's exactly what's being done by more and more large-aircraft operators today. But the small-airplane types are left with a confusing welter of trade-offs, and when all is said and done, the result of detailed planning is little more than a lot of time spent shuffling papers and pushing buttons on a calculator. How much tailwind at altitude makes up for the fuel and time used to get there? Will a high-speed, high-fuel-burn cruise save enough time to offset the additional gasoline used? The questions go on and on, with each situation providing a slightly different answer, and some situations having a *couple* of good answers.

It's mighty confusing, and when all the variables are considered, one inescapable fact emerges: If you want to save fuel in light-airplane operations, *fly at reduced power settings* . . . it's that simple. The airplane is designed to be an efficient transportation machine over a wide range of weights, altitudes, and airspeeds; *power setting* is the key to fuel conservation.

But power setting is also the key to getting where you're going in minimum time, and perhaps you are reluctant to give up all that time to save a few gallons of gasoline. While there are undoubtedly situations in which time *is* worth more than fuel, the book shows some interesting figures when the two are laid out side by side. For example, the Turbo 210 lists 75 percent power as the top line in its cruise charts; the normally aspirated 210 shows 71 percent available at 7500 feet, a reasonable altitude for most trips. Here's a comparison of a 200-mile cruise segment for these airplanes at the highest charted power settings, and at a power setting ten percent lower.

TURBO 210 AT 15,000 FEET	75% POWER	65% POWER
True airspeed	203	193
Time to fly 200 miles	:59	1:02
Fuel flow (lbs/hour)	98	86
Fuel used (pounds)	96	89

NONTURBO AT 7500 FEET	71% POWER	61% POWER
True airspeed	190	178
Time to fly 200 miles	1:03	1:07
Fuel flow (lbs/hour)	89	77
Fuel used (pounds)	93	86

(Similar figures show the same relative savings—and penalties—for airplanes with fixed-pitch propellers.)

If you are one of those who has been religiously flying at reduced power settings and are therefore confident that you are singlehandedly solving the fuel-shortage problem, you'll probably read those figures and weep . . . pulling the power back ten percent saves only about seven percent of the fuel burned at the higher power setting. On the other hand, if you are a "damn the fuel crisis, full speed ahead, haven't got *time*" type, you may well wind up weeping also. It appears that saving three or four minutes can hardly be justified in an extremely fuel-conscious, almost-two-bucks-a-gallon society. Sorry to keep pushing these decisions off on you, but once again, the choice is entirely up to el piloto.

Power setting appears to be the major factor in light-airplane-fuel conservation, and the selection of a manifold-pressure/RPM combination that will produce that power is important. Cruising at the *lowest possible RPM* pays off in terms of less horsepower required to overcome internal friction, a more comfortable noise level, and longer times between overhauls. For reasons that can only be blamed on a failure of the flight-instructor corps, a lot of today's pilots are operating high-power engines at less than optimum RPM settings because they think that instant engine failure will occur if the manifold pressure is allowed to creep beyond the "squared" numbers—one inch of manifold pressure for each one hundred RPMs. If there's a hoary, outmoded concept that needs to be expunged from our business, it's that one, which dates way back to some of the big round engines. They weren't designed to accommodate any more internal pressure than such a "squared" power setting would generate. Today's flat engines are quite capable of handling manifold pressures well in excess of that one-inch-to-one-hundred-RPM situation; the cruise chart for the Turbo 210 we've been talking about indicates power settings of 27.5 inches and 2300 RPM all the way up to 20,000 feet. If it's in the book, it's okay. The engine is *not* going to come apart simply because manifold pressure exceeds RPM.

The benefits of high manifold pressure and low RPM for cruise flight were recognized and taught by none other than Charles A. Lindbergh, whose demonstrations and teaching sessions for combat pilots in the South Pacific resulted in tremendous increases in the combat radius and effectiveness of the Lockheed Lightning, the P-38. Lindbergh said: "The trouble is that the newer pilots, and many of the old ones, cruise their engines at too high an r.p.m. and often leave their mixture controls in auto rich during an entire flight. They have never tried low-r.p.m. cruising and cannot believe that it will not injure their engines—or make such a difference in fuel consumption." (*The Wartime Journals of Charles A. Lindbergh,* Harcourt Brace Jovanovich, Inc., New York, p. 865.) His words are just as applicable today as they were in the 1940s.

If your airplane's inspection intervals and engine overhaul times are determined by a recording tachometer, it makes sense to run the engine at a lower speed whenever possible. Low-RPM cruise extends the time between inspections and overhauls, and reduces the wear and tear on the engine. On top of all this good news, your ears will last longer and your passengers will love you for flying a quieter airplane.

Rather than making your fuel-conservation decision a difficult one, the very presence of all these variables seems to point toward a simplistic approach to the problem; select a power setting that is something less than the top end of the performance potential of your airplane—one that provides fuel savings but which still generates enough speed to make air travel worthwhile to you, lean the mixture properly whenever it's safe to do so, and choose an altitude that results in the highest groundspeed under the circumstances. You'll be doing just about everything possible to help stretch the supply.

And a final word . . . let's keep this information to ourselves, because if the politicians find out about it, they're likely to impose a national speed limit on each class of airplane. How'd you like to be arrested for flying faster than L/D_{max}?

Indianapolis, Memorial Day, and Busy Airports

About the middle of the afternoon, when the 500-mile motor classic is well under way and the field is spread out, there's a steady stream of 200-mile-per-hour traffic around that famous oval. How'd you like to take your VW onto the track and just drive around for a while in the midst of all that? 'Twould be tantamount to vehicular suicide.

Though the likelihood of collision is not so overwhelmingly present, there's a corollary in the little airplane proceeding with nonchalance through the arrival and departure streams that identify a really busy airport. With the high-variety traffic mix that is the hallmark of big-city airports, every pilot who is sincerely interested in personal longevity owes it to himself to know where the "race track" is, and when it's safe to cross.

At the super-terminals, this responsibility has shifted somewhat to the people behind the radar scopes as they administer the comings and goings in Terminal Control Areas and Terminal Radar Service Areas. But a sort of in-between land exists around the airports which are not busy enough to warrant either a TCA or a TRSA, but which nonetheless accommodate everything from biplanes to bizjets and an occasional airliner. It's around this kind of terminal that pilot vigilance needs to be extra sharp.

In addition to keeping your head on a swivel, listen to the ATIS broadcast so you'll know the general direction of traffic flow at least for the IFR types—that's where almost all the high-speed traffic will be. The Approach and Departure Control frequencies can also provide a wealth of traffic information—you don't have to be instrument-rated to *listen*.

The busier the non-radar terminal, the farther away you should begin monitoring the Tower frequency to find out who else is on the track; and check in with the Tower sooner to give them a chance to fit you in and call conflicting traffic to your attention.

If you intend to fly directly over a busy terminal (non-TCA or non-TRSA type), do so at least 3000 feet above the ground to stay clear of the Airport Traffic Area, listen and look. Don't bother the Tower with a request to fly overhead, just go about your business with eyes and ears open—you shouldn't have any major conflicts up there.

Terminals serving air carrier jets will almost always "Keep 'Em High" (that's the official name of the procedure)—maintaining the big jets at 10,000 feet and 250 knots until they're within thirty miles or so, then "dumping" them to lower altitudes for the approach procedure. Knowing the direction of the approach and departure paths (jets climb very steeply to 10,000 feet, then flatten out to accelerate to their best rate-of-climb speed) can go a long way toward keeping you out of these high-risk areas.

2

An Advanced Technique for Crosswind Takeoffs and Landings

SOMETIMES YOU WONDER why it's there at all, and then you remember one of those who-turned-on-the-fan? nights last winter when the only thing that seemed to be standing still on the runway was the centerline. Resolute and loyal despite the twenty-five-knot crosswind pushing sheets of snow across the asphalt, the long white dashes gave you something to line up on, something to keep you out of the snowdrifts.

And you might recall with mixed emotions the few times in a flying career when you had to use the paint-stripe DG on takeoff, straining your eyes out and down until the white lines melted into the fog like everything else, and you were ready to trust the gauge on the instrument panel. Once in his element, an instrument pilot will follow that numbered card without hesitation, but he'll cling visually to the centerline just as long as he can.

Since the number of aviators trying to land on nights like those or trying to take off in fog like that is a very small portion of the total pilot population, is all that white paint really necessary? A yes answer has to be qualified, because centerlines have their useful moments for everybody, at least in the two situations just mentioned, and they are also a big help in separating airstrips from drag strips; but be careful—a lot of home bases for hotrods look like runways from the air, and it wouldn't be good aviation "press" to have one of those funny-looking dragsters with the too big back wheels and no front end at all beat you to the finish line!

Centerlines are no doubt here to stay, at least at airports served by an instrument procedure (standardized runway markings are an integral part of a published approach), and hallelujah! you'd be willing to get out and paint the stripes yourself if they could save your fanny some dark night. But there are also times when those centerline markings might well be ignored by most pilots of small general aviation airplanes. (Spend a little time some day at a busy airport where you can observe lateral displacement at touchdown, and you'll be convinced that last statement is a way of life for some pilots.) The bigger the airplane, either in sheer size or performance, the more important the centerline becomes; but the little guys, who don't have to worry about whether the tread spread will fit the runway, or about dragging an outboard engine pod when a swept wing is lowered into the wind, are maybe too subservient to those white dashes.

Pilots in general are pretty much hung up on making sure the middle of the airplane matches the middle of the runway on every landing, every takeoff, and there are good reasons for the "centerline syndrome." For one thing, it's discipline; it gives the beginner a target he needs, something solid and unmoving in a world that has suddenly become maddeningly mobile in all directions, and all at once. There seems to be a hint of tradition about the centerline too; breathes there an instructor who didn't go through this act at least once on his way to becoming a better teacher?

> "Now we're gonna have a little crosswind from the right this time, so I'll talk you through the approach, and you'll see how we correct for drift. . . . OK, you're lined up real nice on final, centerline looks straight, but see how we're starting to drift to the left? OK, we'll stop that by lowering the right wing a little, that's it, now a little left rudder so she won't turn to the right. . . ."

"But, instructor, sir, I've got the controls crossed, and you said yesterday I shouldn't ever be uncoordinated because . . ."

"I know, but it's OK for right now. . . . More right aileron, we're still sliding left; that's it, and more left rudder now, that's the way. . . . Use all the aileron and opposite rudder you need. . . ."

"But, instructor, sir, you said . . ."

"C'mon now, put some effort into this. . . . More aileron, more rudder; you're still drifting left!"

"But, instructor, sir, you said crossed controls could lead to the worst kind of stall and . . ."

"Never mind that now, just stop the drift and keep the airplane lined up with that centerline. . . . More aileron, more rudder!"

". . . and at this close to the ground, we'd never have time to recover!"

"Look, fella, more aileron and more opposite rudder, and I want that nose lined up with the centerline, and I want the upwind wheel to touch the runway first, and then you fly the rest of the airplane onto the ground, and this is called the wing-down method of drift correction, and it works, and you're going to learn it, and you're going to touch down in the middle of the runway, and that's the way we do it, and now put in some more aileron and some more opposite rudder; and be careful not to get into a cross-control stall this close to the ground or you'll kill us both!"

So another bewildered student develops the ability to straddle the white line on landing and takeoff, regardless of his natural aversion to uncoordinated flight, and all because of the crosswind, which has been giving pilots fits ever since it was invented. Maybe someday man will figure out a way to control the direction of the wind, but the government will probably give it to the airlines, so we're stuck with angling breezes. There are some alternatives; either design airports so that they can be swung around into the wind, or somehow cut down the effect of a crosswind by changing pilot technique, or maybe a ground swell of interest could be generated to develop a series of open grass fields for little airplanes, truly "flying fields," but that wouldn't get many votes either; flying fields in most places except the South and West get soft in spring and fall, are difficult to snowplow in winter and are ravaged by all kinds of animals which dig holes, build mounds and have a tendency to move at the last minute into the spot where you want to land, and stand there contentedly chewing their cuds. Of course, there are re-demptive features to consider; if you can maintain good sod on well-drained ground you can beat the "muddies," and putting skis on an airplane can change your outlook on wintertime flying. Wandering livestock is a natural hazard, but even if a couple of errant milk machines invade your flying field, they always stand with their tails into the wind, and there you are—tetrahedrons with horns, and they keep the grass cut in the bargain.

Despite all the minuses, flying fields have one big plus; even if the wind is blowing in circles, you can line up into the breeze every time and forget about crosswinds. The Navy used to train would-be wearers of the golden wings on huge sodded or paved landing pads, with buckets or baskets or just a windsock to indicate what direction was preferred for going and coming. Why bother learning sideslips and crabs on final?—when you got your wings and were flying with the fleet, you could always ask the captain to please turn the carrier a bit more into the wind, sir.

The "flying field" concept is not going to draw any rave notices from financially beleaguered city fathers either; they know they must provide facilities to accommodate the biz-jets and other fast airplanes which bring money to town, and that means long runways, lined up with the prevailing wind, but still plagued with crosswinds as often as not. The problem could be solved for the little guys by paving a circle large enough to meet their requirements, but can you imagine the monument to the asphalt industry that would result if you set up a circle for the blow-torch set? All of which means that the second alternative, a change in landing and takeoff technique for small airplanes, is in order.

Now before all you crop dusters, bush pilots and other assorted types of working airman get hot under your helmets, relax; the technique is one you've been using ever since Wilbur lined up the launching rail so's Orville wouldn't have to worry about crosswinds—he had enough on his mind to start with. A friend who's been powdering soybeans from the air for more than a few years remembers using farm fields for landing almost at will, of course always angling into the wind to do whatever he could to improve the performance of those Sherman tanks of the air. This practice has largely come to a screeching halt, perhaps because farmers began taking the ag pilots to mayors' courts or calling the sheriff whenever a Stearman planted its stiff legs in the south forty.

At the core of this proposal is the theory that anytime you operate your airplane in harmony with natural forces, the result will be a better operation—more comfortable, more efficient, probably safer. Next to gravity, the most prevalent natural force is wind; sometimes friend, sometimes foe, from whisper to whirlwind. It seems unworthy of the intelligence and adaptability of the modern aviator to accept whatever Aeolus unleashes, struggling into or out of the air at the mercy of the wind. Limited to a relatively narrow strip of pavement or usable grass, and unable to influence the direction of the moving air (unless you've got a direct line to the Great Weatherman), there's only one thing left which you *can* manage—the heading of your airplane during the tag end of an approach and at the start of the takeoff roll.

There have doubtless been days when you wanted to go flying for the fun of it—just get into the air for a while, a few circuits and bumps and then home again—days when a cancellation didn't upset your schedule. Now think of the times when you really needed to go someplace in your airplane and didn't, because of wind direction and force. When surface winds are more than you care to tackle, it's likely that the zephyrs aloft are something else too; and unless your destination was downwind you might have been better off to go by car. But haven't there been times when you canceled a flight because of crosswind reports that were a bit on the marginal side, and winds aloft would not have been prohibitive, all things considered? Do you recall the yardstick you used to make those decisions?—in all probability, it was the runway centerline. When the Tower or ATIS or Flight Service announced surface winds from 070 at 30 knots, and the only runway available had the number 36 painted thereon, didn't your mind conjure up an almost direct crosswind, more than you could handle? A normal reaction, and all because of that single file of white lines marching up and down the runway.

The centerline hangup again; almost to the point of reverence, you've been taught that, no matter what, you must put the nose wheel or the tail wheel on that line and keep it there, and if you can't, cancel the flight—bad winds. There's nothing wrong with joining the hot-stove league in the pilots' lounge, but you didn't come out to talk, you came out to *fly!* Perhaps the local instructors are also indulging in the great coffee-drinking marathon because of the winds, but wouldn't it be refreshing to have an enterprising aeronautical mentor recognize your frustration and offer to show you a better way?

Since a 70-degree, 30-knot crosswind caused the problem to start with, take a closer look at it; you can use a piece of graph paper, or one of the formal crosswind charts, or your navigational confuser (use the square graph at the bottom of the slide on an E6B type, and the wind side of a Jepp). That situation (30 knots crossing the runway at 70 degrees) doesn't help you a heck of a lot in the headwind department, but look at the crosswind component: a husky 29 knots right down the main spar. That may indeed be more wind from the side than you or your airplane can handle, because somewhere in the obscure reaches of your owner's manual, there's a figure that tells you the demonstrated crosswind component for your flying machine. The aerodynamics are simple; since the control surfaces are effective in direct proportion to the amount of air moving over, around and across them, they don't do much for you in zero wind. As soon as you start moving, or as soon as the air moves, ailerons and elevators and rudders can deflect that air and develop controllability— the more air moving, the more control you have—but if the side wind is trying to push you off the pavement with more force than full control deflection can muster in opposition, the wind's gonna win!

Unfortunately, a crosswind has two inherent qualities which decrease takeoff and landing performance; in the first place, some of the control deflection required to keep the machine going in the direction you prefer creates drag, which saps total available energy, helping to make the far end of the runway show up long before you'd like it to. In addition, every wind except a direct headwind or tailwind is really made up of two components, which act in a resultant direction which we label crosswind. Spin your confuser again, and it's apparent that for every crosswind you might experience, part of it can be considered effective straight on, and part of it is acting as if it were blowing right down the wing from tip to root. The crosswind, or sidewind, part doesn't do much in the lift department, since most airfoils are responsive only to those chunks of air moving from front to back— meaning that the more "cross" the wind, the less lift is being produced; and coupled with the increased drag of the deflected-farther-than-usual control surfaces, it may back you into a performance corner you can't fly out of. High-performance aircraft have it even worse, if it's any consolation, because swept wings are obviously more susceptible to the lengthwise airflow, and on most of the big fellas, spoilers are used as well as normal ailerons to keep everything on an even keel during takeoff and landing, and they steal a bit more out of the energy reservoir.

So there you sit, cleared for takeoff, neatly astraddle the centerline, with the crosswind rocking the wings and pecking at the rudder, and you realize that as soon as you release the brakes, controllability will be at a minimum just when you need it most to keep the centerline centered, and that all the while, at least some, probably much, maybe most of the lifting force is being drained away by that sidewind component. There's got to be a better way!

And there surely is. Suddenly, courtesy of the Instant Construction Company, world's fastest runway builders, Runway 5 appears, and the prohibitive crosswind disappears; the component drops to a very acceptable 10 knots. Or if ICC misread its survey stakes and laid down Runway 3 instead, you still might be able to fly in the face of the resultant 20-knot crosswind component. The sidewind numbers for any runway-wind angle decrease accordingly as the wind force lessens; turn down the fan, and you turn up performance. A more normal situation might be a crosswind of 5 degrees, blowing at 20 knots—even if you insist on keeping the centerline under your seat during takeoff on Runway 36, there will be only a 15-knot crosswind component trying to push the airplane off the pavement. If only you could somehow get that runway turned thirty or forty degrees into the wind! As a matter of mathematical fact, *any* turning into the wind will help solve your problem.

Well, you can't turn the runway, and few towers these days will clear you to take off on the grass. So what's left? It's so simple, don't you see, just get away from that dog-gone centerline, and *turn the airplane.* Change your heading during the initial part of the takeoff by lining up in the downwind corner. Blasphemy? Sacrilege? Unsafe? Of course not—it's just a sensible way to get more use from your airplane—there's no law that insists you proceed hi-diddle-diddle right down the middle.

The "out of the corner" takeoff is simple to learn; after you're cleared into position, plan your taxiing so that you end up heading as much as possible into the wind—remembering that every degree you squeeze out of those first few feet of takeoff roll represents a reduction, however slight, in the crosswind component, which translates into fewer feet of takeoff roll. Have the go handle forward, or well on its way to full blower, when you release the brakes, and make a normal short-field takeoff. As soon as you feel solid and safe in the air, set up a crab angle to parallel the upwind edge of the runway, and go about your business. You'll be amazed how soon liftoff happens; if the wind is blowing hard enough to require this technique, there will be more than the usual number of molecules of air racing across the airfoil per unit of time, and they're racing across straighter; it all adds up to more performance.

You'll soon develop a feel for how much distance you're going to need, and there will be times (narrow runway, gusty winds, heavy weight, high-density altitude, etc.) when it's obvious that you'll be out of runway before you're in the air. There's a way to counter this problem too. With airspeed increasing throughout the takeoff roll, the controls are becoming more effective with each passing second, so if the upwind edge is approaching more rapidly than you think it should, start to turn very slowly and carefully down the runway, planning to use up all the pavement's width; it will be a much more positive maneuver than you might imagine, because the airplane is almost flying, and control response should be good and solid.

Everybody knows that there ain't no such thing as a free lunch, and like anything that gives you something, there's a price to be paid; the cost of "out of the corner" takeoffs is increased vigilance and skill. Gusty crosswinds lie in wait for situations like this, when they can give you a shot under the upwind wing, and then things get exciting—especially with the high-wingers. Do the turning (if necessary) with rudder, and control the wings with the ailerons—start flying the airplane as soon as you come off the binders, and don't stop flying it until you're back in the chocks. So what else is new?

A maneuver like this will poke around a bit in some of the unfamiliar or unpracticed nooks and crannies of your airplane's performance envelope, so crawl before you try to walk, or even think about running. Start out with a ten-degree offset on a not so windy day, and gradually work up to as much of an angle as you think you'll ever need. As long as your experimenting doesn't interfere with other traffic (all those unknowing souls out there trying to split the centerline), Controllers will usually let you practice to your heart's content on the crosswind runway. Better yet, find an instructor who knows his way in and out of runway corners, and do your practicing under his guidance until you get good at it.

Engine failure right after liftoff when it's the only engine you've got?—certainly worth thinking about and being ready for, but it shouldn't present problems any different from any other takeoff situation. Sudden silence that close to the ground leaves precious little in the way of things to do, and you'd better be programmed to touch down not in the most ideal place, but to touch down with the airplane completely under control—*how* is much more important than *where*. And, of course, anytime a pilot allows a multi-engine airplane to leap off at less than V_{mc}, he is working with a calculated risk; calculate carefully, and decide if it's worth it at all. In either case, after you've climbed a hundred feet or so, the corner takeoff is not a whit different from a normal one; if anything, you'll be closer to the center of the airport, because you actually used fewer feet in the takeoff roll.

Which brings up another worthwhile benefit of "out of the corner"—*anytime* you want to realize the absolute maximum takeoff performance, line up in the corner, with about a 30-degree angle between your heading and the runway centerline. For this to work, you've got to be lined up in the left-hand corner, so that as power is added, the forces that normally must be overcome with right rudder are permitted to do their thing, pulling the nose of the airplane around to the left, and *voilá!* a shorter takeoff. All right, purists, it uses up the same number of feet, but those feet are now curved instead of in a straight line, and if you bend a line, it will fit into a smaller space, which is really what we're after—you'll use up less of the runway. This neat little trick was a required maneuver for Air Rescue Service pilots when the Grumman Albatross was the go-out-and-get-'em mainstay—at 37,000 pounds, the SA-16 could leave the ground in about 700 feet of runway, using a curved takeoff roll and, of course, rocket assist. (It is also one of the few airplanes that will try to turn *downwind* on takeoff because of the huge slab sides up ahead of the main wheels—it's the world's biggest weathervane!)

If a corner takeoff turns into a can of worms, you can always close the throttle, recover your composure and go back to try again, or quit for the day. But there's something a little more conclusive about landing; once you're up, you've got to come down—there's no way out of it. So the difference is perhaps as much psychological as operational, and there's a way to lessen the control-crossing and wing-downing and final-crabbing and make your return to earth a little easier.

The pattern which precedes a landing in the corner is almost as important as the touchdown technique itself. When there's nobody but you to be concerned about it, fly a circular pattern. Your best friend is a windsock, and the closer it is to your landing spot, the better. From a position opposite the spot, reduce power and begin descending in a constantly curving path toward the runway, putting all your powers of judgment to work as you watch the ground slide underneath. When you reach a heading that apparently stops all drift, you're flying directly into the wind, and that's the course you want at touchdown. It's not lined up with the centerline, but that's the name of this game, and if you can safely maintain that track, touch down and come to a stop within the confines of the landing area, you're playing it right.

It's easy to see why your average tower Controller would come unglued watching an approach like this, and it might be unsafe with regard to other airplanes waiting for takeoff. Trees and towers and tenements outside the straight-in approach path must be considered too, so a pattern curving into the wind may not always be the way to go. When you're locked in to the normal rectangular traffic pattern (or cleared "straight in"), track down final sideways, like a crab, and as soon as it can be done safely, slide over into the corner and land as much as possible into the wind. For the same reasons that applied to the crosswind takeoff, every degree you can turn will produce a better landing, with a shorter roll and less forward speed at touchdown—saves tires and brakes too.

There will be in-between days, when there is enough crosswind to call for cornering, but after you're down, it's apparent that your airborne tricycle is going to run out of pavement before it runs out of steam. There's nothing immoral about using some of the grass, and since most groundkeepers do a pretty good job of maintaining the runway berm, there will probably be no great damage done to either airplane or grass, but boy, is it embarrassing! Once again, pilot judgment comes to the fore, and you should begin turning out of the wind when you see that that will be necessary, increasing the rate to match the disappearing concrete.

With the steering wheel (front or back) firmly on the ground, your forward speed slowed considerably (after all, it was probably a strong wind that started the whole thing, and that means your groundspeed at touchdown should have been *very* low), you should have the beast well in hand, and the turn out of the wind should present no problem.

If you go back and read through this dissertation again, you will notice that it's loaded with probablys, mights, maybes and shoulds; it's a lot like a weather forecast—there are too many variables involved to climb out on a dogmatic limb. The width of the runway, weight of the airplane, condition of the runway surface (long grass or deep snow or mud can wipe out all the good things about the corner technique), strength and direction of the wind, its gustiness, and whatever else might affect the performance of the airplane can make a big difference. But perhaps the most variable of all these factors is the pilot's proficiency level; if you're not *good* with your airplane, don't go out and try this by yourself the first time. Given *your* airplane, *your* airport and its obstructions and peculiarities, and most of all *yourself* and how handy *you* are with stick and rudder, the "out of the corner" or "into" deal may not be a good one.

Neither is it a crosswind panacea—sometimes, using the corner is the wrong thing to try—like the little girl in the nursery rhyme, when it's good, it's very, very good, and when it's bad, it's horrid. Practiced and developed and used properly, the corner technique will do three things for you: first, it will open another door to maximum performance; second, you'll be a more proficient flyer, because "cornering" requires a great deal of skill and judgment; and third, it will make you a more confident pilot, one who knows what he and his airplane can do when the utmost is required. If you can put up with an aeronautical Dutch uncle for a minute, give this some thought—someday, despite careful planning and good intentions, you may find yourself in a situation that will demand all the pilot that is in you, and all the performance that your airplane can generate. When that time arrives, when you're between a rock and a hard place, it's too late to practice; so every now and then, make yourself and the machine really perform—it's good to know what the airplane will do when you need it. "Out of the corner" is just one of many worthwhile things you can use as a whetstone for your flying skills.

Fly Tight Patterns

The "circuit," as our British counterparts know it, evolved from the need to organize all those aviators trying to fly down the funnel at the same time; there's no way but to get in line and take your turn. Another purpose of the traffic pattern is for training, to set up the same situation time after time, so that a budding pilot gets into the habit of seeing the runway where it should be every time he's where *he* should be. Some of those speck-in-the-distance downwind legs you see leave the implication that there's yet another purpose for the pattern: building up flying time.

Wide traffic patterns have several things going for them, none of them good. They put you farther away from the scene of the action and make it difficult for pilots entering a proper pattern to figure out if you're on a crosswind or a cross-country. They encourage low-airspeed, high-power flight 800 feet above airport neighbors who often respond with angry telephone calls . . . justifiably. Wide traffic patterns use up a lot of fuel and time—especially when you're out for a session of self-improving touch-and-go landings, you'll get more practice for the money by flying tight patterns.

In a pattern full of airplanes, you must follow the fellow ahead, but you can place your downwind a bit inside his to keep the pattern from growing. You can also contribute to tight patterns by turning base when the plane ahead of you in the pattern passes abeam on his way to the airport—you'll have adequate spacing on final. When you're the only one out there, set up your own tight pattern—agreed that the faster airplanes will need a little more spacing, but nearly all singles can be landed comfortably from a downwind leg no more than a half-mile from the runway.

There's not an airplane made that doesn't have built-in reference points so you can be the same distance from the runway every time you arrive on downwind—a spot on the wing strut, the wingtip itself, a window sill; there will be something that you can line up visually with the runway. Home-field landmarks (rivers, roads, golf courses, etc.) are great ways of standardizing the pattern, but get in the habit of noticing where the runway appears in relation to your on-the-airplane reference. Elm Street won't go with you to Another Airport, but the wing strut will!

3

Electronic Navigation: VOR/DME/HSI/RNAV

MORE THAN LIKELY, THE AIRPLANE YOU FLY is outfitted with a navigation-communications system—"navcom" in the jargon of the business—half of which is for talking and listening, half for determining where you are or where you're going.

Even though there are newer systems in the offing, VOR remains the most popular radio navigation aid, and it will be a long time before all those omni transmitters are unplugged. But like any source of information, the omni (which is a heck of a lot easier to say than "very-high-frequency omnidirectional radio range") can be of help only to the extent the user understands what it's telling him. Just a little VOR knowledge can lead a pilot down the primrose path: away from the station when he thinks he's flying toward it, or providing course information from a station different from the one he thinks he has tuned.

VORs were set up primarily for IFR use, but since they're on the air twenty-four hours a day, why not take advantage of them? You can lay out those long cross-country flights with more assurance of knowing where you will be because you can fly from one known point to another, and in a straight, predetermined line. In unfamiliar country, it's possible to locate airports, points of interest, whatever you're looking for, more easily and accurately with VOR, but only if you know *how* to use it.

THE SECRET INSIDE THE BLACK BOX

VOR transmitters may be in the middle of a cornfield or the middle of an airfield, but they all do the same thing inside those flat-topped white buildings—they send out a constant stream of electrical energy, available to anyone whose receiver can pick up the signal. There are a couple of antennas, and something about a phase relationship, and if you really get turned on by knowing why things electronic happen the way they do, there are volumes on the subject. But for practical use, be happy and secure in the knowledge that most of the dollars you laid out for the VOR receiver in your airplane bought the capability of interpreting the signals to help you find out where you are. It doesn't happen quite this simply, but imagine a single VOR transmitter radiating an electronic line toward magnetic north, another toward the east, and so on, until every one of the 360 degrees in a complete circle about that station has its own line. In simplest terms, the VOR receiver is able to decode the signal and show you which line you're on.

Suppose that single transmitter were located in Kansas City; you'd know which line you're on, but that's *all* you'd know. If you're headed to or from Kansas City, beautiful; but how about the day you want to go somewhere else? A second VOR in Denver would help, because now you could find out on which of Kansas City's lines you are flying, tune quickly to the Denver station and conclude, "I am here"— where the two lines cross.

More stations, more lines, and the VOR system grew to about a thousand (give or take a few) omni transmitters in these United States. That's something on the order of 360,000 possible lines with which to navigate, and all with one little receiver. Of course, you can't receive all of them at once, but even if you limit each station's lines—wait a minute; let's quit calling them lines and give them a decent name—

even if you limit each station's *radials* to a forty-mile circle, there's still enough coverage to get to or from almost any place by using VOR. Given the availability of all these radials, there are three ways to use VOR for VFR:

1. To fly along the radial that crosses over wherever you want to go; it's got to be down there somewhere.

2. To determine your location on the radials of two or more VOR stations, and draw the radials on your chart; where the lines cross, there you are.

3. When all else fails, tune any VOR with a usable signal, find out what radial you're on, and *stay* on it until you get to the station—then you'll know where you are, and you can start all over again, or quit, depending on the situation.

Your attention please!—a radial is always a magnetic course *from* a VOR station. When flying away from the transmitter, the numbers used to identify both radial and course (track across the ground) are the same. For example, flying due east *from* a VOR, your course will be 090 degrees, and you are indeed on the 090 radial. But when you turn around and proceed inbound on that same radial, the course becomes the reciprocal—you are still on the 090 radial, but the course is now 270—it's a simple matter of adding or subtracting 180 degrees, and it must be done whenever you are flying *to* a station.

WHAT YOU SEE IS WHERE YOU ARE

There are as many ways of presenting the information as there are manufacturers, but all the VOR receivers ever built have three things in common; an omni-bearing selector, an ambiguity meter and a course-deviation indicator—fancy names for the OBS, the TO–FROM indicator and the left-right needle. One at a time then; OBS first, because interpretation of the other two depends on its setting.

The OBS is the means by which you select the reference radial, the one that you'd like the set to interpret for you. There are two ways to use the OBS; first, when you know ahead of time which radial you would *like* to be on, set that

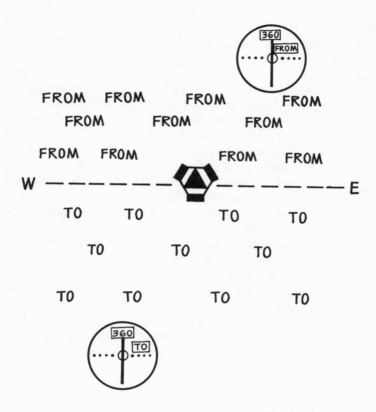

Figure 3–1. The electronic division as "seen" by a VOR receiver. The imaginary line is always perpendicular to the course you select with the OBS.

in the window or on the dial; move the airplane until the left-right needle centers, and you're there. The second situation is the one in which you don't particularly *care* what radial you're on, but you'd sure like to get to the VOR station so you can find out where you are. In this case, center the left-right needle by turning the OBS, and the numbers that appear are the ones you've been looking for.

The TO–FROM indicator lets you know what will happen if you fly the airplane in the direction selected on the OBS—

the alternatives are clear-cut, since you can go only TO the station or FROM the station. The terms TO and FROM need to be amplified a bit—in Figure 3–2, the area around a VOR has been divided by an imaginary east-west line, and this is what your receiver "sees" when you select 360 on the OBS. Because of this electronic division, a VOR receiver set to 360 and located anywhere *south* of that line will indicate TO (wouldn't a heading of 360 take that airplane toward the station?); using the same reasoning, a receiver located *north* of the dividing line would show FROM, which is what would happen if you turned to and flew a heading of 360 degrees.

Up to this point, you probably haven't been very impressed with the accuracy of VOR navigation; the best it has done is locate you within one or the other half-circle, which could extend all the way around the world! But give it a chance, because with the information from the left-right needle, you can narrow things down a bit more. For the sake of clarity, assume that your OBS is set on 360, the TO–FROM indicator shows FROM and you have correctly positioned yourself *somewhere* north of the VOR. If the left-right needle is centered, there's only one place you can be—north of the VOR and on the 360 radial. (Notice that airplane No. 2, south of the station, has the same display with the exception of the TO indication.)

As happens more often than not, the left-right needle begins to creep away from center, or perhaps it's already against the peg on one side or the other when you set up the receiver. If your objective is to get on that centerline, the left-right needle will tell you which way to turn to do it, but the information is valid only when the heading of the airplane is the same as the OBS setting. Whether you do it in your mind's eye or actually lean into the ailerons and turn the plane, get these two numbers in agreement before you read the left-right needle. When the heading-OBS condition is met, the needle will always show the way to the centerline of the course you have chosen. The left-right needle divides the area around the VOR into more half-circles, as in the diagram; if you are in the half-circle to the right of course, the needle will point left, and vice versa.

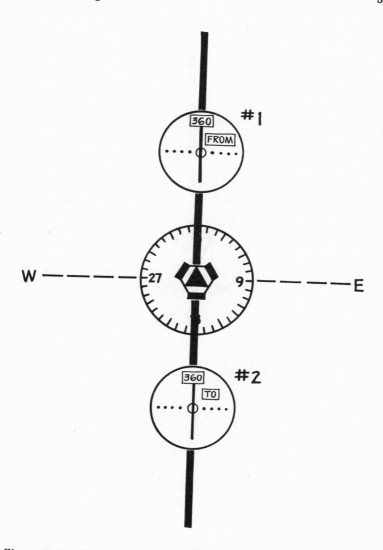

Figure 3–2. Narrowing things down—with the OBS set at 360, a receiver showing FROM with the left-right needle centered must be north of the VOR, on the 360 radial. The TO receiver must be on course, south of the station.

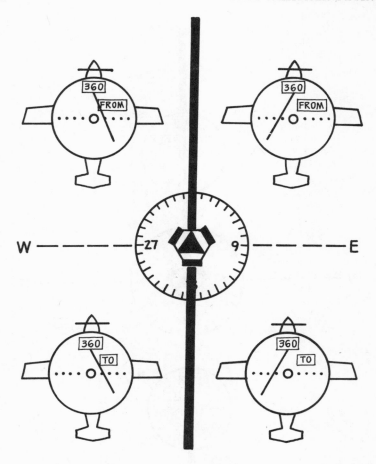

Figure 3–3. Put the receiver in an airplane, match heading and OBS setting, and the left-right needle will always show you which way to turn to get on course.

PUTTING IT ALL TOGETHER

The procedure for interpreting VOR indications can be nicely methodized into three steps:

1. Turn the airplane (actually or imaginarily) or reset the OBS until heading and OBS agree.

2. The TO–FROM indicator will then tell you whether you're coming or going.

3. The left-right needle will let you know if you're on course, or show you which way to turn to get there.

As you fly over a VOR transmitter, the left-right needle will wiggle around for a few seconds, but when it settles down again it will continue to show where the centerline is; the only real change you'll see on the panel is the reversal of the TO–FROM indicator. When FROM pops up (or drops down or slides over) and stays put, make a note of the time— you have passed the station.

So much for understanding what goes on inside the black box and how to interpret what it's telling you—putting the knowledge to work is more important. In the first case mentioned, you intend to navigate along a radial which overheads your destination—call that one the "course-line radial." Keep the left-right needle centered and you're bound to get where you meant to go. With just one VOR on board, you'll have to pick up landmarks for cross-reference as you fly, because a course-line radial provides no distance information.

When you put together enough bucks to buy a second VOR, you should still use terrain features for double-checks, but now you have the added luxury of a second radial for more precise position fixing. Determine which radial from a VOR off to the side of your course passes over the destination, and put that number in the No. 2 OBS (after you've tuned and identified, of course). Fly until the left-right needle on the No. 2 black box moves in to the center, and you're there. This can also be done with one receiver by holding the heading that keeps you on the course-line radial, and tuning up the side VOR for a check on your progress relative to that radial.

The second situation, when you're not quite sure where you are but will know which way to go as soon as you can pinpoint yourself on a chart, requires a bit of draftsmanship. With two receivers at your disposal, set them up on different omnis. (The ideal plot would be from one VOR off the nose or tail and the other off a wingtip. Get a "cut" as close as possible to a 90-degree angle for greater accuracy—if the stations you choose are directly ahead and directly behind, or one off the right wingtip and the other at the left, it's better than nothing, but not much.) Center the left-right needles with FROM showing in both windows so you'll be reading radials; then, with any kind of straightedge, draw these radials from their respective VORs until the lines cross. You said you'd know which way to go when you nailed down your position on a chart, which you have now done, so get going!

Case No. 3: You've exhausted every ounce of your navigational skills, don't have any idea where you are, wouldn't even know which way to turn if you did know. If things ever get this bad (which is not as remote a possibility as it sounds —at night, or maybe on a hazy day over unfamiliar terrain, it could happen), don't forget that every VOR transmitter is constantly tossing out life preservers, as it were, and if you can catch one of them, who cares from whence it came? Don't even worry about trying to identify the Morse code; when you find a frequency that brings the needles and pointers and flags to life, turn the OBS until the needle centers with TO in the window, and fly that heading. Climb if you can to maintain the good signal, and let somebody know of your plight. You'll have time to identify the station on the way there, and you can rest assured that if you can get to a VOR transmitter, there'll be a Flight Service Station within radio range to give you directions to the nearest airport. Having to go through all this is the price you might have to pay for sloppy navigation, but it's a way out of a bad spot, and in this business, that's what counts.

HOW TO INTERCEPT A SPECIFIC RADIAL

Once you've decided which radial you would like to use and have put the proper numbers in the OBS, the fastest way to get to the centerline is to turn and fly at a 90-degree angle—careful, because things happen fast. Facing the good possibility of overshooting the centerline and weaving back and forth in an attempt to catch the needle, you'll do better to make your intercepts at no more than a 45-degree angle, especially when you're relatively close to the VOR station.

WHEN YOU GET ON A RADIAL, STAY THERE

Wind correction is just as much a feature of good navigation when using VOR as it is with any other system, but the omni panel display takes all the work out of it. Once on a radial, drift correction is simply a matter of keeping the left-right needle centered. Start out with no correction at all so you can see which way the wind is going to move the airplane, and as soon as you detect even the slightest positive displacement of the left-right needle, turn ten degrees in the direction indicated. If that happens to be enough of a crab angle to effectively counteract the wind, the needle will stop moving. You might hit the right combination the first time, but more than likely you'll have to cut and try a bit; for instance, ten degrees into the wind may prove to be too much, and the needle will come back to center and keep on going, off to the other side. When this happens, return to the original heading (same as the OBS setting) and wait until the needle once again centers, then put in only *half* as much wind correction.

On the other hand, should the original ten degrees not be enough to keep the airplane on course, the left-right needle will continue moving away from center. As soon as you notice this situation, get busy, because you're moving away from your intended course at a rapid rate—turn thirty degrees back toward the centerline and hold it until the needle centers. Now try twenty degrees into the wind, and watch the needle. Sooner or later you'll come across a heading that will balance the force of the wind, and you can proceed to the station on course.

As you get close to the transmitter and the needle begins to make great larruping excursions across the face of the instrument, just hang in there—stay with the heading that worked most of the way in, and you will cross the station in fine fashion. For safety's sake, make it a habit to turn out when you're several miles from the station and purposely avoid the congested airspace right over the VOR—there are usually a couple of head-in-the-cockpit aviators converging on that point, trying to see if they can fly directly over the little white transmitter shack.

The subject of airspace congestion should be also considered when you're enroute. Flying direct from one VOR to the next is a great way to go, but remember that you are more than likely traversing a federal airway, on which there may be IFR traffic at assigned altitudes. (In general, they'll be flying *odd* thousand-foot levels when eastbound, *even* thousand-foot levels westbound.) Both IFR and VFR people have every right in the taxpaying world to be there, but when you're on an airway, keep the eyeballs moving more than usual—it's not likely that you'll run in to an IFR person, but it only takes once.

WHAT COULD POSSIBLY GO WRONG?

VOR has a lot going for it—prevalence, straight-line accuracy, clear-cut presentation; but it's only as good as the operator who sets it up and does the interpretation. There are a couple of common errors which you should be able to avoid simply by knowing about them.

First, make sure you are working with the VOR you *think* you are—it's not at all difficult to get a strong signal from a station farther away, and the TO–FROM and left-right seem to be right where they belong. This source of error can be eliminated by forming the tune-and-identify habit; as soon as you crank in the first station on a trip, or whenever you change to a new frequency, don't move your hand from the receiver until you have turned up the audio and are certain of the Morse code (sometimes a vocal ident) that comes out of the speaker.

Error No. 2 involves the heading-OBS relationship; *never* use VOR indications to figure out where you are or where you're going unless the heading of the airplane and the number on the OBS are pretty close together. Setting up a cross-check with a radial from some other omni, of course, violates the rule, but on the VOR receiver being used for primary navigation, the course-line radial, the only difference between these two numbers will be wind correction. When you're flying *toward* a VOR station, you should see TO; flying outbound, anything but FROM in the window means that something isn't right.

THERE'S AN EASIER WAY

From the standpoint of making navigational life easier for pilots, the VOR system beat the socks off its predecessor, the low-frequency radio range. But interpretation remains somewhat of a problem (otherwise, there wouldn't have to be lengthy dissertations like this to help pilots understand what's going on!); you must predetermine and preset the desired course, then look to another instrument to determine aircraft heading, then consider your approximate position, and finally come up with a mind's-eye picture of where you are.

This set of mental gymnastics is just about completely wiped out by the Horizontal Situation Indicator (HSI), which is not really a new piece of aircraft equipment, but it's a relatively recent addition to the instrument panels of light airplanes. HSIs have been in use for a number of years in airliners and military and corporate aircraft because these segments of the industry have been virtually the only ones that could afford them. Today's continuing movement toward miniaturization and reduction of cost in avionics has made the HSI a much more frequent feature of light-aircraft installations, and the experienced pilot should have at least a conversational knowledge of this type of navigational display.

At first glance, a typical HSI (Figure 3–4) looks like a directional gyro with some extra features . . . and that's almost exactly what it is. The heart of the HSI is a rotating azimuth card, which indicates aircraft magnetic heading right up at the top, under a lubber line, so that you always know which way you are headed. A course is selected by positioning the large arrowhead to the appropriate number

on the card, and the movable segment of the arrow then becomes the Course Deviation Indicator. In the illustration,
aircraft heading is 150 degrees, the pilot has selected a

Figure 3–4.   Photograph courtesy of Narco Avionics.

magnetic course of 120 degrees, and the display shows that
course off to the right of the airplane; no matter how you
set up this instrument, you can always get to the selected
course by turning the real airplane so that the little airplane
on the display is "flying" toward the line you'd like to be on.

Just like the old-style VOR presentations, the TO–FROM
indication on an HSI (it's the broad white "arrowhead" just
ahead of the airplane symbol) tells you, in this situation,
that if you fly on a heading of 120 (the selected course), you
will be flying toward the station. Arrival over the VOR will
be prefaced by a nervous "needle," and station passage will
be confirmed by a complete reversal of the TO–FROM in-

dicator. In this case, the white arrowhead will show up *be-hind* the airplane symbol.

If the pilot in the illustrated example continued flying on a heading of 150, he'd eventually reach the preselected course; the movable segment is shown in the fully deflected position, which represents a 10-degree (or more) off-course displacement when the receiver is tuned to a VOR signal (full-scale is only 2.5 degrees when a localizer frequency is selected). As the course is approached and the deviation becomes less than 10 degrees, the segment will begin to move toward center, and when it's right under the little airplane, you're on course . . . it's really that simple.

Once on course, wind correction is simply a matter of keeping the airplane symbol centered on the course-deviation bar by means of appropriate heading changes. And when you've turned into the wind the proper number of degrees, you'll once again have a *picture* of the situation—the little airplane will be on the course-deviation bar with the wind-correction angle displayed as it really exists. The station pointer (TO–FROM indicator) will always indicate the location of the VOR—either ahead or behind—in relation to the selected course.

Some HSIs have azimuth (directional-gyro) cards driven by a slaved compass—that is, a system with a sensor that picks up the weak signals from the earth's magnetic field, amplifies them, and keeps the compass aligned with magnetic north without the near-constant checking and resetting necessary with independent gyros. Other systems, in a move to provide the benefits of the HSI at the lowest possible cost, must be matched to the "whiskey" compass, or the runway heading before takeoff, and reset when necessary during flight. Either way, the system is always related to magnetic directions and courses, and makes VOR navigation a snap.

With an HSI, your mind's eye can relax because the entire navigational picture is right there in front of you. It's very much like being able to look down from a great height and watch the changes in your airplane's relationship to a course line painted on the ground; the sooner you begin to think of it that way, the sooner the HSI will really begin to work best for you.

SO, WHAT'S "RNAV"?

To begin with, it's a corruption of the words—"area navigation"—which describe the system; it's also a demonstration of a microminiature computer's ability to provide an instantaneous and continuous solution to a problem of trigonometry. But most important, it's a means of accomplishing radio navigation in straight lines without the necessity of flying from one VOR station to the next. RNAV frees you from the dogleg routes of the VOR system by enabling *navigation* anywhere within the *area* served by a VOR–DME.

Normal radio-nav equipment won't do the job by itself; you must purchase an on-board computer (from a couple thousand bucks to as much as you'd like to spend) which processes the signals from VOR and DME and presents azimuth and distance information to a pilot-determined fix known as a "waypoint." When RNAV was first introduced to general aviation a number of years ago, the marketing folks were fond of referring to waypoints as "phantom VORs"—easy enough to understand, but an exercise in oversimplification. Experienced pilots deserve a bit more.

Refer to Figure 3–5. With the aircraft in the geographic position shown, signals from the VOR and DME inform the RNAV computer that the present position is 12.4 miles from the station on the 210 radial; that information also defines one side—side A—of a triangle. Side B is represented by the predetermined radial and distance of the waypoint, in this case the 300 radial at a distance of 31.2 miles, or the waypoint "address." With this two-sided information available, the little computer rushes through its calculations in the blink of an eye, and figures out the length of side C (distance to the waypoint—36 miles) and the magnetic course from the present position to the waypoint—332 degrees. Simple, *non? Oui.*

The results are displayed as steering information on the CDI or HSI, distance information, and a TO–FROM indica-

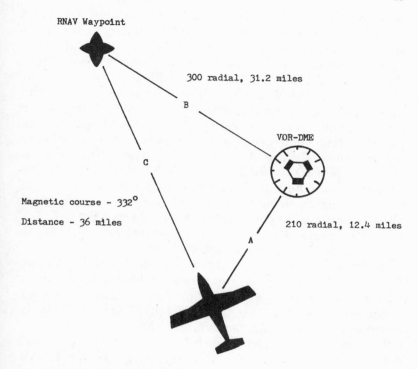

Figure 3–5.   The RNAV triangle.

tion identical to that of a VOR. Once the system is set up
and operating properly, you might as well consider that
you're navigating to or from that "phantom" VOR, because
the indications will be identical. When you drift left or right
of course the needles will let you know, and you'll always
have an indication of how many miles lie between you and
the waypoint. Just like most of the contemporary DMEs, up-
to-date RNAV units will include groundspeed and time-to-
the-waypoint as well.

The pilot's role in setting up and using RNAV is uncomplicated, but requires attention to detail since the output
(azimuth and distance information) is no better than the
input (waypoint address and station tuning). The scientific

term for this is GIGO: Garbage In, Garbage Out. You must be certain that the VOR and DME are tuned to the same station (the more expensive models do this automatically), that the signals coming into the set are indeed coming from the *proper* station (the old rule still applies—tune and identify), and the waypoint address must be correct. The number of waypoints available varies considerably; from a one-waypoint unit at the bottom of the RNAV price scale to airline-type equipment capable of storing more waypoints than you'll likely use in a lifetime of flying. There's even one on the market which "knows" the radial-distance information for a host of airports and calls them up when you punch in the three-letter identifier. Want to go from your present position, to, say, Los Angeles? Simply enter L-A-X on the computer keyboard and the navigation information comes up like magic on the data display.

Return your attention to Figure 3–5 for a moment. Flying from A to B with RNAV equipment on board, a very positive course can be planned and flown by plotting convenient waypoints from the three VOR–DMEs involved. This is possible with any of the aeronautical charts in common use today; but the Jeppesen folks have gone one step farther, with a series of charts designed especially for the RNAV user (Figure 3–6). No geographical features—no towns or cities or railroads—but you'll find all the VOR–DMEs and all the airports, plus restricted airspace and Air Route Traffic Control Center frequencies for your convenience in obtaining radar advisories on your VFR–RNAV flights. Notice that the cardinal radials are provided with ten-mile arrowheads; until you get way out west where the VOR–DMEs are fewer and farther between, you'll seldom have to plot a radial to establish a waypoint . . . this is a *very* convenient chart.

In addition to the RNAV enroute chart, Jeppesen also publishes a directory of waypoint addresses for nearly all the airports in the United States; there are usually addresses provided for two nearby VOR–DMEs, with radial to the nearest tenth of a degree and distance to the nearest tenth of a nautical mile.

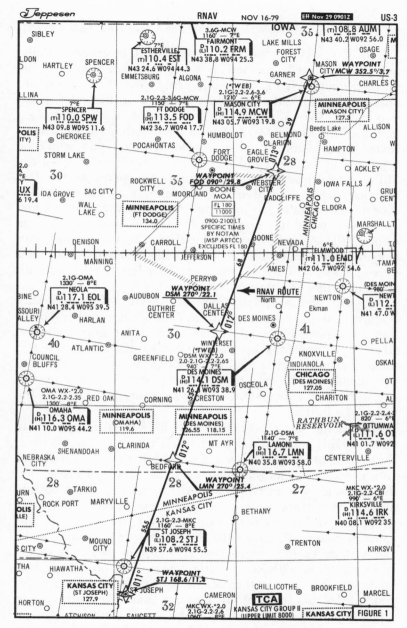

Figure 3–6. Copyright © 1979 Jeppesen Sanderson, Inc., Denver, Colorado. All rights reserved.

Use of RNAV in the IFR environment is growing daily, and that subject is covered in detail elsewhere, specifically, in *Instrument Flying*, by yours truly. But there are other applications for this navigation magic for the VFR pilot; you could, for example, put a waypoint at the southeast corner of the Boone MOA (Figure 3–6), perhaps at the Ames, Iowa, airport, and fly with confidence that you won't be mixing it up with the military fliers doing their thing in the Military Operations Area. Or, put a waypoint at the Des Moines Airport and give the controller a positive position report when you're ten miles out, or whatever. Haven't you often been asked to report "on a three-mile final" at a strange airport? RNAV lets you comply with that sort of request with considerable accuracy. As a matter of fact, when the tower person asks "how far out are you?" it's fun to respond with something like "six point three miles."

Suppose you're flying from St. Joseph to Mason City (Figure 3–6) in something other than ideal weather conditions, and intend to land at Des Moines if things really get sticky. You can look up the waypoint address for the Des Moines airport, set it up in the RNAV memory, and when you decide not to continue, DSM is your instant alternate . . . direction and distance to the airport available at the touch of a button.

The earlier statement that the RNAV steering display (CDI or HSI) is just like a normal VOR was a little bit over-simplified. Most RNAVs are designed with constant-course width, which means that whenever the needle is off center, the airplane is a certain *distance* off course, not a certain number of degrees, as in VOR operations. In most RNAV installations, full-scale deflection of the CDI represents five nautical miles off course in the enroute navigation mode, and 1.25 miles off course when the set is switched to the approach mode (these numbers may vary among manufacturers; be sure to check the specifications before depending on this feature). So you can place your airplane in a position that is x miles from the track you've drawn on the chart, and by keeping the CDI displaced that amount, you can indeed parallel that track.

Besides the convenience, RNAV can save at least some time and fuel by allowing you to fly more consistently in straight lines, which, it's believed, is still the shortest distance between two points. The pilot who flies the most will benefit the most; some devotees who keep good records claim five to seven percent savings in flying time because of RNAV.

HOW MUCH LONGER, DADDY?

Distance-measuring equipment (DME) is finding its way onto the instrument panels of an increasing number of light planes, and if you can read numbers, you can interpret DME. Tuned to a VORTAC frequency, it tells you simply and directly how many miles (nautical, of course) you happen to be from that station. Spend a few more bucks, and you can get a set that will also indicate your groundspeed in knots and the time to the station—time is "nice to know," but an accurate, up-to-date groundspeed is a real help to good navigation. With DME, there's no need to tune a second VOR to get a cross-check, because you can obtain a fix from one station—if you know what radial you're on, the DME provides the distance and there you are—x miles from the so-and-so VORTAC, on the so-and-so radial. This is a much better method of navigation than using two VOR radials; should you be blessed with two VOR receivers *and* DME, it's all the more reason to consider the second radio as strictly a backup. Don't even bother to turn it on unless it's really needed.

Did you know that you can develop a sort of "poor man's RNAV" (area navigation) with the VOR/DME combination you have? Suppose you are planning a trip from *A* to *B;* following the course that goes directly from VOR to VOR would involve a lot of zigzagging, so why not proceed in a straight line? Notice that the course direct from *A* to *B* passes across several cardinal radials of three VOR stations —note these as checkpoints, and make small corrections as you go. For example, when the left-right needle indicates that you are crossing the 180 radial of VOR No. 1, you should be twelve miles away on the DME—if you're a little inside the twelve-mile mark, correct a few degrees to the left. A bit later, you should be over the twenty-two-mile DME fix on the 360 radial of station No. 2, and so on. It's not as accurate

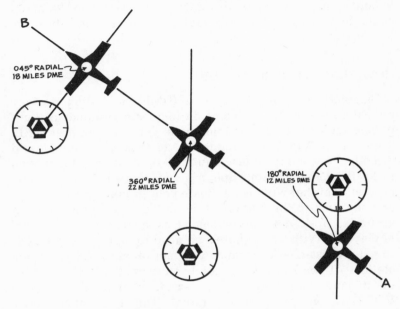

Figure 3–7. Poor man's RNAV. The VOR/DME checkpoints can help straighten a course and save time.

as real RNAV, but it's a heck of a lot less expensive—an instance of getting some additional use out of your equipment by knowing more about it.

That's VOR for VFR—in a nutshell to be sure, but maybe enough principle and understanding so that you can supply the practice. Experiment with the VOR and find out what its limitations are; how far away can you expect adequate reception at the altitudes you normally fly (the higher you climb, the more stations you'll have to work with and the longer you can hang on to the signal of any given station); how accurate is your receiver? There's no legal requirement for VOR accuracy in VFR operations, but why fly around with a bum set? Look into it next time you have access to an official checkpoint and maybe you'll find out why that airport in the boondocks didn't show up under you when the needles crossed.

Modern Airport Manners

PERHAPS THE FIRST AVIATION PEOPLE who moved away from town to avoid noise problems with their neighbors were the Wright brothers. The summer following their successful flight at Kitty Hawk, North Carolina, they carried on flight-training operations in a rented pasture east of Dayton, Ohio, where the clatter of their four-cylinder engine wouldn't bother anyone.

In the years that followed, general-aviation aircraft grew into the need for long, unobstructed areas from which to take off and land, and such facilities were nearly always located comfortably distant from centers of population. Aircraft-noise reduction, even at the smallest airports, didn't become a problem until the inevitable happened: The airports stayed put, but the communities, surging in population, began to spread toward the airfields that had for years enjoyed their remote locations "out in the boondocks."

All of which means that we are operating our aircraft over the heads of more and more people all the time. We've not had to consider whatever discomfort might be visited upon our neighbors, and have largely been able to take off and land using whatever procedures were felt to be proper in the interests of safety and performance.

But now the rules of the game have changed. In addition to the widespread interest in overall noise reduction in our daily lives, the aviation community must be particularly responsible to those who live and work in the immediate environs of our airport facilities. A few suggestions regarding possible noise-reduction procedures seems very much in order.

The problem with which general-aviation pilots can be most helpful is a rather localized one . . . light aircraft taking off and approaching to land over residential areas. While the heavy jets are concerned with noise footprints for several miles after takeoff and before landing, the noise produced by light propeller-driven aircraft is generally offensive only to the folks living in very close proximity to airports.

To help understand the problems, you should be aware that (1) the level of noise (no matter what its source) decreases rapidly with distance, (2) for propeller-driven aircraft, the unwanted noise is generated primarily by the propeller itself, and (3) the amount of prop noise and the degree to which it annoys people on the ground is directly related to the *speed* of that propeller. To combine these principles into a ridiculous generality, you might conclude that all of our problems would be solved by flying at high altitudes until directly over the airport, then shutting down the engine and gliding noiselessly to a landing.

That's hardly practical or safe, and of course completely sidesteps the most troublesome area of all—how to get our airplanes into the air without using high power settings and the high propeller speeds that always result.

Let's consider the problem areas one at a time. First, during the approach-and-landing phase of a flight, we can borrow a page from the large-aircraft operators' techniques by remaining as far above the ground for as long as practical on the approach. Once such a delayed descent is begun, you will find that it requires considerably less power, therefore, slower propeller speed and less noise. Liberal use of flaps and slow descent speeds will reduce noise levels even more. It's the pilots boring in over the rooftops at 200 feet with full flaps and full power (long time exposure at low altitude) that generate most of the complaints.

Folks flying behind constant-speed propellers can utilize the same general approach techniques, but they can go one step farther in making sure that the noise footprint is as light and as small as possible by holding up that final, high-RPM prop adjustment until the last minute. Wait until the aircraft has slowed to the point where the propeller control can be moved to high RPM with no change in actual prop speed. The last two items you should accomplish just before landing—perhaps at 200 feet or so—are a recheck of the landing gear, and prop levers full forward.

At takeoff, most light aircraft require every horse that's built into the engine for safety and acceptable performance; there's just not enough reserve power to allow reduced-thrust takeoffs (larger aircraft, particularly turbojets, use such a technique when they are lightly loaded because they have an ample reserve of power). But once airborne, even the lightest of aircraft can effect certain climb procedures that will move the aircraft—and its noise—farther away from airport neighbors and in a shorter period of time. Climbing at the best rate-of-climb airspeed (or even best *angle*-of-climb for a few hundred feet) will go a long way toward easing the pain on those sensitive residential ears below. With a controllable-pitch propeller, it makes good sense to reduce to a climb power setting, and, therefore, a lower RPM, just as soon as it's safe after liftoff.

If it's practical and safe, it makes sense to continue the takeoff climb straight ahead until 1000 feet or more; every degree of bank robs an aircraft of some of its climb performance, and remember—we are anxious to get the noise away from the ground as soon as possible.

There are several more considerations that will help reduce the overall noise level around a general aviation airport. For openers, the hours between 11:00 P.M. and 7:00 A.M. are considered very noise sensitive; most people just don't cotton to the sound of airplanes during those hours. Whenever possible, pilots should exercise consideration for others and plan their flights during more normal times of day.

Long pretakeoff runups are tough on engines *and* ears, both those inside the cockpit and in the residential areas adjacent to the airport. Particularly offensive here are high power settings for an extended period of time; with a bit of practice a pilot can shorten the time required for mag checks and propeller exercises, and therefore cut down the amount of noise produced.

Intersection takeoffs, except on the longest of runways, may be a practical and efficient technique that we'll have to give up for the sake of noise reduction. While an intersection takeoff eases the pain somewhat for the folks who live close to the approach end of the runway, it inevitably produces flight at a lower altitude and a higher power setting over the heads of the poor creatures who live off the *other* end.

These suggestions can be the framework around which you can develop personal and local noise-reduction procedures and techniques. If there are residential areas near your airport that are particularly sensitive to aircraft noise, identify them and avoid them whenever possible . . . or use noise-reduction procedures if overflight can't be helped. One of our responsibilities as pilots is a responsibility to the communities over which we fly.

We must, of course, be concerned about the safety of anything we do with an airplane; but with imagination, innovation, a lot of common sense and good judgment, we can help reduce the aircraft-noise problem and stay well within the limits of safe flight operations.

Power-off Approaches

At the end of the downwind leg, the objective is to get the airplane on the ground, and the most expeditious way to do that is remove the power—completely. Besides keeping the pattern tucked in tight, the power-off approach is much quieter, takes less time and, perhaps most important, makes you a better pilot. There's a lot more skill involved in powerless approaches and landings, because a great deal of judgment must be exercised way back there on downwind.

Build yourself a base pattern; from an exact altitude and airspeed on downwind, pick a reference that will be universal, and the best one is the runway numbers. Every runway has them, and they make great targets for the remainder of the approach. When the numbers slide under the wingtip or past the strut, reduce power smoothly and completely, extend the first increment of flaps (one notch, one handle pull, ten degrees or whatever it is on your airplane) and don't lose a foot of altitude until airspeed has settled on the number you intend to use for the rest of the approach.

By this time, you will have flown somewhat past the end of the runway, and here's where the judgment comes in—since this first one is on the house, count to five and turn base. Keep going (a good place for the second notch of flaps) until you must turn in order to line up with the runway, and as soon as you're on final, get the rest of the flaps out and see what happens. Airspeed is paramount, so hold it religiously, and watch the bug on the windshield (see Chapter 20)—it will tell you whether you'll be long or short.

If your first experiment puts you right on the numbers, run to the nearest horse track and bet your life savings—this is your lucky day. More than likely you'll wind up long or short, in which case you can adjust your power-reduction point on the next approach. Keep everything else just the same as it was—airspeed, altitude, flap-extension places—the only change will be where you shut off the power. Once you find the "base pattern," go round and round until you burn it into your mind. It will work anywhere, easily adjustable for wind and pattern altitude. If you'd like to really tighten things up (and why not?), you can try extending full flaps right after the power reduction. *Caution*—this will generate a rather steep final approach, and you may have to readjust your perceptions for the different round-out technique that is required.

A pilot who really understands power-off approaches will never find himself in a bind should his engine quit anywhere in the pattern. By virtue of his power-off proficiency, he will also be more likely to walk away from an engine failure outside the airport environs than his counterpart who knows nothing but a powered approach.

5

Leaning Techniques

WANDER OUT TO WATCH the air show some sunny summer weekend, the air show with the World War I fighters chasing around the sky in mock combat. Some of them may be genuine, equipped with the rotary engines popular back then, and you'll notice that power management is an all-or-nothing affair; no throttle, only an interrupter button on the stick which makes and breaks the ignition circuit ... bra-a-a-p, bra-a-a-a-p, bra-a-a-p.

These old engines represented the essence of simplicity in power management; they operated at either one or the other of their two power settings—on or off. So when you're counting your aviation blessings, don't fail to include that piece of motor magic known as the throttle, which provides an infinite number of power settings, and lets you select the amount of thrust you need to get a particular flying task accomplished. But that's only part of the engine-operation story, because the throttle is merely the air valve; that vast range of power settings requires an equally vast range of mixture settings, which means that in order to operate any piston-type aircraft engine properly, you need to understand the fuel-metering system and be able to use good leaning techniques.

IDEAL VERSUS REAL WORLD

The job of the carburetion system in an aircraft engine (regardless of the type—normally aspirated, fuel injected, or supercharged) is to mix fuel vapor and air and deliver it to the cylinders so that it can be burned, releasing the energy contained in the fuel. In order for that mixture to burn and provide power, the proportions of fuel and air must be controlled. Mixtures as weak (lean) as one pound of fuel in twenty-five pounds of air, or as strong (rich) as one pound of fuel in only five pounds of air will support combustion. However, there's precious little power developed in these extreme situations because of the deficiency of fuel in the first case, and the deficiency of air in the second.

At some point in the mixture-adjustment process, an ideal condition will occur . . . ideal, that is, in terms of getting maximum heat release from each pound of fuel-air mixture. This happens at a ratio of about one to fifteen, when each pound of fuel is mixed with fifteen pounds of air; unfortunately, there's not enough energy in that amount of fuel to provide the power to compress the fuel-air mixture in the *other* cylinders, nor to overcome the friction losses within the engine. (This is known as a *stoichiometric* mixture, a ten-dollar description that is derived from Greek and concerns the science of molecular weights. To the depth of understanding we're concerned about here, stoichiometric means that all of the energy in the fuel is being released because the amount of oxygen present in the air portion of the charge is exactly right for complete combustion of the mixture. "Ideal" is an unlikely situation in light of induction-system design and operating limitations.) When all the variables are taken into account, a typical aircraft engine will produce its maximum power when the mixture strength is adjusted so that each pound of fuel is mixed with twelve to fourteen pounds of air, or slightly richer than the chemically correct—stoichiometric—setting.

At very high power settings—for example, during takeoff—when engine temperatures are elevated and the cooling process (airflow over and around the engine) is at a minimum because of the low airspeed, some additional fuel must be introduced to aid in dissipating all that heat. If disregarded, this situation can digress to detonation (*exploding* of the fuel-air charge instead of rapid burning), and probable engine damage, and so all aircraft engines are factory adjusted to a super-rich condition when the mixture control is at RICH and the throttle is opened. A mixture strength of approximately one pound of fuel for each ten pounds of air is normal for full-power operations.

For any given power setting, therefore, you'll find that some sort of mixture-strength adjustment is necessary to extract as much power as possible from the fuel being burned (the so-called best-power condition). In addition to achieving maximum power, there are times when it's wise to lean the mixture a bit more, give up some airspeed and gain some range—this condition is known as the best-economy mixture strength. In any event, a cockpit mixture control (and the knowledge to use it properly) is an absolute necessity if you are to enjoy the benefits of flying with a "properly fed" engine, which benefits include cleaner spark-plugs, better general engine condition, longer range, and improved overall economy.

The operational environment of the airplane—i.e., from sea level to very high altitudes—introduces yet another need for precise adjustment of fuel flow. You wouldn't need a mixture control in the cockpit if you always flew at sea level (some of the older trainers with little four-bangers up front had no provision for a mixture knob, because they were never expected to be flown very high), or if the density of the atmosphere always remained the same. Be that as it may, the physical properties of the atmosphere include a rather constant decrease in air pressure and density with altitude, and since fuel flow remains essentially constant, the fuel-air mixture gets richer as the aircraft climbs. Carried to the extreme, it's conceivable that the mixture would eventually get so rich—too much fuel—that it would no longer support combustion, and the engine would quit altogether. Long before *that* happened, the engine would let you know that all is not well by coughing and spitting and producing progressively less power as you climb. (Your automobile engine has similar characteristics, but it's not a problem because you seldom drive at remarkably different altitudes; motor across the Rockies or up into the High Sierra, however, and you'll notice a significant loss of power and performance. If you're going to *stay* up there, get the carburetor adjusted for the higher altitude.)

When the aircraft powerplant is not supercharged, the *only* way to deal with the altitude problem is to reduce fuel flow with the mixture control so that the desired fuel-air ratio is maintained. And before getting involved in the details of *how* to lean, one of aviation's "old wives' tales" needs to be put to rest, namely, *when* to lean. Our business is plagued with a number of restrictions that persist because "that's the way it's always been"—and one of these which may be costing you money is the "never-lean-below 5000-feet" rule. A lot of pilots have been so impressed with the possibility of engine damage due to leaning, or possibly so intimidated by the engine roughness that almost always shows up momentarily while leaning is being accomplished, that they've taken the easy way out and decided not to lean at all . . . ever. Now, the mixture control is not a snake that's going to bite if you touch it in flight. (Why do all the manufacturers paint it *red,* as if it were a dangerous thing?) It's just another engine control, put there so that you can adjust the fuel-air ratio as required for different power settings and different conditions of flight. The pilot who is spooked by this outdated "rule" and flies at full rich all the time below 5000 feet will use a *lot* more gas, force the engine to run very inefficiently on something other than the best mixture, and will dirty up the belly of his airplane with all that sooty exhaust.

The intent of the 5000-foot mixture no-no has been eroded over the years. It was originally meant to keep pilots from burning up engines when more than 75 percent of the horses were at work, the power setting above which extra fuel is required for adequate internal cooling. Even at full throttle, most small-aircraft engines can no longer develop 75 percent power above 5000 feet because of the reduction in ambient air pressure (except for the turbos, of course, and we'll discuss that special situation elsewhere). Therefore, *whenever the power setting is less than 75 percent, good operating practice demands that the mixture control be adjusted for the best fuel-air ratio, even though your flight altitude may be considerably less than 5000 feet.*

Right away, you should be suspicious of a procedure that seems to solve problems at no cost. And your suspicion would be well founded, because a reduction in the amount of fuel being delivered to the engine *must* eventually reduce the amount of power being produced. You can safely conclude that no unsupercharged aircraft engine can produce the number of horsepower for which it's rated in any atmospheric condition other than that which exists at sea level on a standard day. Whether the reduction in power output is due to a too-rich mixture caused by lowered air pressure, or the reduction of available energy when the mixture is leaned by the pilot, there's a price to be paid . . . and that price is extracted in overall performance (see Chapter 18, "Aircraft Performance").

MIXTURE-ADJUSTMENT PRINCIPLES

Once established in a cruise configuration, the method of moving the mixture control toward LEAN until the engine runs rough, then easing the knob or lever forward a bit until the roughness disappears is the least complicated technique of adjusting the fuel-air ratio. And it's just as good as gold when you're working with a small, uncomplicated engine. You'll never damage such an engine (low horsepower, normal carburetion system, no fuel injection, no supercharging) by leaning to a point just short of roughness, but there are some considerations which, if understood, may help you to get even better performance from the airplane.

In this simple powerplant, the fuel-air mixture is distributed to the cylinders through the intake manifold, an arrangement of pipes which must of necessity bend and turn to fit into the confines of the engine compartment. The system must be designed to deliver a mixture rich enough to not only support full power when the throttle is opened, and provide the internal cooling mentioned earlier, but enough fuel must be added to insure that the cylinders downstream from the carburetor are fed a diet they can live with in consideration of the "plumbing" losses along the way. So when you level off at cruise with the mixture knob still snuggled up tight against the instrument panel, the engine is swallowing considerably more gasoline than it needs for proper combustion.

Just as soon as you make the first move with the mixture control toward LEAN, things start to improve. No longer at full power, the engine doesn't need extra fuel for cooling (the increased airspeed at cruise is picking up some of that load as well), and because of the reduction in ambient air pressure, the optimum fuel-air ratio can only be achieved by cutting down on the amount of gasoline being ingested.

At some point in the leaning process, the mixture arriving at that cylinder which is farthest from the carburetor or which suffers most from bends in the intake manifold (in some engines, it's possibly more than one cylinder) will reach ideal strength—that cylinder is now producing its maximum power—and any further leaning will cause it to misfire. Enter engine roughness. With no fuel-flow instrumentation, you've done as good a job as is possible when the mixture is leaned to the point just prior to the onset of rough-running; and the only way to determine this point is to *find* the roughness, then eliminate it by enriching the mixture. Crude, simple, but effective.

On the other hand, the pilot who wants to go one step further with the leaning process (I hope that's at least *one* of the reasons you bought this book!) has some additional tools to work with, namely, the manifestations of power output when that elusive point of optimum fuel-air ratio is reached. These tools are the tachometer for an airplane with fixed-pitch propeller, and the airspeed indicator for an airplane with a constant-speed prop. Once the mixture is leaned to the point of maximum RPM and/or airspeed increase, you have a happy choice: Leave everything as is and enjoy the benefits of higher speed; or throttle back ever so slightly to the engine speed or airspeed you expected without this fine-tuning of the mixture, and burn less fuel. Either way, it's a bonus.

Suppose the mixture that produces a higher airspeed or RPM *also* produces a rough-running engine? This unhappy coincidence is no doubt best resolved by enriching the mixture just enough to eliminate the shakes; a reciprocating engine has enough built-in vibrations trying to shake the accessories loose (alternators, pumps, wiring, and the like) without your adding more.

There's one more fuel-adjustment principle that, on a hot day, may apply to even the smallest of aircraft engines. As the amount of gasoline in the mixture is gradually reduced, and, therefore, is no longer available to carry away some of the heat of combustion, internal engine temperature will rise. Now, the greater cooling burden is borne by airflow around the engine as well as the air being exhausted from the engine, and if the outside air temperature is high enough, engine temperature indicators will start moving toward red-lines . . . your concerns here must be to prevent abnormally high cylinder-head and oil temperatures. (Bear in mind that it generally takes a *really* hot day and prolonged high-power settings to set up this vicious circle in a small engine, but it *can* happen.)

You've several options: Reduce power, enrich the mixture, increase airspeed by reducing pitch attitude, or some combination of the three. The larger the engine, the greater this problem becomes. (Engine overheating may turn into a critical limiting factor when you're flying a heavy airplane in mountainous terrain on a hot day. Unlike the flatlands, where you can drop the pitch attitude a few degrees, pick up several knots for more airflow, and still not be concerned about running into the real estate, mountain-country flying (especially IFR) sometimes demands a rate of climb which can't be obtained without overheating the engine. Depending on the situation, you may have to choose another route, circle while climbing at the required higher airspeed/lower rate of climb, or at the extreme, delay your departure until the air cools enough to support the operation. Inconvenient, but it beats the hell out of trying to move a mountain!

ADIOS, CARBURETOR

When fuel-injection systems were introduced to the light-aircraft fleet, a couple of good things happened with regard to the mixture-control problem: First, each cylinder receives a precise charge of fuel which is injected under pressure just upstream of the intake valve—no carburetor involved—and the process becomes much more efficient and exacting; second, since fuel flow is now measured much more ac-curately, it's possible to install fuel-flow indicators on the instrument panel, providing pilots with good information about the amount of gasoline actually being used by the engine. If the system is working properly, the pilot of a fuel-injected airplane can refer to a power chart to find the amount of fuel (in terms of pounds or gallons per hour) re-quired to produce a certain percentage of power, and leaning can then be accomplished by carefully adjusting fuel flow to the corresponding figure.

This method is seldom used by itself, since many of these fuel-injected engines are also equipped with EGT gauges (that's coming up next), but nevertheless it's a step upwards in the leaning process. When using fuel flow as the primary source of mixture information, you *must* refer to a power chart of some sort, and the outside air temperature *must* be taken into account. In most cases, the manifold pressure provided on the power chart for a particular power setting is the manifold pressure to be used when the temperature is *standard*. And there will always be a note to the effect that you must adjust the throttle setting slightly when air tem-perature is at some other value; a reduction when the air is colder than standard (more dense), and an increase when it's warmer (less dense). Such a change in throttle position, of course, affects the amount of fuel being injected, and fuel flow will also need to be readjusted to obtain the best mixture for that power setting.

HOTTER IS BETTER . . . UP TO A POINT

We have seen how leaning the fuel-air mixture results in more power being produced by a reciprocating engine, and how that extra power was manifested in higher RPM or airspeed, or both. Some of the big radial-engined aircraft that proliferated before jets stole their thunder had systems that actually measured the power output; as power increased, the additional twisting movement (torque) applied to the propeller shaft was translated into a reading on a very sensitive oil-pressure gauge known as TOP, or torque oil pressure. Using this instrumentation, pilots and flight engineers could set throttles and prop controls for a particular power, then lean the mixture until the TOP gauge showed its highest reading (as mixture strength got so lean that power began to drop off, the TOP would show a reduction). This system provided a direct reading of power applied, and, therefore, the ability to arrive at desired power settings very precisely. For the purposes of this discussion, the TOP gauge permitted accurate and dependable mixture settings for very complex engines.

Torque oil-pressure technology never made it into the ranks of low-powered engines, for reasons that are not at all important—although they probably revolve around dollars and weight and complexity. But there is a way to take the measure of power output in our small engines—at least indirectly— and it has to do with *heat;* more specifically, it concerns the temperature of the exhaust gases flowing out of the engine.

Back up a moment to our description of the stoichiometric mixture, that condition in which there is exactly enough air in the mixture to cause the complete combustion of all of the fuel, thereby releasing all of its heat energy . . . an ideal situation that doesn't work in practice because of friction losses and the additional power required for compression in the other cylinders. The importance of optimum mixture strength lies not at the point of perfection, but on either side; at least, from a temperature standpoint.

Consider the situation when the mixture is too *rich,* when there's more fuel coming into the engine than can be burned; some of the unburned particles of fuel are exhausted, taking heat with them, and resulting in a cooler exhaust. On the other hand, if the mixture is leaned to the point where all of the fuel is burned and there's still some air left over, the exhaust temperature will once again be cooler than it would be in a stoichiometric situation . . . now, there's excess *air* available for cooling.

Either way, it's obvious that if exhaust temperature can be measured and displayed on a gauge in the cockpit, it would be possible to watch the temperature rise, reach a peak, then begin to fall as the mixture is leaned from the full-rich condition. The fellow who figured out such a system and patented it is Al Hundere, chairman of the board of Alcor Incorporated, the San Antonio firm that manufactures such a device. The full-blown name of the process is "inflight combustion analysis," but for now, let's go with EGT, for Exhaust Gas Temperature.

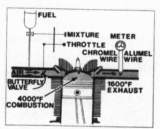

Figure 5–1. A typical EGT system installation.

The heart of the EGT system is a thermocouple, a probe that generates an electric current when heated. Mounted in the exhaust line not far from the exhaust valve (Figure 5–1), it registers temperatures almost instantaneously on a gauge in the cockpit. The thermocouple is completely self-powered, and is totally independent of the airplane's electrical system; in other words, it always works.

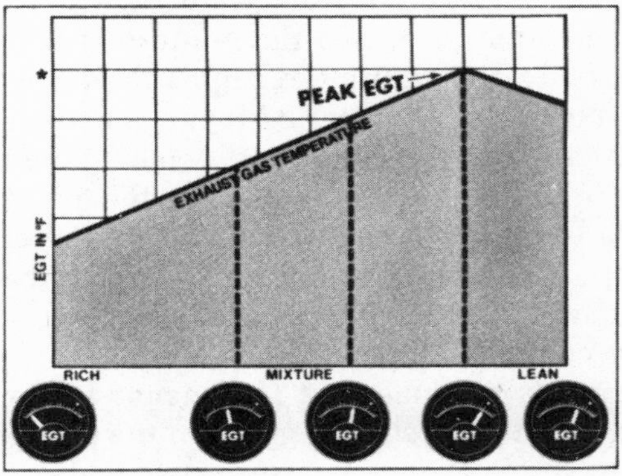

Figure 5–2. Mixture strength vs. EGT.

Figure 5–2 illustrates the relationship between mixture strength and EGT. Starting from the left (FULL RICH), the mixture is leaned, and EGT increases because the excess fuel and its cooling capability is gradually being removed. At some point, *all* of the excess fuel will have been leaned out of the fuel-air charge, and EGT will "peak." If the mixture is leaned further, the exhaust gases will grow cooler because of the excess air, and, of course, the engine will be producing less power. The condition that exists prior to reaching the peak temperature is known as operating "on the rich side of peak," and when the leaning process is continued past peak EGT, it's called the "lean side." Most engines begin to complain when you get more than a very little past peak EGT; this is "lean misfire," it causes the engine to run rough, and it's what you are looking for when leaning a small engine without an EGT gauge.

Although the EGT meter is a very delicate and responsive instrument, there is a slight lag between sensing the temperature of the exhaust gases and displaying it on the cockpit gauge. Patience, therefore, becomes the byword for successful use of an EGT system. You must follow the manufacturers' recommendations for mixture setting during climb, and when you level off in cruising flight, don't be in a big hurry to back off the mixture control right away. A good rule of thumb is to allow five minutes at cruise power for engine temperatures and pressures to stabilize. You'll get much better results by following this procedure.

Okay, five minutes have gone by, it's time to lean. Move the mixture control toward LEAN ver-r-r-r-y slowly, giving the system plenty of time to accommodate the changing temperature (that's too fast, slow it down!). If you'll *really* take it easy, the engine will probably never reach the rough-running stage. You'll notice the subtle changes in engine sounds, a decrease in RPM if yours is a fixed-pitch propeller, and—after you've used the system for a while—a definite "feel" for the peak. The idiosyncrasies of various engines produce flat peaks in some (the EGT rises as though it were connected to the mixture control, then stays put for some time while you continue leaning), sharp peaks in others; you'll get to know what to expect from your engine in short order.

Right about here, it's necessary to consider a key point in this method of mixture control: *It is hazardous to your engine's health to lean beyond peak EGT at power settings above 65 percent.* The problem lies in the inability of the exhaust valves to handle the heat produced by higher power settings. Check the *Pilot's Operating Handbook* for your airplane, or the operator's manual for your engine, and you'll find that when operating at power settings higher than 65 percent, there is a specific limitation imposed . . . something like a requirement to operate at an EGT 50 or 75 or 100 degrees on the *rich* side of peak, just to keep the exhaust valves from burning, or perhaps to prevent super-heating inside the cylinders and the resultant detonation. Those are very definite hazards to the health of an airplane engine.

So, the balance of this discussion will be limited to power settings of 65 percent or less, when it's safe and proper and rather economical to lean to and operate at peak EGT. As was pointed out earlier in regard to the simplest of leaning methods, there is a noticeable increase in performance (in this case, cruise airspeed) when the mixture strength is leaned to the point of near-total combustion, or peak EGT. But because some of the heat energy in the fuel must be used by the engine to provide the power for compression and driving accessories and to overcome friction losses, there must be a mixture strength that provides excess fuel for cooling, accounts for internal losses, *and* moves the airplane at maximum airspeed for that power setting. Keeping in mind that at peak EGT you will be deriving the best *economy* from the powerplant, that slightly richer point on the mixture-strength scale where maximum airspeed occurs is known as the best *power* setting.

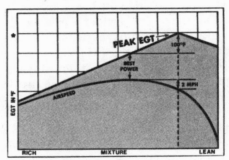

Figure 5–3.   Effect of mixture strength on true airspeed.

Check Figure 5–3, in which an airspeed curve is superimposed on the EGT graph; it's apparent that airspeed rises slowly as the mixture is leaned from full *rich* toward peak EGT, and that it drops off rather rapidly after that. The greatest spread between the two conditions occurs at approximately 100 degrees on the rich side of peak; and for most small engines, this is the best-power-mixture setting. Your *Pilot's Operating Handbook* will more than likely show cruise performance (range, airspeed, endurance figures) in terms of one or both of these conditions. The phrase "recommended mixture setting" (or words to that effect) is usually defined as peak EGT and therefore "best economy," and there will often be another set of performance figures based on the best-power setting. It's not much of an airspeed increase—only two mph in the example—but if speed is more important and therefore more valuable to you, fly at best power. It's a nice choice to have.

Speaking of economy, Alcor ran some tests on a typical light airplane with an 0–470 engine at 65 percent power, at 10,000 feet MSL with the mixture leaned to peak EGT, and assuming a fuel cost of two dollars per gallon. Figure 5–4 tells the story.

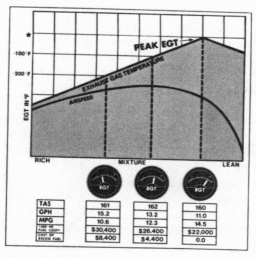

Figure 5–4.   Fuel savings possible with an EGT system.

There's nothing automatic about setting the EGT (at least, not yet!), and certain situations require that the pilot readjust the mixture control once the peak is discovered. The most obvious change is a change in power setting, and the most *dangerous* situation is the one in which power is *increased*. When operating at peak EGT (or any properly leaned condition, for that matter), it is absolutely imperative that the mixture be enriched before additional power is applied; otherwise, you are running the near-certain risk of causing detonation in the engine, or burning the exhaust valves . . . neither of which is calculated to extend the life of the engine.

A reduction of power, as in an enroute descent, doesn't necessarily call for a change in mixture strength, since pulling back on the power reduces both the internal temperature and the exhaust-gas temperature. If anything, the mixture should probably be leaned *further* for a descent at reduced power.

There are five limitations to be applied to the use of an EGT gauge for mixture control in light-aircraft engines:

1. Always move the mixture control *very slowly* when searching for the peak (lean one engine at a time on twin-engine aircraft) to allow for the slight, but important, lag in the indicator. Rapid movement of the mixture control will produce false peaks.

2. Some engines (most turbocharged ones) have an absolute EGT limit marked as a red line on the temperature gauge. This is to protect the exhaust system from excessive heat, and the limit *must* be observed. If the needle moves into the red on the way to the peak, *don't go any farther.*

3. Never lean the mixture to peak EGT at power settings above 65 percent. Consult the *Pilot's Operating Handbook* for the procedure to be followed at higher power settings.

4. Peak EGT is a *relative* setting; changes in outside air temperature, power setting, type of fuel, engine condition, etc., can result in today's peak being different than yesterday's, or last week's, or maybe even the peak you obtained on the last flight.

5. The ultimate leaning limit for *any* engine is defined by cylinder-head temperature; if internal temperatures begin to push the CHT needle into the red, you must reduce engine heat to prevent possible detonation or failure of the engine structure, and the most effective way to cool things down in a hurry is by adding more fuel to carry away heat. If peak EGT results in too-high cylinder-head temperatures, you'll have to accept the penalty of a slightly over-rich mixture until the problem is solved.

An EGT system goes a long way toward optimizing mixture control, but there's a serious shortcoming: With just one exhaust-temperature probe (the simplest of the systems available today), it's anybody's guess as to which of the cylinders is in fact the leanest, and that when the probe is inserted in a particular exhaust stack, the resultant indication of EGT will reflect the true condition. As a matter of fact, tests prove that the actual strength of the fuel-air charge reaching individual cylinders varies considerably from engine to engine, at different altitudes, and at different throttle settings.

There's relief from this problem, though; a probe can be mounted in *each* exhaust stack, and with a selector switch on the panel, you can read the EGT for *all* cylinders, determine which is the leanest, and adjust the mixture strength accordingly. Such a system also enables a certain amount of engine diagnosis, because a change in the combustion pattern due to faulty valves, spark plugs, or carburetion will alter the EGT readings.

Going one step further, a system that senses both EGT and cylinder-head temperature for each cylinder provides a unique method of analyzing the combustion process in considerable detail. The merit of such a trouble-shooting tool should be obvious.

The march of technology will no doubt bring more exacting and comprehensive methods of mixture adjustment, but for now, the use of an EGT system provides a better way of doing business for light-plane pilots.

LEANING FOR THE DESCENT

Here's another of aviation's "old wives' tales." Probably sprung from the equally fallacious "rule" that says you must never lean the mixture when flying below 5000 feet, this one claims that whenever a descent is commenced, the mixture control must be moved to the FULL RICH position.

In a word, baloney.

Consider an engine properly leaned for cruise at 65 percent

power; there's enough fuel to pull the airplane through the sky at that power setting, plus enough fuel to provide internal cooling and keep exhaust-valve temperatures within limits. When power is reduced, engine temperatures decrease, thereby decreasing the need for both combustion and cooling. It's quite possible that the mixture-control position set for cruise will be adequate for the new, lower, descent-power setting. No matter, for the pilot of a simple-engined airplane, one which is leaned by the "rough-engine" method, can continue to monitor his powerplant for the "shakes" during descent: a process that would tell him that it's time to readjust the mixture control. At power settings less than 65 percent, there will be no damage done even if the mixture gets so lean that it proceeds all by itself to the lean side of peak; of course, you'll know it when the engine begins to misfire. This is nothing more than a reversal of the process you went through when you leaned at cruise. Engine rough? Squeeze the mixture a bit toward RICH until the roughness disappears, and wait for the misfire to show up again.

Don't forget that air pressure builds as altitude decreases, and if you don't adjust the *throttle* now and then to keep manifold pressure or RPM at a constant descent-power setting, the engine will gradually produce more power, and mixture strength must be adjusted appropriately. Ignoring this practice can get you in trouble, especially with the larger engines, if power should build up to and beyond 65 percent with the mixture strength unchanged . . . remember the super-hot exhaust valves, and the possibility of detonation? Could ruin your entire day.

The key to good mixture management in a descent is recognition of the power setting to be maintained; if you choose to descend at cruise power, fine, but be certain to accomplish the necessary throttle adjustments on the way down, and change the mixture strength as required to keep the EGT on peak (or the proper number of degrees on the rich side, as required by the *Pilot's Operating Handbook*). For those who would rather let down at a lower-than-cruise power setting, the drill is to reduce power, recognize that the cruise mixture setting is adequate for descent power, and watch for the signs (engine roughness, rising EGT) of increasing power due to increased air density at the lower altitudes.

A blind, slavish adherence to a full-rich-for-every-descent philosophy hurts your engine (and your pocketbook!) just as much as never leaning below 5000 feet.

Maybe the FAA should mandate a change in the certification rules that would require all bright-red mixture-control knobs to be repainted green; at least, it might change pilots' perceptions of that engine control from something dangerous to something put there to save you money.

Don't Let Your Life Be Ruled
by a Wind Tee

Here's another of those sacred cows of the aviation business—always, *always* you must take off and land into the
wind. Nothing wrong with that in the training and early-
experience phases of flying, when a new pilot shouldn't turn
his back on anything that will help. But haven't there been
occasions when you dutifully taxied clear to the other end of
the airport because the wind tee (or the Tower) indicated a
light movement of air in the appropriate direction?

Of course, airport discipline (i.e., using the same runway
as everybody else) is the inevitable price of a burgeoning
aviation population; it's asinine to request a downwind takeoff when there are a half-dozen airplanes waiting nose-to-tail
at the other end of the runway. But how about those times
when there's no one in the pattern, and you'd much rather
land, turn off and taxi to the ramp the *short* way, even if
you'd have a bit of tailwind in the process—or the days when
a downwind departure would let you be on your way directly,
straight out, no time-consuming turns? All you need do is ask;
unless your request compromises safety, most Controllers
couldn't care less which way you land or take off.

There are a couple of things to be considered when going
with the wind. Takeoff distance will grow, and height above
obstacles off the far end will shrink because you'll experience
a flatter climbout. On landing, the approach will be less steep,
and groundspeed will be as much greater as the velocity of
the wind. On the ground, you'll notice a slight but occasionally
significant deterioration of control as the airplane slows down
and the wind from behind bites the control surfaces backwards. (The deterioration could be significant on a slippery
runway—bad time to even consider a downwind landing.)

When you go out to see what downwind operations are like,
pick a long runway—there are traps on both ends of any
landing strip, but a short field is worse. Approaching downwind, the increased groundspeed heightens the impression of
closing rapidly on that little bit of runway, and there's a strong
temptation to slow down—that's the stall-spin trap, and its
jaws will slam shut on what may have been, in truth, your
final approach. A downwind takeoff from a short runway has

obvious consequences if you can't gain enough altitude to clear whatever lies in your path; the same trap awaits when you execute a downwind go-around.

Even the avid performance-chart readers will have to sharpen their powers of judgment and common sense in a downwind situation, since few if any light-plane charts calculate tailwind performance. It's another way to get a little more out of your airplane, so when it's safe and sensible, be gone—*with* the wind.

6

Toward Better Communications

What a wonderful thing is the aircraft radio; it expedites traffic, saves lives, broadcasts weather information and lets you call for a cab on a rainy night. . . . It also lets the whole world know when you've made a communicative ass of yourself.

ANONYMOUS

FELLOW BY THE NAME OF James Clerk Maxwell closed the first switch in the development of the radio-telephone by discovering radio waves, Heinrich Hertz devised an apparatus for generating them and Guglielmo Marconi demonstrated a practical application of the radio concept in 1895. One year after the century turned, Marconi astonished the scientific world by sending the single letter S all the way across the Atlantic without benefit of submarine cable.

When aviation came alive in the 1920s, the more affluent flyers had wireless sets in their airplanes, but those early rigs were far too heavy to be practical. Lindbergh, super-conscious about extra weight, left the radio behind in lieu of more gasoline and had to throttle back and holler to a fisherman, "Which way's Ireland?" That was a long, long way from the black boxes we take for granted today. Our modern electronic wonders allow us to communicate across remarkable distances with a quality that wouldn't have been believed just a couple of decades ago. Even the most inexpensive contemporary aircraft radios would boggle a Marconian mind.

Everybody who flies these days becomes a communicator —not by choice, but by regulation. Maybe your world of flight is the first thousand feet of air above a grass strip and you never venture within an electron's throw of a radio facility—even so, you will probably have to show that you can cut the communications mustard on a certification check ride or a biennial flight review, whichever comes first.

If we take the word "communications" at face value (which, saith Webster, is "the imparting or interchange of ideas, opinions, sentiments, etc."), it won't take much listening on the aviation band to come to the conclusion that we've battered the original purpose pretty badly. (And that's only on ATC frequencies—tune your black box to unicom some Sunday afternoon . . . it's worse than the Hopkins Corners party line the day after the preacher ran off with the choir director!) The number of interrupted messages, the "say agains," the unintelligible and unnecessary transmissions make it clear that either some pilots will never make the grade as communicators or they've been poorly taught. Since aircraft radio work is not all that difficult, the heaviest odds are on the latter premise.

But that's not all bad; a problem that exists because of lack of education is easily overcome in a society which holds learning in high esteem. We've *got* to get better at talking—unless we pilots teach ourselves to cut down on needless chatter and time-consuming transmissions, we're going to talk ourselves right out of the sky. It could happen physically (there won't be enough frequencies available for all that talking) or economically (you won't be able to afford the all-new equipment to fit into the system)—even if the forecasts of general-aviation growth are only *halfway* out in left field, there's going to be more vocal traffic than the system can handle.

Interested in keeping general aviation alive and well?—one of the biggest contributions you can make is to become a better communicator.

A PROBLEM WITH TWO PARTS—MAYBE THREE

Whether you're the captain of an airliner or an Ercoupe, all successful radio communications depend on these two qualities: saying exactly what needs to be said, nothing more and nothing less, and saying it so that the person on the receiving end gets the entire message the first time around. We'll assume that you have radios of adequate quality and that those to whom you direct the electrons are similarly equipped: Lindbergh may have done a smashing job of shouting "Which way's Ireland?" (you can't put such a momentous question much simpler than that), but the fellow on the fishing boat may have been hard of hearing or didn't speak English, or both—it's got to be a two-way street. That's the interchange of ideas that defines communications.

"Noise" is many things to many people. Hard rock is noise to the over-thirty music lovers who'd just as soon listen to Wayne King; a jackhammer breaking up the pavement outside is noise to an office worker; the signal distortion that makes your VOR needle jump all over the dial now and then is "noise" to an electronics man. In short, when speaking of the science of communications, anything that interferes with the transfer of a message from transmitter to receiver is noise, and it can enter a communications channel at the transmitter, enroute, or at the receiving end. If the guy who does the talking says the wrong thing (or the right thing improperly), the message doesn't stand a chance. Likewise, comprehension is zero when someone breaks into a message in transit, if the fellow on the receiving end is distracted or doesn't have his equipment set up properly, or any one of a thousand combinations of message and noise . . . if there's more noise than message, forget it.

PART ONE: WHAT TO SAY, WHAT NOT TO SAY

You've taken a giant stride toward the solution of the first part of the problem when you elect to use standard words and phrases in frequently encountered, aviation-wide situations. When a couple of well-chosen words will do the job of a five-minute dissertation, use the well-chosen words and do your bit to unclog the system. This is really the fine art of voice compression.

Stock communications fit stock situations, which means that you can fill your communications shelves with standardized reports, requests and replies, to be taken down and used whenever they'll reduce the noise in your communications. Load your paper airplane with a generous supply of standard jargon, and see how often it can be used on a VFR flight from a large airport to another large airport with all facilities available at both ends and in the middle. To begin with,

EVERY AIRPORT HAS AN ATIS

. . . which broadcasts a continuous stream of information to let you know the weather, winds, runways in use, altimeter setting and whatever else the Controllers feel is applicable to flight operations at the airport. *Every* airport has one?— sure does, whether it goes by that name or not. It could be disguised as Ground Control, where you can listen as someone gets "the numbers" ahead of you, or it could even be unicom. Wherever you obtain the information, make notes and set instruments, and when you're ready to taxi, tell the man (if there's a man to tell) you have "the numbers"; okay, so it's not always Automatic—but it's still Terminal Information Service. With "the numbers," you're almost ready to request taxi clearance, except at Big City Muni, where you must first contend with

CLEARANCE DELIVERY

. . . which is your entree to "poor man's IFR." Stage III terminals (so called because of the level of radar assistance offered to VFR folks) are so busy the Controllers need an electronic handle on flights arriving and departing—it's a function of airport-traffic-area saturation, and you should figure on encountering Stage III more and more in your aerial odysseys. It provides separation from other locally controlled aircraft within the Terminal Radar Service Area (TRSA) but is an exercise in voluntary participation—it's a good deal when there's a lot of traffic, but a time waster when the skies are empty—if you feel you can proceed safely on eyeballs alone, let the Controllers know on your first transmission that you are "non-participating."

But let's participate for the sake of illustration. With the ATIS numbers duly noted, "Big City Clearance, Barnburner 1234A, VFR westbound, with Hotel" (or whatever letter lets him know you listened to ATIS). Stage III departure clearances vary all over the lot, but he'll come back shortly (maybe immediately—be ready) with a heading, an altitude, a frequency for Departure Control and quite likely a transponder code. It's an official clearance, and must be acknowledged, so save more time when you confirm it—for example, "34A, heading three six zero, two thousand five hundred, one two three point eight, three three zero one"—just the numbers; that's all he wants to hear to be sure he gave you the right ones, and that you copied them correctly. When Clearance Delivery rogers your readback (this is a lot like IFR operations, and it's good practice for instrument work), you're ready for the next facility:

GROUND CONTROL

. . . which is interested in four pieces of information: *who* you are, *where* you are, do you have your *clearance* and *what* do you want to do.

Now here's where you can go to extremes in the interest of being proper: "The William B. Hartsfield–Atlanta International Airport Ground Control, this is Barnburner November 1234 Alpha, parked on the first ramp south of the fourth hangar from the left on the west side of the airport. I have listened to the information contained in Automatic Terminal Information Service broadcast Sierra. I have received the necessary clearance out of the Terminal Radar Service Area from The William B. Hartsfield–Atlanta International Airport Clearance Delivery. I will be northbound under Visual Flight Rules, destination Nashville, Tennessee, and I am ready to taxi."

Phew! . . . All the good stuff was in there, along with a lot that wasn't so good. It could have (and should have) been cut down to perhaps: "Ground [what other Ground Controller would you be calling except Atlanta?], Barnburner 34 Alpha [the last three characters in your call sign and the type of airplane will identify you quite nicely] Hangar Four [he knows where things are on the airport], with Sierra and clearance, ready to taxi, VFR."

On the way to the runway in use, you may be held short of another runway; when the Ground Controller asks you to whoa, acknowledge with a simple "34 Alpha," and stop. When he clears you across, there's really no need to talk back, just add a little power and start moving—that's the most positive acknowledgment in the book.

Remain on Ground Control frequency until you're at the runup area, and when everything's checked out and ready to aviate, you're ready to contact

TOWER

. . . the Controller who has been waiting for you to call and who is responsible for fitting your departure into the traffic flow in his sandbox, the airport traffic area. With Stage III and the TRSA, the Local Controller has a special "strip" in front of him with your identification, your destination and your clearance—the only thing he doesn't know about you is: Are you ready to go? So when you call, just say, "Tower [it's still Atlanta; you wouldn't be calling anybody else], Barnburner 34 Alpha, ready on one five." If he comes back with "Hold short," acknowledge simply with "34 Alpha." When he says, "Taxi into position and hold," acknowledge simply with "34 Alpha," and taxi into position and hold. But when he says, "Cleared for takeoff," or "Cleared for *immediate* takeoff," do it!—don't bother with the radio. He'll see the airplane start to roll and can then turn his attention to other things, such as using the communications time you *didn't* use to talk to someone else.

Procedures will vary until you're out of the terminal area,

depending on local policies, the altitude you requested and whatever else bears on efficient control of all the airplanes using the system. If the Local Controller hangs on to you electronically for a while, and asks you to turn right or left, or maintain an altitude, you've already been introduced, so your acknowledgment need be only "34 Alpha." Then do whatever is required.

Sooner or later, you'll be asked to contact

DEPARTURE CONTROL

. . . and likely as not, the frequency won't be mentioned—that was part of your clearance and you should have written it down somewhere. Again a simple "34 Alpha" will acknowledge the request, and when you tune the new frequency and are certain no one else is on the line, hold it; stop and think before you say a word—the Departure Controller is probably vested with the responsibility of controlling only VFR traffic participating in the TRSA. Therefore he too knows who you are and where you're going, so just make him aware of your presence: "Departure, 34 Alpha, one thousand five hundred." Until you spend all those bucks for an altitude-encoding transponder, altitude is the only thing his radar doesn't tell him about you, so confirm it—he feels better when he *knows*. Heading-change requests should elicit just "34 Alpha" followed by the execution of the turn, and if the Controller clears you to another altitude, let him know by saying, "34 Alpha cleared to four thousand five hundred, leaving two thousand five hundred"; straightforward, clear as a bell, and no one has any doubt about what you're going to do.

Once outside the Terminal Radar Service Area, Departure Control's obligation is satisfied, and you'll frequently hear "Barnburner 34 Alpha, nineteen miles northwest of Atlanta, radar service terminated, squawk the appropriate VFR code, frequency change approved, good day." Which means that he's finished helping you avoid other traffic, and that you're free to contact Flight Service, unicom or Center, or turn your radios off if you wish—*do* turn up the right numbers in the transponder and get off the Departure Controller's scope.

If you want to use *all* the ATC facilities you're paying for, request a Center frequency from Departure Control before he gets away. This needn't be a long, drawn-out question—just "34 Alpha, request a Center frequency north-bound." Departure knows why you want it (radar advisories en route) and he also knows the frequency Atlanta Center uses for that purpose, so he'll probably come right back with the number—remember it for the areas you use most frequently, and save yet another transmission on future flights by going directly to that frequency.

THE AIR ROUTE TRAFFIC CONTROL CENTER

. . . is primarily concerned with IFR traffic in its area, so the first call-up should be a brief one—"Atlanta Center, Barnburner 1234 Alpha, VFR." That lets him know you're there, that you're not an instrument flight for which he's responsible, and when he can take time from his other chores, he'll answer. *Now* tell him where you are and what you want: "34 Alpha, twenty northwest of Atlanta, four thousand five hundred, squawking one two zero zero, landing Nashville, radar advisories, please." And if he has time, he'll have you squawk ident (which is where you don't say a word, just press the ident button), let you know you're in radar contact and advise you of other airplanes in the vicinity. Should he ask you to use another frequency for advisories, thank him and go through the same routine again.

From time to time, Center will point out traffic which might present a conflict. If you're doing a good job of scanning, you should see the targets before the Controller calls, and if this is the case, answer immediately "Tally ho" or "In sight"—make it short and sweet. When you don't see the traffic right away, say "No joy" and keep on looking.

The Center Controller may ask you to contact his counterpart on another frequency as you fly into a different sector or perhaps the next Center. In this case, the two Controllers will almost certainly have communicated internally, the next man will know what's going on, so you need say only, "Atlanta Center, 34 Alpha, four thousand five hundred." Nine times out of ten, the response will be "34 Alpha, squawk ident," and that's all—unless you hear otherwise, you are to assume that you are in radar contact. Handoffs like this may continue throughout the flight, but when you're within about thirty miles of your destination, it's

ATIS TIME AGAIN

. . . so crank up the appropriate frequency and begin listening. When ATIS first hit the market, it was almost always broadcast on the localizer frequency; but that's a directional signal, with most of the signal strength beamed along the extended centerline of the runway. There are now many terminals whose ATIS frequencies are up in the communications band, like 125.9, 132.65 and so on—some have two ATIS facilities, one for arrival and one for departure. When it's available, always use the higher frequency for the best reception—you'll be set up for your approach long before you can see the airport.

And here's a trick of the trade that will bring the ATIS broadcast into your loudspeaker long before you can *hear* the airport . . . normally. All contemporary aircraft radios are equipped with squelch controls, with which you can reduce the amount of static (bacon frying) and therefore enjoy a remarkable improvement in sound quality. Squelch controls come in two varieties—adjustable and automatic—but the idea is the same. The squelch feature can actually be used to extend the range of your receivers, if you're willing to put up with some noise long enough to get the information you want.

Try it next time you're in the air; pick out an ATIS broadcast so far away that you can't hear a thing when the proper frequency is tuned, then open up the squelch (or remove it entirely if your radio has the automatic feature—it's labelled TEST) until you can hear the communicator's voice. *Still* can't hear anything? Wait a few minutes and try again; sooner or later you'll be close enough to hear bits and pieces of the broadcast, and it will happen at a distance much greater than that which results from keeping the receiver squelched and waiting for a nice clean voice to come through. Give a little (sound quality), get a lot (distance) . . . and don't be surprised at reception distances of 80, 90, 100 miles, even at altitudes below 10,000 feet. If all that you are able to determine through the static is weather conditions—IFR or VFR—or the runway or approach in use, you've gained important planning information and the time to put it to good use.

If there's no formal ATIS, listen on Tower frequency for a while to pick up the wind and weather, altimeter setting and runway in use. Let the Tower Controller know on the first call that you're aware of traffic flow, and tell him what you intend doing—"Nashville Tower, Barnburner 1234 Alpha, ten south with the numbers, will report left base for three one"—if he would rather you did something else, he'll let you know. Most of the time (if you've analyzed traffic flow properly and have decided on an entry that will fit) you'll hear merely "Barnburner 34 Alpha, roger." When ATIS is available, substitute the alphabetical designator for "with the numbers." A Stage III airport, with the attendant TRSA, will close its ATIS broadcast with instructions for VFR flights to contact

APPROACH CONTROL

. . . on a specified frequency, a discreet one set aside for the control of arrivals and overflights. With no prior notice, make your first call like this: "Downtown Approach, Barnburner 1234 Alpha, eight west with Kilo." As soon as you're in radar contact, the Controller will vector you right up next to the airport. Heading changes and new altitudes should be acknowledged, but only with "34 Alpha" unless you have some doubt about what you thought you heard, or if that heading would put you in a cloud—you're *not* an IFR flight, and it's your responsibility to maintain proper VFR clearance from the white stuff, to say nothing of other airplanes.

Most Approach Controllers will hold your hand until

you're within a few miles of the field, aim you toward the landing runway and ask you to get in touch with

THE CONTROL TOWER

. . . for your sequence in the lineup for landing. Not much for you to say here, because once again the Approach Controller and the Local Controller in the Tower have gotten together, and Tower is expecting you—"Downtown Tower, Barnburner 34 Alpha, four southeast"—he knows everything else he needs to know. Ere long you'll be cleared to land, which should be acknowledged with another "34 Alpha." Since almost all

GROUND CONTROL

. . . facilities are set up on one twenty-one point something, a good sharp Tower man will say, "34 Alpha, Ground point nine clearing," as he observes you safely on the ground and ready to turn off. This is one you don't even need to acknowledge—you've still got your hands full of airplane. When you're past the double yellow lines that separate runway from taxiway, be sure you know where you want to go on the airport, and describe it in the simplest possible terms. "Ground, 34 Alpha to the transient ramp" or "to the terminal" or "Ground, 34 Alpha, directions to the general-aviation ramp, please." Don't be reticent about asking directions at a strange airport; it will save everybody time in the long run, and don't forget to thank the Controller for his help when you get there.

PART TWO: HOW TO SAY WHAT
YOU'RE SUPPOSED TO SAY

If you've never heard of a throat mike, you may wonder why the pilots in those World War II films of air combat always put a hand on their throats whenever they talked on the radio. The ear-splitting air and engine noise inside military aircraft of that vintage never made it to the silver screen, but it was there in real life, and it made communication with a hand-held mike almost impossible. By strapping two small microphones around the neck so that they pressed against the voice box, ambient noise was eliminated, and the pilot had a hand free in the bargain. Except the movie-star pilots, who applied a slight additional pressure just above the white silk scarf—it may have improved sound reproduction a bit, and also gave the actors something to do with their hands.

Throat mikes were a little uncomfortable and required a separate press-to-talk switch, which may be why they're extinct today; but they produced great sound—pure, right-from-the-source sound, undistorted by physical characteristics of mouth and teeth and lips. It was impersonal sound, but easily understood; something like the quality you'd expect from a mike strapped to an organ pipe. Nor did a throat mike require much volume, since all that had to vibrate was the air in your throat—once you learned how, you could communicate in a voice that wasn't really a voice at all, just a rumble.

It's not likely that throat mikes will ever come back, but the theory of "throat talking" can be used with today's hand-held mikes. They are super-sensitive—you'll be amazed how softly you can talk into them and be heard clearly at the other end. As a matter of fact, you'll be heard *better* when you speak at a low volume, so the first rule to improve *how* you communicate is, talk softly.

Which works only if you put the mike right up against your lips, minimizing the length of the column of air that has to vibrate to produce sound. When you've decided what you want to say, think of a cat purring—you can *feel* the sound—and try to make your voice do just that. In the noisy environment of even the most soundproofed airplanes, everyone needs to talk louder than normal to make conversation. But when you talk like that into a microphone, think of the poor guy on the other end in the quiet (relatively speaking) of a Control Tower cab. As a guide, when you can hear yourself talking, you're talking too loudly. If more of us played see-how-softly-you-can-talk-and-still-get-the-point-across, we'd put the aspirin people out of business.

Abide by rule number two, talk slowly, and you'll find
that "Say again?" will seldom be aimed your way. A slowly
spoken but instantly understood message takes less time
than a rapid-fire recitation that must be repeated two or
three times. If you're a fast talker and know it, force yourself to slow down; you'll find communications improving
instantly.

Rule three, think before you speak—not so much about
how this next transmission will sound, but in terms of how
effective it will be. If, after a moment of reflection, you decide that what you were considering shouldn't be said *at all*,
that's working toward more efficient communication. Listen
—someone else may ask your question for you, or a Controller may solve your problem with a transmission to another aircraft. A lot of what we say on the air is self-serving;
a lot of that precious communication time could be saved
by just shutting up unless something really needs to be said.

Listen before you go on the air, rule four. That particular
frequency is yours only when someone else is not using it—
first come, first served. Now and then you'll hear only one
half of a radio conversation because of line-of-sight limitations; wait until the half you hear sounds like the end of a
discussion, then do your thing. When somebody gets cut out
in the middle of a transmission, everybody has to wait while
the receiver goes through the "Say again, you were cut out"
routine—communication time being poorly used in repetition.

Using your receivers properly is the fifth rule, and it begins
with setting the volume so that it's comfortable in terms of
the facility that's most important to you at the time. When
the volume is turned down to keep one of those bombastic
talkers from hurting your head (there's another good case
for not shouting into an aircraft mike), you might miss a
traffic advisory or landing instructions from a transmitter
farther away. Put up with the momentary audio discomfort,
and remember how it sounded the next time you pick up the
mike.

The squelch control on most modern receivers is there for
a purpose, to adjust the noise level of incoming messages.
Always set the squelch just short of the bacon frying, and

you'll get the most out of your receiver. One setting won't do for all frequencies, since distance makes a difference—whenever the radio is retuned, squelch should be readjusted.

Once you've identified a VOR or an NDB, turn the sound completely off. Unless you're listening to a weather broadcast or using the VOR as a communications receiver, a navigation station's noise can do nothing but distract you from other, more important things. That's communications "noise" at its best—guaranteed to get in the way of your thought processes.

If you've an audio switch panel that allows selection of any one or all of the receivers on board, stick with one. It's like watering the lawn—the sprinkler system performs well when the only opening in the hose is at the sprinkler head, but poke some holes along the way and sprinkling gets less efficient. Likewise, most small-aircraft audio systems work best with only one signal being amplified. Try it some time; notice the increase in quality and volume through the speaker when those unnecessary holes are plugged—besides, who can listen independently with each ear? "Noise" again.

Don't reply with a click of the mike button—to Controllers all clicks sound alike. 'Nuff said.

Use one radio—period. The only time a fair-weather pilot *needs* a second communications radio is when the first one rolls over and dies. If you have a pair, keep number two for a spare. The pilot who dazzles folks with his fancy fingerwork on the audio panel will inevitably flip the wrong switch and break up someone else's transmission. It's inefficient, time-consuming and embarrassing.

Every now and then it's bound to happen—an unknowing Controller asks you to do something and you just don't have the time to answer. If the something is "doable," start doing it, but let your electronic response wait until you have everything under control. The standard phrase that tells the guys on the other end of the microphone that they've caught you at a busy time is "Stand by one"—the universal signal to "Wait a minute, I'll call you back when I get all the pieces picked up." In a nutshell, there's *nothing* that's more important than maintaining control of the airplane.

PART THREE: THE PERSONAL PROBLEM

Being the part of the communications problem that you know best, this should be the easiest to solve, but it may mean a bit of pride swallowing; that's why it was originally headlined as the "maybe" part. Some pilots were apparently born with silver tongues, and their mellifluous tones sing across the airwaves like a network announcer's. Their perfectly enunciated rumblings leave little to be desired in communicative quality, and some of them grow up to say on the PA system in a voice two octaves lower than Orson Welles's lowest, "This is the captain speaking."

But, alas, most of us suffer from built-in voice problems, and the average pilot could stand some improvement in diction and elocution—in short, voice management. If you *know* that there are weak areas in your speech patterns, make an effort to do better—if you have a machine-gun mouth, slow down; if you know that your voice is high-pitched, try to lower it; if people hold the telephone at arm's length when they know it's you calling, turn down your volume whenever you pick up the mike—all these little things are magnified over the air and will ultimately cost communications time.

The most revealing test of your vocal efficiency is a tape recording—it may well be a brutal blow to your ego as well, for few people are less than appalled at the sound of their own voices. Not sure of your grades in communications school? Take along a recorder next flight, and it's likely you'll find a few habits to break and some weak points to strengthen. Self-analysis is the first step in self-improvement.

Voice management means doing a good job with what you have, but it also implies constant improvement. There's an easily effected rule for becoming a good talker: be a good listener. A lot can be learned by eavesdropping—along with better ways to communicate, you'll hear a lot of things that you'll be glad *you* didn't say!

There's something contagious about good radio discipline; when you really bear down on speaking slowly, softly and sensibly you'll notice others picking up the habit, and the entire system works more smoothly. Whenever a situation comes up that tempts you to reply with an oration that would do justice to a campaigning politician, remember this: if God intended that we should talk more than we hear, He would have given us two mouths and one ear.

Special VFR—a Good Deal . . . Sometimes

The poor man's IFR—designed to accommodate those pilots who aren't instrument-rated, or even the full IFR types who for some reason or another don't want to wait for an all-the-way instrument clearance. Anybody can request a Special VFR clearance (except, of course, student pilots, and nowadays you must be instrument-rated to get one at night), which represents ATC's OK to proceed into or out of a Control Zone in some general direction, as long as you can stay clear of the clouds and see a mile. To keep you from running into IFR traffic at higher altitudes, a ceiling is almost always imposed on "Special" flights. There are some airports where the press of bona fide IFR business won't permit the generalized wanderings of a Special, and those terminals have Control Zones outlined on the charts with big Ts or heavy dashed lines. Don't bother to ask; there's no way they can clear you unless you're IFR-rated and IFR-equipped.

To use Special VFR safely, you'd best be knowledgeable in two major areas—the terrain and obstructions over which you're flying or intend to fly, and the weather characteristics of the same chunk of geography. An inbound Special is usually not much of a problem, as long as you know the major landmarks that will help you find your way to the airport; when you spot the landing field, your troubles (if you had any to start with) are over.

The dangerous kind of Special VFR is the outbound one, especially in an unfamiliar part of the country. Now you're proceeding away from things that can help, into an essentially unknown weather situation—it's a lot like leaving the boat dock in a heavy fog and heading for the other side of the lake. You may *hope* the weather improves to basic VFR very shortly, but what if it doesn't? There you are, illegal as hell, and quite likely just as *concerned* if the visibility gets worse or the ceiling lowers, or both. Without a good idea of where you are and where the tall things are, you may wish you had never heard of Special VFR.

Use the Special with care and in moderation. When you know you'll need one, let the Ground Controller know when you call in ready to taxi. Better yet, file a flight plan so the Controllers know ahead of time what you want to do—chances are they'll have a clearance ready when you call. Be ready to copy a clearance, because that's what a Special is—you'll receive a direction in which to fly, an altitude restriction and, depending on the facilities available, a transponder code and maybe a Departure or Approach Control frequency. Same thing in reverse when you're inbound.

Above all else, remember that when you accept an outbound Special, the Controller assumes that you have checked the situation and will be able to maintain VFR conditions once you're outside his Control Zone—you can really bollix things up by getting halfway out and then deciding to do an about-face. What are you going to do if the Controller tells you to maintain VFR and he'll be back with you in a minute?

7

Cabin Pressurization

UNFORTUNATE BUT TRUE . . . the fact that most of the general-aviation community operates in airplanes limited to relatively low altitudes, which means that most of the time you'll be flying *through* whatever weather happens to exist between departure and destination. The ability to fly *over* the weather is an awesome thing, but is found only in the airline and corporate jet fleets, where rapid climbs and descents through the murk often make it difficult for those pilots to get enough actual weather time to stay legal.

It will likely be many moons before the average general-aviation pilot will have at his disposal the kind of flying machines that permit such storm-topping excursions. But the promise of at least a "sometimes" capability to get above the weather brightens with each new technological development in light aircraft. One of these advances is cabin pressurization, almost taken for granted in cabin-class twins, and now moving rapidly into the high-performance single-engine ranks as well.

Strictly a creature-comfort consideration, cabin pressurization is expensive, adds weight, introduces another system to be maintained, repaired, and adjusted, and in itself does not enhance aircraft performance. As a matter of fact, the extra weight and engine power to provide pressurization detract from useful load and ultimate performance of any aircraft, unless more horsepower is installed to accommodate the increased demands. Cabin pressurization will probably never pay for itself, but the ability to fly well above high terrain, the advantages of high-altitude tailwinds, and the superb safety factor of being able to see and circumnavigate most of the nasty weather are plusses that are hard to deny. You'd have a hard time convincing a pressurized pilot that he should give up that system and sink back down into the weather and low-groundspeed regimes of the lower altitudes . . . you get spoiled in a hurry!

In essence, cabin pressurization does nothing more than provide an artificial environment for the occupants. It's accomplished by sealing up all of the air leaks in the cabin except one, then introducing more air into the cabin than is allowed to escape. The need for pressurization at higher altitudes is founded in physiology and physics; your body requires a certain amount of oxygen in order to function properly, and while the atmosphere at virtually any level contains the same *amount* of oxygen (approximately 21 percent), the pressure exerted by the oxygen drops off at the same rate as the total air pressure. At 18,000 feet, for example, the pressure available to push inhaled oxygen through the lung membranes into your bloodstream is just about one half what it was at sea level. But if great volumes of that 18,000-foot air are pumped into a nearly sealed aircraft cabin, and very little is permitted to escape, the resultant increase in pressure does the job; oxygen is once again absorbed into your bloodstream, and the life processes continue in a normal fashion.

Contemporary light-aircraft pressurization systems are dependent on the supercharger, which make it possible to operate piston-powered aircraft at altitudes that require enhanced life-support systems (turbojet passenger aircraft, because of the remarkable increase in operating efficiency at very high altitudes, were pressurized from the very start— there was no other way). Some of the high-pressure air

produced by the supercharger is bled off through ports leading to the inflow valves, thereby quite literally pumping up
the cabin. An outflow valve, usually located at the rear of the
passenger area, may permit all of the incoming air to escape
(an unpressurized mode of operation), or may be programmed
to restrict the egress of air so as to maintain a given pressure
level inside the cabin.

There are limits to the amount of cabin pressure that can
be developed or maintained. The first of these would obviously be the amount of pressurized air that can be delivered
by the turbosupercharger; increases in available pressure
are self-defeating in terms of overall performance, for every
pound of pressure bled from the supercharger is a pound
of pressure that cannot be used to maintain high engine power
at altitude. The second, and perhaps more significant limitation, centers on the economics of building a cabin strong
enough to withstand the difference between pressure inside
and pressure outside.

Consider a sealed cabin very shortly after takeoff from a
sea-level airport—the pressure inside (sea level) is exactly
the same as pressure outside. Assuming that this particular
aircraft can maintain a cabin pressure equal to sea level
throughout its climb, that zero pressure differential at sea
level will have changed drastically as the airplane progresses
through 18,000 feet, the halfway point in the pressure atmosphere; the pressure inside the cabin is now *twice* that
outside. And without the appropriate restraints in the form
of strengthened windows, fuselage skin, and structural members, the airplane would literally come apart at the seams.
If this hypothetical aircraft were still able to produce and
contain enough pressurized air to maintain a sea-level cabin
at 34,000 feet, every square inch of the pressurized portion
would be trying to move outward with a force of slightly
more than eleven pounds.

Turbojet aircraft, which *must* operate at these high altitudes in order to realize their potentials of speed and fuel
efficiency, must of necessity be constructed to such toler-
ances. You'll find that most of them operate at pressure
differentials in the neighborhood of eight or nine psi, which

maintains a cabin pressure equal to that experienced at about 8000 feet, even at operating altitudes of 35–40,000 feet. But the piston-powered aircraft, the overall efficiency of which begins to wane rapidly once it's climbed out of the teens, can ill afford the weight and performance penalties of a structure beefed up enough to withstand these significant forces. The pressure vessels of most light aircraft, therefore, are built to withstand maximum differentials of three to five psi, sufficient to maintain a cabin pressure equal to that experienced at 10,000 feet (generally considered to be the maximum safe without supplemental oxygen) when the aircraft is actually flying at 20–25,000 feet.

The chart in Figure 7–1 illustrates the cabin altitude/aircraft-altitude/pressure-differential relationship of a light twin engineered to withstand a maximum differential of 4.6 psi. To understand the workings of this typical system, consider the pilot setting up the pressurization controls so that the outflow valve begins to close at a point 1000 feet above takeoff elevation (this is necessary because structural considerations prohibit pressurization on the ground).

From liftoff to 1000 feet AGL, the outflow valve remains wide open, and the pressurization system is doing nothing more than ventilating the cabin—air is pouring through the inflow valves and escaping just as freely through the outflow valve. But when the aircraft climbs through 1000 feet, the outflow valve closes just enough to maintain cabin pressure at the preset 1000-foot level; and as the aircraft continues to climb, the pressurization controller senses the change in cabin pressure and causes the outflow valve to move toward the closed position.

At some altitude in the climb, the outflow valve will have closed all the way as the controller attempts to maintain the preset 1000-foot cabin-pressure level. Let's say that when this occurs, the pressure differential is 3.0 psi on an aircraft with a limit of 3.75 psi. If the airplane continues to climb, pressure will build inside the cabin—still maintaining the 1000-foot pressure level—with the outflow valve fully closed, and now the pressure differential continues to increase until the limit is reached. (Referring again to Figure 7–1, this situa-

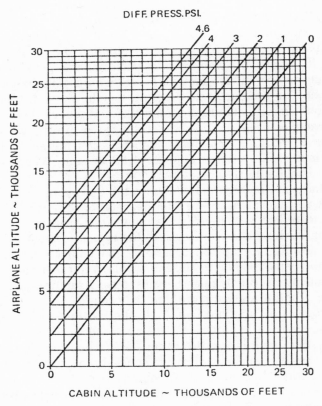

Figure 7–1. Cabin pressurization schedule for a typical light twin-engine aircraft.

tion would occur at approximately 11,500 feet.) Assuming that the airplane continues its climb, with the outflow valve tightly stoppered and the pressure differential at its maximum, the cabin pressure must be relieved, since outside air pressure continues to decrease—there's no way to do this but open the outflow valve somewhat again, and allow the cabin to climb with the aircraft.

Eventually, in such a pressure-differential-limited airframe, the cabin altitude would reach 10,000 feet. In our example, this situation takes place at 25,000-feet flight altitude; if a higher altitude is necessary, oxygen masks should be used, and there will be a warning light or sound to alert the pilot to that condition.

In addition to the weight-and-power penalties mentioned earlier, the pilot of a pressurized aircraft must remain alert to the possibility of malfunctions in the system. There are three situations that should be considered hazardous, or at least potentially dangerous: decompression (slow, rapid, or *explosive*), overpressurization, and pressurized-air contamination. Whether it's the result of a slow leak in the system or a rapid loss of pressure due to a window or door departing the aircraft in flight, cabin altitude is going to arrive at aircraft altitude sooner or later—sooner in the case of a door or window failure, later in the case of a slow leak. In either event, when aircraft altitude goes above 10,000 feet, supplemental oxygen must be considered, or an immediate descent to a suitable altitude must be commenced. At the least, that's frustrating; at the worst, it could involve a descent into the very weather conditions that you're trying to avoid.

The terms that describe the speed with which the cabin loses its pressure are important, because the rate at which this happens will usually determine the action to be taken by the pilot. A *slow* decompression is a hint of things to come . . . in other words, it's a clear warning that you will probably need to use supplemental oxygen sooner or later if you're on a long trip, or that you'll need to plan a descent before long. The cabin-pressure differential will decrease with altitude, and the slow leak may cure itself—but it should put you on notice that there's something wrong in the system! If you notice the cabin altitude creeping upward and the differential is not "on the peg," you may be able to solve the problem at least temporarily by programming the system for more pressure . . . and again, it's only a temporary fix.

On the other hand, a *rapid* decompression is one which takes place in just a few seconds, and usually calls for a very quick descent or "right now" donning of oxygen masks if the airplane is operating above 10,000 feet. You'll no doubt feel the pressure change in your ears, and you owe it to yourself and your passengers to get to a lower altitude as soon as possible. It may not be an emergency yet, but it's right next door to one.

Finally, the *explosive* decompression presents serious and immediate problems to the pilot of a pressurized aircraft, for two reasons: first, there has been a major rupture somewhere in the pressure vessel; and second, all the ingredients for a panic reaction are present. Cabin altitude will rise to aircraft altitude in very short order when all the pressure has vanished through a missing door or window, and there will probably be a great rushing of wind, lots of strange noises, charts and papers flying around the cabin . . . a sudden and alarming change of environment. Emergency descent procedures must be started immediately, and the pilot's welfare must be placed at the top of the list of concerns, for if you are unable to function, survival of your passengers is academic.

The second potentially dangerous situation—overpressurization—would certainly have to be considered a much more serious problem, although it's much less likely to occur. The certification rules (as well as the laws of common sense) dictate a pressure-relief valve built into the system, spring loaded to a preset position, which will cause the valve to open as necessary to relieve any pressure differential above the certified maximum for the airframe. But valves have been know to fail, and if an unhappy circumstance like this were allowed to prevail, it's possible to overpressurize to the point of structural failure . . . then you've got the decompression problem all over again.

In the third case, consider material failure in the ducting between the turbo and the cabin, or an engine fire, allowing contaminated air to enter the cabin. This could be manifested as toxic fumes, dense smoke, excess heat, or all three. All pressurization installations have valves—usually operated by large T-handles or knobs prominently placed in the cockpit—with which the pilot can isolate pressurized airflow from either or both engines. If that procedure solves the problem, your troubles are really not over with, because very few recip-powered pressurized aircraft can generate enough airflow from one engine to maintain the relatively high pressure differential necessary to keep the cabin at a safe altitude when the airplane is flying high. It's likely that you'll have to put up with a higher cabin altitude or descend to lower, denser air . . . perhaps both.

The same predicament would prevail if either engine fails, or has to be shut down as a precaution against imminent failure. The *Pilot's Operating Handbook* for pressurized aircraft will list detailed precedures for countering all of these emergencies, and the pilot of such an aircraft must be thoroughly familiar with those checklist provisions. He must also be capable of executing them in a very rapid and positive manner. A flight procedure unique to pressurized aircraft is the emergency descent, designed to get the aircraft and its occupants to a safe, lower altitude as rapidly as possible following a sudden pressurization failure; the emergency descent usually calls for throttles closed, props to full high RPM, gear down, and head for the ground at V_{le}—maximum gear-extended airspeed.

Under normal circumstances, the management of a pressurization system in a light, piston-powered aircraft is not very difficult. It's usually a matter of making sure that the system is set to begin pressurizing at some altitude *above* departure airport elevation, and prior to beginning descent, resetting the system to an altitude that will insure touchdown in an unpressurized condition.

Because nearly all descents in a pressurized aircraft will be made at relatively high rates, more feet per minute than most people's ears can comfortably stand, some advance planning should take place. For example, if you are cruising at 17,000 feet and anticipating descent to a sea-level airport at an average rate of 1500 feet per minute, the descent will require a bit more than 11 minutes. Using the chart in Figure 7–1 to illustrate, a flight altitude of 17,000 feet puts the cabin at 5000 feet, so a cabin rate of descent of only 442 fpm would do the job . . . and nearly *anybody's* ears can put up with that. By adjusting the cabin-rate controller to a round figure of 500 fpm, you're assured that the cabin and the aircraft will arrive at the same altitude at the bottom of the descent. In general, the higher you fly and the faster you intend to descend, the more you need to plan ahead; failing to take this into consideration will mean large, uncomfortable, high-rate changes in cabin altitude at the last minute; or flying-around-in-circles delays while the cabin comes down to meet the airplane.

One of the pleasant offshoots of pressurization is the even heating it provides within the aircraft. Although aircraft in this class will also have combustion heaters installed, the pressurized air coming from the turbos is warm enough to do the entire heating job most of the time; a heat-control lever or knob allows you to adjust the operation of an intercooler to provide the amount of heat you want. Of course, there will be days when you don't want any more heat (many pressurized aircraft are also equipped with air-conditioning systems), and the drill here is to delay the start of pressurization, allow ram air to ventilate and cool the cabin until later in the climb.

All of these benefits of pressurization carry a price tag in addition to the extra dollars when you take delivery of the airplane, and that additional price is the exposure to a hostile environment. All of the warnings about hypoxia and hyperventilation can come home to roost when something unpleasant happens "at altitude," even if it's only 15,000 or 20,000 feet above sea level. The only way you'll know what it's like is to experience the sensations firsthand, and the only safe way to do that is to enroll in the one-day physiological training course offered at a number of military installations throughout the country, and at the FAA's facility in Oklahoma City. These courses consist of an intensive classroom session followed by a "ride" in an altitude chamber, during which you will be given the opportunity to experience those symptoms of hypoxia unique to you . . . everyone reacts in a slightly different manner to lack of oxygen. For five bucks, these courses are one of the best bargains in aviation today.

Nearly any pressurization-system failure or malfunction handled properly in a light airplane flying at 20,000 feet or so will be little more than an inconvenient interruption in an otherwise routine flight. But the next time you're flying in the company jet or on an air carrier at Flight Level 390, give due consideration to the flight attendant's briefing on emergency oxygen equipment. If a window or door should fail at this altitude (it *has* happened!), you will be suddenly gasping for breath in the rarefied atmosphere of 39,000 feet, and the time of useful consciousness—the time available to make a rational analysis of what's happened and do something about the lack of oxygen before you pass out—is only a few seconds.

8

Night Flying

IMPRISON an engineer-inventor-craftsman on an island, tell him he can't leave, and he'll come up with some way to break the restraints. Daedalus, the ancient Greek architect, found himself in just such a fix, and figured the only way out was to fly —the fact that flying hadn't been invented yet didn't stop him for a minute. He scrounged enough bird feathers and beeswax to make wings for himself and his son Icarus, and with no dual to speak of, the flight of two launched from the island of Crete. Daedalus, the older and wiser of the two, made it; but Icarus got intoxicated with the joy of flying, ventured too close to the sun (how 'bout *that* for a service ceiling!) and bought the farm when the wax melted. They were good wings, but Icarus' foolishness created such bad PR that the wax-wing people have never been able to overcome it.

Had Daedalus given his escape a bit more thought, he might have waited until sunset to fly the coop. In addition to becoming the first persons to fly at night, the father-son formation would have gotten better performance in the cooler air of evening, and sunset over the isle of Crete was probably a spectacular sight. But the safety considerations of a night flight overshadowed any physical or aesthetic benefits—who can deny that, all other things being the same, Icarus would probably have made it to the mainland had it not been for the heat of the sun! And some clever myth writer would have come up with a different ending for this classic tale.

There are times when flying at night is a pleasant diversion, other times when it's the only way to get a job done and still other times when it shouldn't even be considered. You probably know pilots who are convinced that if they leave the ground after sunset in a single-engine airplane, it's preordained that they shall suffer an engine failure and fall to the ground. That risk is always there, daylight or not, and it's true that your choices are somewhat restricted when a nighttime emergency comes up, but there are enough *good* things about night flying so that you shouldn't arbitrarily stay away because it's dark outside.

For example, the aesthetics alone make it worthwhile to fly around in the dark every now and then. When the lights aren't browned out by smog, our cities are a mass of diamonds spread out on black velvet—truly beautiful. (I've personally never seen a mass of diamonds spread out on black velvet, and I know that description lacks novelty, but every time I see a big city from the air at night, that's what I see.) Some cities become horizon-to-horizon lights, some soft, some glaring. Fly over Las Vegas on a clear night, and you'll understand why Hoover Dam is where it is—they couldn't possibly pump that much electricity any farther away! The stars take on a new dimension when you climb away from the sour air we live in; there's a new world of visual pleasures waiting for you. It's usually smoother and cooler and, in general, more comfortable flying at night.

BUT IS IT SAFE?

Your airplane doesn't care one whit whether the air that makes it go is light or dark; engine power is dependent on how much air it ingests, lift is dependent on how fast that same air moves across the wings, and barring a major mechanical problem, there's no reason why the airplane shouldn't continue to fly just as reliably as it does during the day. To be sure, an engine failure at night presents some unique problems (like, where do I land when I can't see the ground?), but conservative flying and plenty of knowing-what-you're-doing will obviate a great deal of your concern in that department.

There are some things about night operations that are different, as you'll see when you start on your first nocturnal venture with an airplane. There are enough things different for the FAA to require new pilots to jump through several hours of night-training hoops if they want an unrestricted certificate—otherwise, your ticket will bear the limiting words NIGHT FLYING PROHIBITED, and you'll not be able to take advantage of all the good things about night flight.

Given a reliable vehicle which operates under the same laws of physics and gravity at midnight as at high noon, the only change that could occur when the sun goes down is in the operator—the pilot. What makes you a different animal when the sun disappears in the west? The most significant changes occur in what you see—or *don't* see, depending on circumstances. Owls and bats and other natural-born night flyers are eminently prepared for their work after dark—we're not, and therein lies the problem. Our eyes must adapt to the condition of darkness, and the human mind must adjust in order to interpret these new inputs properly. So a discussion of the safety of flying at night must revolve around the limitations of the human body and mind—like any other flight situation, the more you know, the safer you'll be; and the whole operation will be more pleasant.

THE EYES HAVE IT

Right off the reel, you've got to realize that night flying is a lot like instrument flying. The big difference lies in the *number* of visual clues available—when you're on the gauges, it's assumed that you can't see outside at all, and are completely dependent on the instruments to tell you where you are and where you've going. You've gotta have faith that there's no one else out there in front of you. But under night VFR conditions, there will be *some* outside references—

otherwise, you're illegal—which provide a measure of visual orientation for you. Some nights you'll find a wealth of clues, as over a heavily populated area; but on other nights there's nothing out there but a few stars and barnyard lights, and that can be the worst of all, as we'll see later.

Just having a bunch of lights on the ground doesn't always solve the problem either, because your brain is capable of switching those visual inputs until what you *think* you see can be dangerously far from what is actually going on; some training in interpretation is needed. Every foot of altitude you put under you is detrimental to night vision and interpretation, and unless you have an oxygen-equipped airplane there's nothing you can do about it—except *know* about it, and realize that you have some limits at night.

So the eyes have the key to all the unusual properties of night flying; if they can't pick up enough light to let you see what's going on, you're in trouble, and if you don't know how to interpret what little information they are furnishing in the dark, you're not much better off—maybe much worse. In the pages that follow are a number of tips and techniques relative to flying safely at night; they've all got to do with your eyes, and how to make them work more effectively for you.

AT NIGHT, ALL CATS ARE GRAY

To begin with, you have a hole in your eye, whether you think that's a good deal or not. At the center of the field of vision, there's a spot which contains no "cones," the receptors that distinguish colors, and which do their best work in bright light. Since they are almost completely insensitive to the lowered illumination of a night situation, the cones create a blind spot. When you look directly at an object in the dark, it appears to disappear—squint for all you're worth, you won't see an airplane coming at you from dead ahead as long as you try to find it by looking at it. The name of the night-vision game, then, is to look *past* something you want to see. A watch face that glows in the dark (i.e., one with phosphorescent numbers and hands) can be used to demonstrate this phenomenon and also to train yourself to look to the side of dimly lighted objects. In the dark, fix your gaze on one of the numbers and observe the sweep second hand as it goes around the dial—it will disappear as it passes the number and reappear shortly thereafter. From this, you can get some idea of the size of your personal nighttime visual limitation. Remember that the watch face is only inches away from your eye—as you look for things farther and farther away, the effective size of the hole in your eye grows remarkably, and could hide a pretty big airplane or TV tower or any one of a number of things that could ruin your evening.

On a really dark night, your eyes are super-sensitive—a source of light as insignificant as an ordinary match has been seen at a distance of twenty-five miles (keep that in mind should you ever find yourself in a situation where you need to be found—light a match and even a one-eyed search pilot twelve and a half miles away ought to pick up your signal)—but you've got to provide some optical assistance in the form of a methodical scan of the visual field. The rods (that part of the retina most sensitive to low light levels) are concentrated around the periphery of the eye, and unless you shift the focus occasionally and hold it for at least a few seconds, you may never see objects which are hiding in the blind spot. There's an added danger in the light source which blends into the pattern of ground lights or stars, and which may never be identified as the lights of another airplane or obstacle until it moves . . . right into your cockpit. With even more discipline than your daytime scan, train yourself to look outside the airplane frequently, fix your gaze on an object or an area of the sky and hold it there for a few seconds; you'll likely see things jump out of your blind spot or appear as potential hazards because they're moving. Think for a moment on this: when you're on a collision course with another object, it will appear to stand still in your field of vision; if that lack of motion buries the intruder in the ground lights or hoodwinks you into thinking it's a star, school may be out shortly.

Know where hazardous towers and buildings are located, and listen to what's going on in the airspace around you. When someone else checks in with the Tower and gives his location, take a look; pay attention to the approach and departure patterns in use and make yourself scarce in that neighborhood. When you're cleared to land and the final approach lies over city lights, there's nothing wrong with lining up a bit to one side and scanning carefully as you fly down the chute—anyone else in there with you will appear to move, and relative motion is one of the secrets of effective night vision. If you suspect that you have company anywhere in the pattern, make him "move" by changing your heading or altitude or speed or all three. There aren't many street lights or billboards that change position—a moving light is probably fastened to another airplane.

Almost as dangerous as the lights that *are* moving but don't appear to be, are the lights that *aren't* moving but seem to be. Confusing?—yes, until you realize that your night vision will play tricks with your perceptions of a stationary light source and cause it to wander all over the sky. A truly spooky phenomenon, it's called autokinetic movement—the appearance of movement by a fixed light source in an otherwise dark field of vision. A classic accident involved an airline captain who executed a violent diving turn to avoid what his eyes told him was another airplane on a collision course—as it turned out, autokinetic movement was the villain. Knowing what it's all about and having some idea of who is in the air with you can go a long way toward preventing accidents like this. Scanning is the answer, since apparent movement won't happen when the perceptions are constantly changing—it's a fixed stare that will do you in.

WHICH WAY IS UP?

You're a couple of jumps ahead when you concede that night flying is a shirttail relative of full-blown instrument flying. In addition to the increased possibility of flying into unexpected low-visibility conditions (this is the *only* time a pilot is "caught" by weather), a particular set of nocturnal circumstances can inject you into an IFR situation faster than you can say "Where's the horizon?" The ingredients are a starry night over sparsely populated country, with no moon and just enough ground lights to make it easy to confuse

earth and sky. It doesn't even take a turn to develop a
three-way mental race between what you see outside, what
you see inside (on the instruments) and what you feel in the
seat of your pants. Actual horizon says you're turning, artificial horizon says you're not, seat of pants says yes you're
turning but in the opposite direction, and the conflicting
perceptions begin to hurt the head.

Depending on which sensation you choose to believe, you
may roll into a turn, roll out of a turn or worsen a situation
that's already a bad one. When your poor tired brain tries to
make sense of all that conflict, the mental gyro may tumble,
and you've got vertigo—in spades. It could be that you and
your airplane can fly inverted for long periods of time, but
more often than not the confusion that results from trying
to tell the difference between a few stars and a few ground
lights leads to complete disorientation and, not infrequently,
complete disaster.

There's an easy way out—recognize a potential disorient-
ing situation, and stop it before it starts by referring to the
instruments. They are quite likely the only reliable source
of attitude information, and although you may wind up
sitting sideways in the seat thinking you're in the middle of
a Lomcevak, the airplane will be straight and level when the
gauges say so. After a while, when your eyeballs stabilize
again and you can determine the real horizon, do your VFR
thing. But be super-aware of what caused the problem, and
don't let it get started again.

WHEN YOU FLY AT NIGHT, FLY HIGHER

For all the usual reasons, the higher you fly the better
you'll like it, and especially at night; smoother air, less traffic,
better true airspeeds and frequently better winds. But there
are other reasons when the sun has gone over the hill, and
the list is headed by time—more time to make a rational
decision should an engine failure or some other emergency
alter your original plans. In addition to the extra time, the
higher you are when you holler for help, the more people will

hear you, and when you don't care from what quarter help might come, it's good sense to let everybody within earshot know you're in trouble—you never know who might come up with an idea that could save your skin; there's nothing to lose by trying.

Night flying in a familiar area is no problem altitude-wise when you know the height of obstructions and stay well above those levels. On a cross-country trip, why not use the airways with their published safe altitudes (Minimum Enroute Altitude on the IFR charts) and *know* you're high enough? Off airways, be sure you're well above all obstacles and terrain within several miles of your intended course—things can get a little confusing at night, and the next pilot who wanders off course into a mountain won't be the first. Your navigation is never as good at night as it is during daylight hours, and on a dark night you won't see the mountain until it's too late.

Stay high until you're in the terminal area and are close enough to land power-off if you have to. As long as there's a prepared landing surface within gliding distance you've nothing to worry about, but a low, dragged-in approach could prove embarrassing if the engine gives up—look out, downtown, here I come.

Filing a VFR flight plan is optional, as it should be, except for long cross-country trips at night, when common sense and a deep respect for your well-being and that of your passengers makes it imperative that you let *somebody* know where you're going, when and what route. There's nobody better equipped for this than the Flight Service Station, who can and will alert the proper parties when you aren't heard from within a reasonable time. At least they know where to start looking.

EVERY GOOD DEAL HAS ITS PRICE

. . . . and when the good deal is flying high at night, the price is reduced night vision. The retina, that super-sensitive piece of film that covers the back of the eyeball and "sees" things for your brain to interpret, is more susceptible to lowered oxygen content in the blood than any other part of the body. When hypoxia comes to town, it knocks on the retinal door first.

Any lowering of air pressure has its effect on your night vision—even taking the elevator to the cocktail lounge on the top floor of your office building. There's less pressure up there, consequently less oxygen in your blood stream, and the retina feels the pinch, albeit insignificant. This is not to imply that when you fly high at night you'll go blind, but climbing to only 5000 feet puts some restrictions on the things you can see, and how early and how well your eyes pick them up. If you take off from a mountain town and have to climb even higher to clear terrain, you're behind the eight ball right from the start.

The top-of-the-building cocktail lounge can play hob with your night vision in other ways too, since there are activities and commodities available there which can reduce your cat's-eye powers even more than the lack of oxygen pressure. Smoking, fatigue and alcohol make large dents in night vision; the effects of these three show up as insidious and persistent thieves of the oxygen-carrying capability of the red blood cells. Smoking three cigarettes in a row makes your sea-level night vision just about the same as if you were at 8000 feet, the equivalent of a 25 percent reduction in visual sensitivity. *Now* get aboard your aerial steed and head for the heights; the old eyeballs think they're much higher, and there will be other people out there you won't see. Let's hope that they see *you.*

Supplemental oxygen makes a difference you won't believe until you take a couple of whiffs on a night when you've been at altitude for a while; it's as though someone turned up a rheostat on the world below—you'll see lights appear where there were none a moment ago, at least to your oxygen-starved eyes. There are a number of small portable oxygen bottles on the market which are prohibitive neither in size nor in price—consider the wisdom of carrying one in the airplane if for no other reason than to perk up those retinas just before a night landing.

SEE AND BE SEEN

There's nothing that will jump out of the sky at a pilot like another airplane's landing light; you know that the only time you can see that touchdown torch is when the other plane is coming right at you. In an effort to reduce the hazard of mixing aircraft of vastly different speeds in the same terminal area, military and airline pilots turn on the landing lights when they are in a congested area, and it seems just as sensible for pilots in other segments of aviation to do the same. Not hiding your light under a bushel is effective anytime, but particularly at night, when navigation lights, even rotating beacons and strobes, are easily obscured in the mélange of ground lights around an airport.

You can use your landing lights to good advantage for identification by Controllers too. When you are within sighting distance of the Tower, give them a call: "Tower, 34 Alpha five east with a light, landing." Have a spare finger poised over the landing-light switch, and when you come to "with a light," flick the candles on. Nine times out of ten the Controller can pick out the flash of light, and you're identified; leave the light on until after landing, and everybody else in the pattern will know you're there. Worried about the cost of landing-light bulbs?—they're a heck of a lot cheaper than either people or airplanes, or both.

WHAT YOU *THINK* YOU SEE IS NOT NECESSARILY WHAT YOU GET

The transition from a relatively bright runway environment to almost complete darkness can really cross up your perceptions immediately after a night takeoff. Instead of the familiar slow dropping away of the surface, you may suddenly find yourself suspended in a black void, with little or no ground reference. Of course, if the takeoff path goes right down Main Street, it isn't so bad—the transition is more gradual—but don't count on it, because sooner or later you'll leap off from a country airport at night and it'll be blacker than the inside of a chimney out there.

Ever since you started aviating, you have built up a memory bank of information that translates into: "Whenever the visual references appear diminished or few and far between, that must mean I am very far above the ground." Unless you consciously overcome this mental programming, the natural reaction will be an attempt to descend, or at least to arrest the climb; neither is recommended right after liftoff. There are several ways to combat this strong urge: seat-of-the-pants works for a lot of people; the sound of the engine isn't all bad as a climb indicator; but why not learn and use a method that works every time?—begin introducing a touch of instrument flight into your night takeoffs, and be sure. Pay some attention to the flight instruments, realize what they're telling you and do what has to be done.

There's an equally consistent, though not quite so dangerous, problem associated with what you think you're seeing during final approach to a night landing. It's bad enough when you fly a normal traffic pattern and give your eyes a chance to adjust to the changing sights, but a long straight-in approach at night is guaranteed to produce something other than your best landing effort unless you know what's happening and do something about it.

The problem is depth perception and the false indications it generates. Approaching a narrow runway, your final will almost inevitably be too low and too fast—your eyes fool you into believing the surface is farther away than it really is. The wider the runway (or the farther apart the lights—you can't tell the difference at night), the higher your final will be, and you'll try to round out many feet above the surface.

Both these situations are the result of locking on visually to a single set of light clues—the runway lights themselves—instead of scanning around the horizon during the approach and tempering the runway lights' appearance with other lights in the immediate area. The total picture is much more important than those two rows of white lights, and if there were ever a chance to stump for the standard-pattern, spot-on-the-windshield technique, it's right here. When you realize that eyes alone will let you down at night, it makes good sense to settle down and fly by the numbers—the numbers you developed during the daytime, and which have been producing good, safe, consistent approaches and landings. Just like the assurance of a positive climb after a night take-off, a disciplined final approach to a night landing gives you a peg to hang your proficiency hat on—it's the *sure* way.

If your airport has installed a VASI (Visual Approach Slope Indicator), get familiar with it and use it every time. A VASI should be flown just like a spot on the windshield—set up an attitude for the final approach airspeed you want, and "keep the lights" with power, not pitch. There are several variations of VASI, with different colors and different interpretations—but as long as you know how it should look when you're on a safe glide path to the runway, the name of the system is totally unimportant.

DON'T EXPECT TOO MUCH TOO SOON

Your eyes need just as much time to adapt to nighttime conditions when you sit down in your airplane as they do when you sit down in a darkened theater; it will probably be thirty minutes before you're the owl you think you are (ever sit on someone's lap in what you thought was an empty seat at the Bijou?). In days gone by, the rule was to wear red goggles or sit in a red-lighted room to shorten the night-vision adaptation time, but perhaps you've noticed the apparent contradiction in the new airplanes equipped with *white* instrument lights. Red lights are now old-hat, due to the current thinking that the color of the light doesn't matter as much as the brightness. In any event, if your night vision is normal, after thirty minutes in the dark you should be able to see a light ten thousand times dimmer than what you could see right after you left the bright lights. This being the case, continue turning down the panel lights as adaptation improves, until you have them so low you can almost count the twists in the filaments—that in itself is hardly important, but the lower the light level inside the airplane, the more objects your eyes will pick up outside, and that *is* important.

BUT WHAT IF THE ENGINE *DOES* QUIT?

A pilot who is deeply troubled by the thought of engine failure at night should give serious consideration to limiting his aeronautical excursions to daylight hours. If he's preoccupied with this concern, he's probably not able to devote enough attention to flying the airplane properly while the engine *is* running. To be sure, it's a calculated risk, but given the reliability of today's aircraft engines and associated systems, there's little justification for losing sleep over this kind of emergency.

Okay, so there's a chance, suppose your number *does* come up, and you are suddenly at the controls of a night glider that was never even intended to be a day glider? There are some helpful things you can be doing while the ground comes inexorably closer. Knowing where you are is a big help, so you can immediately head for the nearest airport; if there's no airfield within gliding distance (boy, would a little more altitude be worth its weight in gold right now!), head for the nearest open country. Even more than in daylight, fly a single-engine airplane from one emergency landing field to the next—always have somewhere to go.

As in any airborne emergency, there are some actions that must take precedence; doing the first things first may make the difference, and there's absolutely nothing more important than controlling the airplane. Your reaction to a sudden engine stoppage should be airspeed-oriented—don't lose a foot of that precious altitude until the airplane has slowed to the best gliding speed. If you don't know that number as well as you know your own name, find it out and imprint it on your memory. Better than that, imprint it somewhere on the instrument panel. The few feet of altitude you conserve, or the extra eighth of a mile you are able to squeeze out of a glide by flying at the most efficient airspeed, might be the margin between attainment and interment.

In an airplane with a controllable-pitch propeller, move it into the high-pitch, low-speed position for less drag. When you've plenty of time (altitude) and it's obvious that the engine isn't going to restart, might as well stop the engine by slowing the airplane until the prop stops. A windmilling propeller is just the power source for an air compressor, sapping energy that you can convert into time and/or distance. You'll glide farther with a stilled engine, and the cockpit will be a lot quieter—you have a better chance of hearing that still small voice if it speaks to you. (*Caution*—prop-stopping airspeed is probably right up against stall speed; unless you are *very* proficient, *very* confident and very sure that the extra distance or altitude is worth the risk, hang on to that good glide speed and accept the air-compressor penalty.)

Get on the horn when you get into trouble. Even a calmly delivered "Mayday" on 121.5 will energize a large corps of assistants, and if nothing else, someone will know which way to point the search parties.

Now that you're headed toward what you've decided is the best place to go under the present circumstances, have attained the best glide speed and have let someone know of your predicament, start trouble shooting in the hope that you can find the glitch that kicked off this whole messy situation. Check the fuel selector first; more than a few airplanes make unscheduled landings with a tankful on the other side. Make sure you haven't brushed against the mag switches by accident, or that the guy in the right seat hasn't kneed the mixture control to OFF. Turn on fuel boost pumps if you've got them—perhaps an air bubble in the line is the culprit (don't ever switch tanks without the applicable boost pump operating, especially at higher altitudes). Carburetor heat can't do any harm, and there's an outside chance of enough heat left to solve the problem, but don't count on it if the intake system *is* iced up—you should have used carb heat much earlier—sorry 'bout that! Try everything!—try *anything!*—what have you got to lose?

When everything's tried and nothing's worked, get ready to land. You may have little to do with *where* it's going to happen, but you're still in charge of *how*, so fly the airplane all the way to touchdown. Just as in any other landing, you'll probably walk away from it if you touch down at the lowest possible forward speed and while you still have complete control. Unless you hit the vertical face of a mountain, you'll make it if you do the hitting slowly. Get the wheels down if you can; they'll absorb considerable energy as they're torn off. To heck with the airplane, look out for yourself—think in terms of decelerating with the least possible damage to Number One—YOU. Save the battery for that last few hundred feet, then turn on the landing lights to help evaluate your landing site, and steer around the big, solid obstructions. Keep flying the airplane right down to impact if possible, then cover your face with your arms and hope for the best.

THE NIGHT JUDGMENT DAY ARRIVED IN OHIO

Do you have any idea how quietly a J-3 Cub can slip through the night sky with the prop stopped? Ask someone I'll call John Smith, who's been around general aviation in the Buckeye State for a long time, building up a repertoire of the salt-and-pepper experiences that keep this business from ever becoming dull.

John had a good friend whose forte was the trumpet, and in addition to being aware of the almost noiseless qualities of a powerless Piper, they found out that a particularly zealous religious group would be winding up a hellfire-and-brimstone session with a night meeting at a nearby country church. The wheels of mischief began to turn, and when it was dark, off they went in John's Cub, climbing into the moonless night until they were high over the church—the hallelujahs and praise-the-Lords could almost be heard through the open side of the little airplane.

When the meeting-house doors finally burst open and the highly charged congregation streamed out into the night, John shut off the engine, stopped the prop, and the town trumpeter leaned out the door, shattering the night with Gabrelian notes that must have made believers of even the most doubting of Thomases.

Whether the evangelist crossed a palm or two, we'll never know—the trumpeter remains anonymous, and John's not talking.

BON VOYAGE, AND HAVE A GOOD NIGHT

Get started in night flying the way you should get started in weather flying—a little at a time, with a good instructor. Dusk flights are among the most pleasant of all, and they serve as the best introduction to noctural navigation by air. You can experience some of nighttime's sensations without the full effect of them all, and begin to accustom yourself to being aloft when you can't see the ground.

Be insistent on a super-clean windshield before every night flight, and get used to the reflections of instrument and cabin lights. Know which interior lights to turn off when you need maximum outside visibility.

It won't matter how owl-eyed you are if the light level inside the cabin drops to zero. Your eyes can't do something with nothing, so ALWAYS CARRY A FLASHLIGHT; a fully charged, fresh-batteried one that's stored where you can get to it in a hurry. A couple of spare batteries and an extra bulb wouldn't be a bad idea either. If you can fly at night without a flashlight and not feel antsy, you've a strong constitution; turn out all the cabin lights some night (come on now, *all* of them) and see if you can handle the airplane in total darkness. Of course you can't, because you can't *see,* and it's been proven that a fully fueled cigarette lighter lasts only a few minutes longer than a book of matches—if either happens to be on board in the first place. When the lights go out inside, you're forced to rely on visual inputs from ground and sky, and the stage is set for disorientation and vertigo. Don't ever leave the ground without a flashlight that you're willing to bet your life on; you may have to.

Flying at night can add another dimension to your aviation world; besides, there aren't many other endeavors in which you can be a "fly by night" and still have something to be proud of!

How to Look for Bogies

We don't use that war-spawned term any more. Although "squawk" and "tally ho" and some others have survived, "bogies" have turned into "traffic" on today's radar scopes. Regardless of the name, radar advisories keep airplanes from running into each other, and there's nothing wrong with that.

Now that the fellows in front of the radar scopes have altitude information on many of the targets they're watching, you'll get fewer advisories, as long as the Controller also knows your altitude. Why clutter up the airwaves telling you about another flight that can't possibly represent a traffic conflict?

When the Controller doesn't know the altitude of an airplane moving your way, he'll sing out, "Traffic at ten o'clock, two miles, slow-moving, altitude unknown," or whatever information he can develop. Right away, look out your window at the ten-o'clock place, and at your altitude—that's the area of greatest concern right now. As soon as you're satisfied that no one is hiding behind the windshield post or that big spot on the window, enlarge your area of search up and down through ten o'clock; not much up and down, just enough to be sure that there's no one encroaching on your chunk of airspace. During a climb, be especially watchful above; when descending, it makes sense to pay attention to who's underneath.

Another radar limitation with which you should be familiar is the fact that a Controller sees only two blips tracking their respective courses across his flat glass world. He sees tracks, not headings, and that's the way he calls 'em—it's up to you to adjust your scan to accommodate any drift correction in use at the time. Every "o'clock" is thirty degrees, so look for the bogies in relation to where you're going, not where you're headed.

Which is akin to the two cross-eyed fellows whose cars collided in the middle of the street—the first one jumped out and yelled, "Why don't you look where you're going!!" And the other guy came right back with "Why don't you go where you're looking!!"

9

Flying in Turbulent Air

JUST ABOUT HALFWAY BETWEEN Detroit and Buffalo on Lake Erie's
southern shore sits the city of Cleveland; heavy on industry
and highly dependent on air transportation. To ease the load
on Cleveland's big airport and in recognition of the needs of
the business community, farsighted planners created Burke
Lakefront Airport to be one of the most convenient in the
country—within walking distance of "Wall Street" in Ohio's
biggest city. Its runways point a little north of east and a little
south of west because that's the way the lake shore runs, and
given the prevailing westerlies of northern Ohio, you'd expect
the wind to be down the centerline most of the time. Not quite
so—if a poll were taken of Burke's regular aviation customers,
you'd soon find out why it's known in the business as "Cleveland Crosswind Airport." The wind can be blowing from two-
four-zero everywhere from Chicago to Chautauqua, but when
you turn final at Lakefront, it will shift—that's as safe a bet
as two dollars on Secretariat at the county fair.

And when Cleveland winds blow vigorously from the
south, aviators are confronted with turbulence from the
picket fence of downtown buildings just a few blocks up-

stream of the runway. Air moving across downtown Cleveland gets pretty badly torn up and vents its anger on airplanes; the turbulence is always at least light, sometimes moderate and consistently uncomfortable. There are other airports whose traffic patterns get a little lumpy for the same reason; like Chicago's Meigs Field, also on a lake shore, and also in the lee of a line of buildings—you can get your timbers thoroughly shivered at Meigs every once in a while. The dirigible hangar at the Akron, Ohio, municipal airport creates interesting wind currents, and the big flat-topped hangars on the southwest side of Detroit's City Airport don't do much for aerial tranquility. If you'll flip back through your flying memoirs, it's not too hard to remember certain landing fields whose turbulence-producing surroundings made takeoffs and landings something less than the graceful goings and comings you wanted them to be.

The point is that turbulence is here to stay, and like everything else in our aeronautical world, the more you know about it, the better you can handle it, or avoid it if it's more than you care to try handling. Our counterparts in sailboats haven't much choice—when there's no wind, there's no sailing—a calm day puts them out of business. Sailors put up with the pitching and rolling that always accompany wind in exchange for the benefits the moving air provides, mainly locomotion. But we pilots don't depend on the wind to get where we're going; while tailwinds are always happy things, and headwinds cost something in time and/or money, we can operate whether there's wind or not. It's another in the continuing compromise that is aviation—when the air is rough, we give up a little comfort, a little time, and work a little harder to enjoy the utility of our aircraft. We don't need the wind, but neither should we cancel a flight just because it's there. The turbulences produced by surface winds (as well as the several other types) are a pilot's enemies only as long as they remain unknown and unflown. Lumpy air is a way of life in aviation—to know it is not necessarily to love it, but an understanding of how turbulence is produced and how to navigate your airplane through an uneasy atmosphere can go a long way toward more satisfying flying experiences.

A BUMP IS A BUMP IS A BUMP, BUT . . .

The buildings in Cleveland, Detroit and Chicago that interfere with the normal flow of air and make things uncomfortable create *mechanical* turbulence. Although the effects are the same, there are other ways in which turbulence can be caused—knowing the conditions likely to produce rough air gives you the upper hand if you want to stay clear of it. There is the turbulence of convection, when a sun-warmed surface generates rising columns of air—*thermal* turbulence. When the velocity of the wind changes more than a few knots for each thousand feet of altitude, areas of disturbed air will show up as *shear* turbulence. And the other general class of rough air is analogous to the frothing water that follows any boat—airplanes leave wakes too, and the turbulence that results is aptly named: *wake* turbulence.

Is yours an investigative personality? Then line up for Runway 24 at Cleveland Lakefront some day when it's 95 in the shade (thermal turbulence), there's a moderate south wind (mechanical turbulence) blowing ten knots faster at five hundred feet than on the surface (shear turbulence), and you're a half-mile behind a just-landed jet (wake turbulence)—your final approach may come out a bit wrinkled.

THERMAL TURBULENCE

Rough air that has gotten that way because of rising columns of warm air (thermals) is probably the easiest to avoid because it's nearly always visible. Those cauliflower-topped clouds on a hot summer day are really the caps of thermals—each of them supported and being pumped up by a column of air warmed at the surface and nowhere to go but up. When you fly through the resulting updraft, you'll feel it; maybe a soft push, or maybe a good hard kick in the ribs—depends on how fast you're going and how fast the thermal is rising.

It's not the air within the thermal column that's rough, it's the up-and-downdraft combination that makes the lumps; for every cube of air that is lifted in a thermal, a cube of air must descend to take its place. The sudden change from upward-bound air to downward-bound air results in the turbulence, and the faster you fly through it, the rougher it gets. But it's a different kind of rough when you're really moving—slow aircraft (below maybe 200 knots or so) tend to wallow and pitch rather slowly in turbulence, while the speed merchants get much the same effect as in driving a car down a railroad track, hitting more ties per second as speed increases. High speed may provide a slightly more comfortable ride in terms of queasy stomachs, but don't count on it to help your airplane withstand the shocks! In general, the airframe's ability to come through lumpy air with all the parts fastened together is enhanced by slowing down, preferably to the maneuvering speed.

The hallmark of thermal disturbances in the atmosphere is instability, or the tendency of air to continue moving upward whenever a lifting force is applied. Air classified as stable will indeed be lifted somewhat by solar heating, but when it gets higher it has cooled to the temperature of the surrounding air and has no tendency to move higher. The result?—some soft lumps at lower levels, but nothing like the days when *unstable* air is kicked upstairs by strong heating and, when it gets there, continues on until the energy is exhausted. If the air is *very* unstable, the story is often titled "Thunderstorms and Other Interesting Meteorological Phenomena." It's easy to visualize what happens in an unstable situation by thinking of the air as a kettle of water at room temperature—no currents within the water, because the temperature is stabilized—all the water particles in the kettle are quite happy with their thermal relationship with the water particles which surround them. Now put the kettle on a hot stove, and the heating from below increases the buoyancy of the water particles in the lower levels; expanded by the heating, each particle now requires more space for the same weight, and the only place where this situation can be reconciled is somewhere higher in the kettle, so the particles start up. Gentle, slow warming (such as generally occurs early on a summer morning before the sun gets high enough in the sky to really turn on the heat) means gentle, slow upward currents, not at all unpleasant. But come high noon or someone flipping the burner switch to HIGH, the particles coming off the bottom of the kettle can't cool fast enough to get acquainted with their neighbors on the way up, are always warmer than the air through which they are rising and are always trying to find a higher level where the temperature is more to their liking—that's instability. Moist air is usually unstable, because the water vapor slows down the cooling process, and tends to keep that kind of air slightly warmer than its surroundings, hence more unstable.

Thermal turbulence is easy to avoid when the updrafts are made visible by cumulus clouds, and there is also a vertical limit because the up-currents run out of gas sooner or later. When the air is very unstable and thunderstorms are blossoming, the altitude at which they stop rising can be 50,000 feet or more; on those days, it's impossible to top all of the thermal turbulence. But the normal, everyday updrafts begin to run low on energy at levels which can be topped by most light planes—something on the order of 5000 to 8000 feet or so. If no cumulus development is visible to give you a cue, look for the top of the haze layer, since it often defines the point at which vertical movement stops. Expect the smooth level to be considerably higher around big cities because of local heating.

Either by circumnavigation or by climbing above it, thermal turbulence should be avoided whenever possible and practical. On some very short trips, it just isn't worth the time and trouble to climb to smooth air. But though it may require another five minutes to get there, your passengers will appreciate your consideration when you take them to where there are no lumps. It's amazing that people will talk about how smooth is was at altitude (even though they were

up there only ten minutes of a thirty-minute flight) and tend
to de-emphasize the bumpiness on the way up and down.

By climbing at a high rate and at a low airspeed, you kill
two birds with one stone—you get up to smoother air sooner
and reduce the hard knocks on the way by virtue of the
lower airspeed. Remembering that vertical currents are more
often than not the product of a hot day, keep an eye on
cylinder-head and oil temperatures; if they start to go overboard, you've no choice but to speed up, increase the flow of
cooling air through the engine, apologize to the people and
give up a little of that climb rate.

On the way down, plan your descent to compromise two
things: a low-airspeed/high-rate descent and the passengers'
ears. Stay in the smooth upper levels until the last minute,
then come downhill in a hurry—with gear and flaps hanging
out, if necessary. Pick the "blue holes," open-sky spaces
between updrafts, because they usually represent the downdrafts that supply cool air to the lower altitudes where con-
vective currents have done their work. In addition to being a
little smoother, the blue holes are going the same way you
are, and will help get you down even faster. Be careful not to
pull the power all the way back for an extended descent;
engine bearings are designed to carry the load under power,
and long-time idling with the prop pushing the engine re-
verses the stress.

At the graduate-school level of thermal turbulence is the
atmospheric unrest caused by a thunderstorm. Operation in
a thunderstorm is covered by a single four-letter word of
advice—DON'T—which should be expanded to include flight
operations near a thunderstorm. It's generally accepted that
the clear air between two well-developed storm cells may
contain severe turbulence—even when the storms are as
much as thirty miles apart! Put as much distance as you can
between you and any thunderstorm.

Just as the ground swells of an approaching sea storm begin pounding the beach well in advance of the storm itself,
a heavy thunderstorm will announce its presence in the form
of heavy, rolling turbulence in the air close by. Whenever
you are in thunderstorm country and get the feeling that a

giant hand is toying with the airplane, slow down and turn carefully away from the pile of clouds that's causing it— you never know when the widow-maker might be just behind the next lump.

SHEAR TURBULENCE

The trout fisherman floating his favorite fly downstream hopes that the roil out there in midstream is the watery signature of a record rainbow. The astute student of fluid dynamics would recognize the swirl as evidence of different flow rates; sluggish near the bank, faster out in the middle. In like manner, the air through which we fly develops whorls as it flows along the surface of the earth, and wherever velocities differ, there's the likelihood of turbulence. If, for instance, the wind's moving over *East* St. Louis at ten knots at the same time there's a twenty-knot breeze over *West* St. Louis, you can count on at least a little turbulence where adjacent streams of air are moving at different velocities. This is *horizontal* wind shear, and seldom causes problems at low altitudes because of the relatively great distance over which the change occurs.

Going to the other extreme, when high-altitude winds gather together into a recognizable river of air moving at 100, 150, sometimes 200 knots or more, the resulting turbulence can be literally very upsetting to a pilot who wanders into its path. These "jet streams" are relatively narrow and shallow, and since the wind force increases remarkably in a vertical plane, this type of turbulence is generally blamed on *vertical* wind shear—velocity changes much more rapidly per thousand feet of altitude than it does across the same horizontal distance. When they were discovered by high-flying bombers late in the Big War, it looked like a bonanza, but pilots soon found out that the unpredictable paths and intolerable turbulence made jet streams something to stay away from.

In between the distance-diluted bumpiness of horizontal wind shear and the sometimes devastating forces of jet streams (often called CAT, or Clear Air Turbulence) is low-level vertical wind shear. It's usually found whenever the winds aloft are moving at considerably greater velocities than surface winds. In general, you can expect considerable turbulence when vertical wind shear is more than four knots per thousand feet—that's all it takes.

A commonly encountered winter situation has warm air flowing briskly northward over cold surface air. There may be a bump or two going through the relatively narrow vertical band of rapid wind velocity change, but once through the interface (which almost always will be announced by a rapid rise in temperature, or "inversion"), it's usually smooth sailing, and if you're headed north, you'll have a dandy tailwind to help you along. Southbound?—well, c'est la vie. The important thing is to recognize that the turbulence will usually be in a rather narrow band of altitude, and can be traversed in a hurry by means of a rapid climb or descent.

Except some shear turbulence when high velocities are forecast at the upper levels of the atmosphere (upper in terms of your operating environment), and, as always, it's the old compromise game—you give something to get something— because to take advantage of the beneficial winds, you might have to climb through some rough air. Take all the factors into consideration and decide what's best for this trip, this group of passengers. You might want to give up some of the groundspeed for comfort; you may be fifteen minutes late, but you won't have to clean up the inside of the airplane.

Experiment with different altitudes when shear turbulence is having a field day; often a change of just a thousand feet or so will work wonders in smoothing out the ride. Temperature is often the key to what's going on, so note the readings on the outside-air-temperature gauge as you climb— if the turbulence is due to a strong inversion, you can probably stay clear of the rough levels on the basis of temperature.

MECHANICAL TURBULENCE

Meanwhile, back in the city, the wind blowing across the office buildings is creating what used to be called "air pockets"—probably invented by an aspiring journalist in the early days of flying whose lack of knowledge about the behavior of moving air led him to believe there were indeed "holes" in the air. When you're sitting in an uncomfortable cane seat in a noisy, hot trimotor and the bottom suddenly falls out of your world, don't talk about downdrafts and mechanical turbulence, brother; you've just hit an *air pocket!* Perhaps the reason that the expertise of fluid dynamics was a mite slow permeating the aviation community was the very invisibility of the air—scientists were well aware of the characteristics of atmospheric currents, but the passengers (and many of the early pilots) who couldn't see what they were flying through knew only that, when they hit a bump, whatever was supporting them had suddenly given up—once coined, "air pocket" stuck like glue in aviation lingo for a lot of years.

Even over a smooth, unbroken plain, anything more than a gentle zephyr will stir up some mechanical turbulence close to the ground. As air moves across the landscape, the friction between air and ground slows the lowermost layers, and what really develops is another form of vertical wind shear. The difference between this and the shear turbulence discussed earlier lies in the method of production—different velocities due to atmospheric conditions versus different velocities due to surface friction. As the terrain gets rougher (therefore more friction) or the wind speed picks up, the slowing-down process becomes more pronounced and builds to higher levels. When there's a strong surface wind over RUFF TRRN (as they say on the teletype machines), you may feel the effects of mechanical turbulence for several thousand feet above the ground. An overwater flight on a windy day is almost always smoother than a flight over land under the same conditions (barring turbulence because of unstable air); the surface of the water is necessarily smoother, therefore the mechanical turbulence will be less intense. It's the same principle that drives race-plane pilots to spend agonizing hours on the other end of a shine cloth, polishing the skins of their machines to shave-in-the-cowling smoothness, decreasing surface friction. That translates to more knots per horse, which is the name of the airplane-racing game.

When the TRRN proceeds to get *quite* RUFF, as in mountains, and wind speeds increase significantly, mechanical
turbulence takes on yet another characteristic form—standing waves—and the associated bumps can go beyond uncomfortable; they sometimes get into the damaging category.
You can see standing waves in nearly any fast-moving
stream, and one that's particularly impressive is the Niagara
River, just above the falls of the same name. Approaching
the edge of the cataract, the water accelerates until some of
it simply can't continue to move at that speed and still fill
the voids created by rocks and logs and other things on the
stream bed. The lower layers turn back on themselves and
become rapids in shallow areas, but where the river is deep
enough, the rest of the water takes note of the disturbance
and goes rushing on. In the process of "noticing the disturbance," the top layers descend a bit, then climb upward again
as the stream is deflected by another obstruction, and soon
standing waves are formed. The water moves forward as
before, but there is a rhythmic up-and-down wave created
which will continue until the stream slows down or dissipates
the energy over a long distance, or until it roars over the lip
of the chasm, as in Niagara Falls.

It's a good analogy, because fast-moving air behaves iden-
tically. Instead of the Niagara River flowing over its rocky
bed, consider the prevailing westerlies moving at high speed
across the Rocky Mountains, or any of the local situations
that might affect your flight operations (the airstream couldn't
care less whether the disruptive influence is Pike's Peak or
the First National Bank Building). If there is enough moisture
in the air to cause clouds to form, they'll be of a lenticular
shape ("lennies," as the soaring trade knows them) and will
sit atop each wave. But frequently the air flowing across the
hills is quite dry, and no clouds will develop—rest assured
that even though there's nothing to be seen, the waves and
the accompanying turbulence are there whenever high winds
and high hills get together.

The low-level pilot should understand that whenever mountain waves are in the weather picture, there is some rather
violently disturbed air filling in the void on the downwind

sides of the hills, and trying to fly at or below the elevation of said hills will probably result in a very rough, very uncomfortable, possibly unmanageable situation. If you've got to go that direction, climb to an altitude roughly half again as high as the hills (7500 feet over a 5000-foot range, for example) and you'll *probably* miss *most* of the heavy turbulence. Emphasis on *probably* and *most*, since there's no guarantee that rough air won't exist at all altitudes around or over a particular peak or range. If your mission calls for flying toward the lee (downwind) side of the mountain, for heaven's sake don't approach it head on; fly at a 45-degree angle so that if you encounter a downdraft that exceeds the climb rate of your airplane you won't have to turn more than 45 degrees to keep from topping a few pine trees. If your airplane is severely limited in climb capability (and what light plane isn't?), work your way up the slope in a series of zigzags, turning away from the face of the ridge at the end of each traverse. Coming up on the wave producer from the other side, take advantage of the free lift, and let it boost you over the mountain and on your way—never look a gift horse in the mouth.

For the most part, a higher flyer will be above the rough air. Although turbulence has been experienced at very high altitudes in a mountain-wave situation, there will usually be some point in the vertical development where the airflow is quite smooth as it rides across the standing waves. When you can find this level, you'll get a super-smooth ride. Now, there's a choice—either stay in the stream and go up and down with it, or maintain altitude and fly in and out of the air river. If you elect to go the altitude route, don't be surprised when the airspeed indicator goes back and forth from near-stall to near-redline; you're fighting the elements, forcing the airplane to "climb" when it encounters the down side of the wave, and pushing the nose over as soon as you enter the updraft on the other side. There's also the possibility of getting into a touch of the turbulence that might exist under or over the stream itself.

On the other hand, if the air in which you find yourself is nice and smooth, what's wrong with staying put? As long as the undisturbed air clears the terrain, hang in there—you can do it by maintaining a constant airspeed and letting altitude go where it will. You'll also become a weather researcher, because you'll find out how deep the wave is, for whatever that's worth. Might make interesting conversation at the next cocktail party.

Even at relatively low levels, the wave will often be smooth as glass for a couple of thousand feet vertically. Experiment with altitudes, and if you've a long way to go upstream, staying in the middle of the river may be the smoothest way to go. And since you're flying at a constant airspeed in a constant-velocity wind situation, it seems the most efficient way to go as well.

WAKE TURBULENCE

The only mystery still surrounding wake turbulence is: Why did it take so long to discover the real nature of the beast? It wasn't too many years ago that aviators were labeling the disturbance behind a moving aircraft "prop wash" and putting up with the associated discomfort because it was apparently one of the prices to be paid for flying. Even when jet power eliminated the props, the bumps remained, so we cleverly changed the name of the phenomenon to "jet wash" and went about our aeronautical business, expecting to be tossed and rolled about whenever it was encountered. (Instrument pilots who judge the accuracy of their hooded 360s by the thump of their own prop wash two minutes later have something going for them, but it's not prop wash.) Bigger airplanes created bigger problems, and when aviation-safety interests decided something had to be done, the resulting in-depth studies came up with some rather astounding conclusions.

Right off the reel, let's put things in proper perspective; there's *wake turbulence* and there are *wingtip vortices*—although the two go hand in hand, the causes and effects are quite different. Wake turbulence is just another form of disturbed air, but wingtip vortices are somethin' else!

With the same certainty that a wake will be produced by a boat of any size moving through the water, you can count on some turbulence whenever an airplane cleaves the atmosphere—no matter how streamlined, it displaces air as it moves along, and since any natural system returns to equilibrium just as soon as it can, said air will try to get back where it was before the airplane showed up. When your airplane gets in the way as the disturbed air tries to return from whence it was pushed, there's going to be a bump or two.

There's not an exact parallel between an aircraft's wake turbulence and that produced by a boat, but they're similar enough for this discussion; so if you're in a canoe, would you rather cross the wake of a garbage scow or a Gold Cup hydroplane? The garbage hauler is chugging along with its broad-beamed, deep-bellied hull pushing water out of the way like gangbusters, and the wake that results as the same amount of water tries to return behind the boat gets pretty fierce. Meanwhile, the hydroplane skims across the surface flat out, almost flying on its sponsons and about half of the prop, and leaving practically no wake at all—very little disturbance, very little wake.

Crossing speed counts too, because a small boat hitting the garbage scow's five-foot wake broadside at thirty or forty knots becomes unexpectedly airborne—flying through the air in a small boat isn't a bad deal, but the lack of control may get you into trouble.

Suppose that your boat happens to be bigger than the garbage scow—a different story, because you can probably handle the waves he's creating without even spilling your drink.

That should be enough to draw some conclusions regarding wake turbulence:

1. Avoid flying behind large, slow-moving aircraft.
2. If you have to cross an airplane's wake, slow down.
3. If you're about to fly through the wake of a smaller airplane, don't sweat it.
4. Watch out for garbage scows.

WINGTIP VORTICES

The other half of the always-there pair is by far more bothersome, and in certain situations can be downright lethal —wingtip vortices, the pretenders that have gone around all these years dressed as prop wash. They changed into jet-wash clothes when the time came, but they're still there, and until the aeronautical sciences come up with an inexpensive way to create lift without wings, they're going to stick around. The crux of this discussion is that wingtip vortices are generated by *every* lift-producing body—some more than others, but if lift is there, the vortices are there. Having resigned yourself to their omnipresence, your best defense is knowing when, where, how severe, and how to stay away from them.

The investigation of the causes and possible solutions of wingtip-vortex·problems has intensified in recent years; not only are they dangerous, they also represent a great deal of wasted energy which if recoverable or reduceable, might allow greater speeds or loads with the same power—there's an economic push behind all this interest too. In general, we conclude that wingtip vortices:

1. Are created by all aerodynamic (lift-producing) shapes when they're doing their thing.

2. Assume the characteristics of horizontal tornadoes.

3. Spin clockwise off the left wingtip, counterclockwise off the right wingtip (viewed from behind the airplane).

4. Move downward and away from the aircraft's flight path.

5. Grow in strength, and therefore potential danger, as aircraft size increases.

6. Can ruin your whole day.

Fly directly behind a larger airplane at the same altitude and you may experience only a shudder from the wake turbulence, but drop down a few hundred feet, and the gyrations of your flying machine may become interesting indeed. What will likely take place depends on the direction you are moving in relation to the generating aircraft—flying directly across his wake from right to left or vice versa will probably result in a strong upward displacement followed by a very strong downward thrust, and finally another weaker updraft as you exit the two rolling columns of air. If there's nothing hard at the bottom of that vigorous downdraft in the middle, you'll probably be able to wipe the coffee off the ceiling, pull the kids out of the headliner and go about your business.

On the other hand, should the ground interfere with your sudden descent, you will make an unscheduled landing—probably a very hard one. This result is also available to those who fly directly between the vortices, in trail with the generating airplane—the next plane that is thus slammed viciously into the ground on takeoff or landing won't be the first one.

The reports of wake-turbulence and wingtip-vortex accidents seldom come from little airports, because aircraft of similar size can usually absorb the energy of their kin—that's why the mix of sizes that takes place around larger terminals creates such a problem. Although the up-and-downdrafts are capable of writing finis to a smaller airplane's flight, the rolling moments of the twin tornadoes are of far greater concern. Don't run right out and test it, but there's a rule of thumb that will give you some idea of how well your aircraft can withstand flying up somebody else's wingtip vortex; it's based on wingspan, and says that if the following aircraft's wings are as long as or longer than those of the generating aircraft, the rolling moment can probably be offset by control deflection. In other words, should you find yourself right in the middle of one of those whirling funnels of air from a *littler* guy, full aileron into the roll should be able to stop it. Uncomfortable maybe, but you'll stay right side up.

Now let's switch sides and have you follow the larger airplane; since a bigger airplane creates stronger vortices (as the weight to be lifted increases, so must the lifting potential and therefore, generally, the size of the wing), the rolling movement he is setting up will no doubt be greater than your controls can overcome. If you get into the thick of it, *you will roll,* even with the wheel or stick hard over. Now, you may be of the opinion that rolling an airplane is a hazard no matter how it is accomplished or where it occurs, but when it happens right after takeoff or just before landing . . . well, you'd best leave that kind of flying to the people who get paid for it. With no aerobatic training (let's face it—if you limited the next pilots' meeting at your airfield to those who would react instinctively and properly to a sudden roll, you wouldn't have to rent a very big hall), most flyers will do the worst possible thing when the windshield is suddenly filled with earth instead of sky—the eyes tell the brain, "Get away from the ground!" and the only response available to the gray matter is to tell the arms, "PULL!" Obediently, they pull the airplane right into the ground; in air-show talk, a Split-S—more likely, the first *half* of a Split-S.

Vortex-encounter remedies are limited; you can have enough presence of mind and aerobatic ability to continue the roll and fly out of trouble, or you can not be there at all. The latter is by far the more reasonable and practical, and can be easily accomplished by putting your knowledge of the phenomenon to work. If vortices are not generated until lift is produced, there can be no problem until the bigger aircraft rotates on takeoff, or after its nose wheel touches down on landing. So simply stay out of the airspace under the biggie's flight path, and you're out of trouble. The situation is weighted in your favor since a big airplane will usually gobble up most of the runway on its takeoff roll, and will touch down just as close to the threshold as safety permits— most of the runway is relatively free of the vortex problem, giving the light-aircraft operator plenty of working room.

Intersection takeoffs or departures on crossing runways are subject to a standard three-minute delay imposed by the Controllers, but that's just a sop to theory—the twin tornadoes have been known to persist for fifteen to twenty minutes. If you don't think that's enough time to let the energy blow out, wait as long as you care to, or ask for another runway. Even though you can climb above the turbulent area, don't forget that the vortex on your side of the generator's flight path is moving toward you at about five to ten knots in calm air—how embarrassing, when you've planned carefully to climb above the vortex cores, to encounter the monster just as *you* rotate! When in doubt, wait—if you're still uneasy, wait some more.

The continued emphasis on wake-turbulence/wingtip-vortex avoidance during takeoff and landing has somewhat overshadowed the enormity of the problem at altitude. Concern close to the ground is justified, because when the roll associated with the vortex core is encountered, altitude in which to recover is the key item; but the same invisible monster exists up high, and it's there in spades. A big airplane flying at high speed really tears up the atmosphere; keep your eyes on a sharply defined and persistent contrail against a deep blue sky some day, and watch as it is ripped into shreds and great convoluted loops, all because of wake turbulence. The vortex cores are there too, just as strong as they are on approach or departure (maybe even more wicked, if some students of turbulence are to be believed), and every bit as much a hazard to your operation. It's now standard practice for ATC Controllers to provide at least 1000 feet vertical and five miles horizontal separation from the "heavies" (aircraft with gross weight capabilities of more than 300,000 pounds), and those are good figures to start with.

When a crossing is unavoidable, try to make it happen with you on top; if that's out of the question, get as many feet between you and the bigger airplane as practical, and by all means avoid crossing just under its flight path several miles back—that's where the bad guys are.

A VORTEX BY ANY OTHER NAME . . .

Words of wisdom on the subject of wake turbulence run to great lengths on the generation, strength, behavior, and avoidance of the hazard, but precious little is said about what to do if you get caught. Want to experience wake turbulence safely? Make a date with an instructor at the nearest soaring school, and have him demonstrate the downdraft and both vortices as you explore the wake of the towplane; it's not *much* of a wake, but the characteristics are the same, and you can get some of the feel of the phenomenon. Or, you might talk to a military pilot who has flown troop-carrier or aerial-refueling aircraft, with takeoff intervals of as little as fifteen seconds, and identical climb profiles; wingspans are the same and therefore control is adequate, but such a pilot will be a vortex veteran—that's the way it has to be.

Such experience shows that a pilot's first action must be *immediate* control response to counter the rolling moments of the vortex. Once a roll starts, remember that it will cost you some altitude, so you might as well crowd on the power; since all vortices descend, the additional thrust can't help but start the airplane moving upward, the fastest way out of the problem area. If you're not at all familiar with the aero-dynamics of inverted (or nearly so) flight, remember that every degree of bank is a lift thief, and if the situation gets extreme, be ready to override the pullback instinct; you'll likely have to shove the wheel farther forward than ever before.

Should you encounter a vortex that's literally bigger than you or your airplane, when full control into the roll has no effect, you have no choice but to complete the roll. In most nonaerobatic airplanes, this is the maneuver that generated the phrase "easier said than done." Never been upside down in a flying machine? You might consider investing a few bucks in an aerobatic demonstration just to see what it's like.

The downdraft at the heart of a large aircraft's wake can increase your rate of descent remarkably, and in an en-counter close to the ground, there's no sensible choice but to add all the power available and go around; if you get into the downwash so close to the runway that full power won't stop the descent, push the go-handle anyway and cushion the touchdown as much as possible.

Unlike acquiring experience through training, as we do in instrument-flying and engine-out procedures and other pilot operations, it's pretty tough to teach proper responses for wake turbulence encounters. But we can all learn what causes the problem and where it's most likely to show up . . . and

armed with that knowledge, it's not at all difficult to stay out
of harm's way.

HOW TO HANDLE YOUR AIRPLANE IN TURBULENCE

Under certain conditions, there's nowhere to go within the
performance capabilities of your airplane that will put you in
smooth air, but it's usually possible to find an altitude that's
at least a bit more comfortable. Given the states of the atmosphere that produce low-level turbulence, climbing will more
than likely provide your quickest "out" where the air gets
lumpy. But in order to smooth the ride for yourself and
your passengers, you're going to have to fly through some
roughness. Rather than just accept whatever happens, use a
bit of technique which will make things more pleasant for all
concerned and might someday become a safety factor if you
get into air that's full of really *big* lumps.

Very seldom does turbulence happen right now, like flying
into a brick wall; there's almost always some warning, some
indication that the air is going to get rough. It may be in the
form of turbulence-torn clouds up ahead, obvious signs of
strong surface winds, or billowing cumulus clouds all over
the sky. Whenever the opportunity presents itself, prepare
yourself and your passengers before the cabin begins tossing
—if you expect anything more than light turbulence, have
everybody take up a notch in his seat belt and "bottoms up"
so that there won't be globules of coffee or Coke floating
around the cabin. (Why do pilots always wait until you
have just poured a steaming-hot cup of coffee, full to the
brim, to announce impending turbulence? A passenger who
can come through moderate turbulence with a half-full cup
and unburned lips should apply for a master juggler's
license.)

Pull a little tighter on your own seat belt, because the
more your body bounces, the harder it will be to read instruments—eye cameras have proved that in really heavy
turbulence your eyeballs jiggle around like the instruments,
since they're both shock-mounted—do yourself a favor, cut

down the movement of the "panel" (your body) by strapping it firmly to the seat. Loose things can become missiles in severe turbulence, and even if it doesn't get that bad, anything flying around inside the airplane will surely take your attention from flying the airplane. Put flashlights in the glove box, computers in your pocket, thermos bottles back in the picnic basket; get them out of sight, out of mind—you have more important things to do.

Preparing the airplane consists mostly of slowing down. This will have considerably different implications depending on the type of airplane, but most light planes cruise at something in excess of recommended "maneuvering speed." That's one of the V speeds you had to learn when you were becoming a pilot, and chances are you haven't thought of it, much less used it, since. Very simply explained, flying at maneuvering speed gives you the best chance of surviving an encounter with a really severe updraft or downdraft, because an aerodynamic stall will occur before the structural limits of the airplane are exceeded. You've got to admit that it's easier to recover from a stall than from a structural failure—when the wings come off, the decision-making process becomes a rather sterile effort.

"VERY SIMPLY EXPLAINED" ISN'T GOOD ENOUGH

. . . at least not for the serious pilot, so here's a more detailed explanation of maneuvering speed.

The name says little of what this speed means, and perhaps most importantly, says *nothing* of what it means to you with regard to flight in turbulent air . . . it would be a lot more significant if it were called "maneuvering and turbulent-air speed." But we're stuck with the term as is, so we'll use "maneuvering speed" for the rest of this discussion.

Nearly all general-aviation airplanes are designed to stay in one piece with a load factor of 3.8; in other words, during a very steeply banked turn, or a vigorous pullout from a high-speed dive, or upon encountering a *really* strong vertical gust, your airplane's weight can suddenly be increased 3.8 times without structural failure. There's a safety factor built in—you'd have to put a load factor of 5.7 on the airplane to actually bend the airframe—but it's very unlikely that would happen in the normal course of events. In the first place, that much G-force is most uncomfortable, and chances are good that anything more than a momentary exposure to that kind of load factor would cause you to black out (blood tends to rush to the lower extremities, and vision is progressively "tunneled" until you can't see at all—vision returns immediately and totally as soon as the G-load is reduced). Secondly, in order to put a load factor of 3.8 or more on your airplane at normal speeds, you'd have to pull a lot harder than you'd like on the control wheel. And in the third place, even if you pulled that hard, the wings would probably stall before the maximum load factor was reached. This high-speed stall is most important, and deserves more attention.

Any maneuvering of the airplane in order to generate high-load factors requires increasing the angle of attack, whether it's pulling out of a dive or adding back pressure in a steep turn. And you know that when the angle of attack is increased beyond its critical value, a stall takes place; the wing doesn't care how that happens, but it *will stall whenever the critical angle of attack is exceeded.* Now, imagine an airplane flying level at its stall speed—very low airspeed and very high angle of attack. If the angle is increased *at all,* the wing will stall (this is what you should shoot for when performing that training operation known as "Maneuvering at Minimum Controllable Airspeed," or what used to be known as "slow flight").

But the important thing is to note that when the stall occurred, the load factor was exactly *one;* when you applied back pressure to cause the stall, it happened instantly, with no Gs being applied to you or the airplane. Now imagine the same airplane being flown level at some higher airspeed; the angle of attack will be lower than before because the increased airflow over the wing serves to develop additional lift. If, in *this* condition of flight, enough back pressure is applied to cause a sudden stall, you'd find that in the process of changing the angle of attack, there was some acceleration involved, some load factor applied to the airplane and to you, and you'd feel it in the seat of your pants. The effective weight of the airplane would increase momentarily, and that would cause the stall to occur at a higher airspeed than before. If this exercise is carried out at higher and higher speeds, the load factor present when the stall occurs will also continue building, and at some airspeed, you'd discover that you were pulling 3.8 Gs in order to make the airplane stall.

Check Figure 9–1, which is a typical maneuvering-envelope diagram for a light airplane (no particular airplane; this diagram is strictly hypothetical). The curve which runs through points A and B was developed by noting the G-loads imposed on the airplane when it was stalled at various airspeeds and provides two critical points in the airplane's performance envelope: first, Point A, which represents the airspeed at which a one-G stall takes place; and Point B, which is where the "stall curve" intersects the 3.8-G structural limit line . . . this, of course, is the airplane's maneuvering speed *at a certain gross weight.*

If you were flying this airplane at the "heavy" weight, and at the maneuvering speed indicated on the diagram, you could haul back on the wheel and expect that the wings would stall and relieve the load on the structure without exceeding the 3.8-G limit. Fly at an airspeed faster than that, and the back pressure required to produce a stall would be enough to exceed the structural limits of the airplane. For example, at an airspeed of 125, this airplane (Figure 9–1) would not stall until the G-load reached nearly 5, and the potential for bending some of the metal would be very great.

It's safe to say, then, that at any given weight, there's an airspeed at which the airplane will stall and relieve itself of the added load before the structural limit is exceeded. Anytime you are flying at an airspeed *less* than maneuvering speed, you can pull on the wheel as hard as you are able, and the worst that can happen is a stall; but fly at some airspeed *above* maneuvering speed, and the same hard pull may cause the wings to come off. More likely, it will be the tail that will separate, but at that point, who cares? It's a nonrecoverable disaster either way . . . chances are you won't want to try it again.

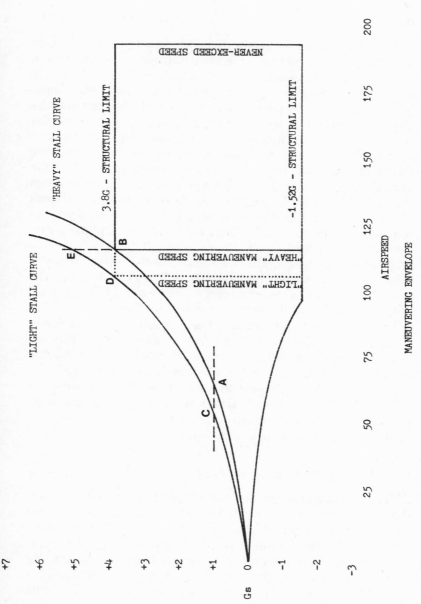

Figure 9–1. Maneuvering envelope diagram of a typical light airplane.

To this point, we've been talking about pilot-induced loads on the airplane structure—the result of excessive back pressure—but there's another way in which angle of attack can be increased. Suppose you are flying level once again right at the stall speed in perfectly calm air. All of a sudden, the airplane enters a severe updraft, and as a result of the instantaneous change in relative wind, the angle of attack is increased. It doesn't take much; remember that you were flying *at* the stall speed, therefore, hovering close to the critical angle of attack. If the small change of angle due to the updraft is enough to *exceed* the critical angle, a stall will occur. And just like the pilot-induced stall when flying at the stall speed, there will be no loading of the airplane structure—it's a 1-G stall.

Should that same updraft be encountered when flying at some higher airspeed, the updraft will try to displace the entire airplane upward, but inertia will resist the movement, with the result that the load factor will increase and the stall will occur at a higher speed. Once again, higher airspeed produces higher load factors when a gust is encountered, and the wings will stall and unload themselves at increasing load factors until that magic number is reached where the load is enough to exceed the structural limit. Instead of maneuvering speed, here is where we should add "turbulent-air speed" to the definition, because the pilot didn't do any maneuvering at all to cause the problem.

HEAVY, LIGHT OR WHO CARES?

Pose this question in the pilots' lounge some rainy Saturday afternoon. Which airplane (same type, of course) will be in greater danger of shedding some of its appurtenances in heavy turbulence—one loaded to the gills or the one with only the pilot's fanny and two gallons of gas? The engineers will make strong claims one way, filling the blackboard with convincing algebraic solutions, and those who have flown both situations in rough air will line up against the opposite wall, and the argument could last well into the night. The large transport-category airplanes, jets in particular, are extremely critical when it comes to selecting the proper turbulence-penetration speed because of the range of weight versus stalling speeds and the usually catastrophic aftermath of picking the wrong one; but for most light airplanes, changes in gross weight due to loading or fuel burn in flight are not large, and don't make remarkable changes in maneuvering speed. The manufacturers quote one speed which applies safely to a range of aircraft-loading situations. But for the record, take another look at Figure 9–1, the maneuvering envelope, and notice that the 1-G stall speed for a light airplane (Point C) is lower than that of the heavier airplane (*that* shouldn't be a surprise!), as is the maneuvering speed . . . Point D, where the "light" stall curve intersects the 3.8-G limit line. The lesson is a simple one: Maneuvering speed always varies directly as the weight of the airplane, or in other words, as weight goes down, so must maneuvering speed. (There's also a simple formula that underscores the direct relationship between weight and maneuvering speed: maneuvering speed = stall speed × √load factor. Stall speed decreases with weight, and, therefore, decreases maneuvering speed.)

Unless you're really into aerobatics (which requires an airplane stressed for a much higher load factor), you are probably not going to go out and throw your airplane around the sky with so much force that the maneuvering portion of the definition will apply. But when you encounter rough air, rough enough to produce some anxiety about whether your aluminum bird is going to stay together, remember that the airspeed published in the *Pilot's Operating Handbook* is valid only for that airplane loaded to its maximum gross weight. If your airplane is exceptionally light on the day in question, slow down . . . your concern is for structural damage, and the worst that can happen at some lower airspeed is a stall. When the airplane is very heavy, go to the published maneuvering speed; but *no faster,* because an airspeed increase at *any* weight pushes you closer to both limits . . . stall *and* structural failure.

Of particular concern is the pilot flying a very light airplane, and who just doesn't feel comfortable about slowing down when he encounters turbulence. That's why Point E was added to the maneuvering-envelope diagram. Suppose the "heavy" maneuvering speed is being used for the "light" airplane; a truly vigorous updraft could conceivably load the airplane to more than 5 Gs before relief shows up in the form of a stall. And 5 Gs is asking the airframe to bend a long way without breaking. It's just about a sure thing that you'll need to take your flying suit to the cleaner after an experience like that!

SOME TIPS FOR TURBULENCE

You might as well be satisfied with hitting the target instead of the bull's-eye, because if the turbulence gets much more than moderate, your airspeed indicator may be bouncing off the pegs on both ends of the scale. It's of the utmost importance, then, to know what power setting and pitch attitude will produce maneuvering speed. Next time you fly in smooth air, find out what these settings are, and if you *should* come up against that brick wall suddenly, you can at least make an intelligent move in the right direction.

When things get to the point where you feel like the bone in the turbulence terrier's teeth, there is one thing to remember that will do you more good than anything else—maintain a level attitude. Once you've powered back and pitched up to maneuvering-speed conditions, hang in there, and do your utmost to keep the wings level and the nose on the horizon. Forget airspeed and altitude (unless you're about to meet a mountainside, in which case you'll have a hard time ignoring your height above the ground), don't change power unless it's absolutely necessary and don't manhandle the controls. All your control inputs, especially to the elevator, should be moderate ones; just enough to stop the excursion, and the pressure should be eased off as soon as the excursion stops.

Your objective in turbulence becomes an "average" attitude, where the rolling and pitching movements are permitted up to a certain point (set your own conservative standards here), then they're stopped and the airplane is returned as nearly as possible to level flight attitude. You'll never be able to make the airplane hold completely still in turbulence, so why fight it? As long as you're going through or toward the desired attitude, you're doing okay. When you need to turn or climb or descend, increase the pitch or roll excursions a little more in the appropriate directions, and don't let them go as far the other way.

The proper use of trim, especially elevator trim, is more important in turbulence than in smooth air, where it does little more than relieve the pilot of pressure loads in order to maintain a desired attitude. When things get rough, trim will help you return the airplane to what you know is a safe, flyable attitude. During violent departures from normal attitudes, it becomes difficult to apply control pressures in the smooth, even manner you normally use, but when the airplane is properly trimmed, much of the work is done for you; it's sort of a memory bank for the controls.

A well-trimmed airplane will *try* to return to that sought-for average attitude, and all you need do is help it a little. Use rudder as required, but mostly to keep things as coordinated as you can. Making that little black ball stay put in turbulence is out of the question—apply rudder pressure to keep the nose from swinging wildly and let the ball take care of itself.

Trim for maneuvering speed and then leave the trim wheels or switches alone—there's a safety consideration here. A husky updraft which appears bent on pushing you to a new altitude record persuades you to roll on a few turns of nose-down trim—no sooner is this done than the airplane flies into an equally ambitious downdraft, at which point you're looking at the ground instead of the sky. The next maneuver—commonly known as "Let's get the hell out of this dive!"—is frequently a heart-stopping performance.

GEORGE, THANK GOODNESS YOU'RE HERE!

The eternal question: autopilot on or autopilot off in heavy turbulence? The answer (if indeed there is one) depends on a number of things—the intensity of the turbulence, the type of airplane, the type of autopilot, your ability to hand-fly the machine, the sharpness of the gusts, what else you have to do at the time and enough other considerations to pretty well muddy the waters on this point.

After some experience in turbulent air, you will probably develop a good hand at rough-air flying, and chances are that you can control the airplane better than George. All autopilots control by reaction, which means that nothing happens until something happens—*when* it happens, the airplane may be in one of those out-of-trim situations, and the next something could just as easily occur in the opposite direction. Not to imply that a human pilot won't have the same troubles, but after a while you'll find yourself sensing turbulence a split second before it hits—almost a sixth sense —sounds weird, but it seems to work that way. Besides, hand-flying the airplane keeps your mind off the unimportant things, and you have a built-in excuse when the guy in the seat behind you wants to play another hand of gin rummy—"Are you kidding? I've got my hands full just keeping this thing right side up!"

To thine own self be true—a realization that you're not certain you can handle the situation should be followed by an immediate autopilot engagement. If the situation gets to that point, George will do at least as good a job, probably better, and you'll have time to fall back and regroup. Perhaps a few relatively quiet moments when you have time to think about what's going on will generate a solution—a way to fly out of the bad stuff instead of slogging all the way through. When in doubt, let George do it.

REPORTING TURBULENCE SO THAT OTHER PILOTS
KNOW WHAT YOU'RE TALKING ABOUT

Isn't it interesting that the two most pucker-muscle-tightening airborne hazards are reported within the aviation community in the most unreliable terms? Turbulence and icing (the troublesome twins) mean so many different things to different pilots—a trace of light ice on a 747 may be a ship-sinking load of the white stuff for a 100-horsepower trainer. There's a psychological problem too, with the pilot who is asked, "How's the ice situation up there?" and who doesn't want to admit that he's into something he can't handle—"A little clear ice, nothing serious"—when in fact he's shuddering along on the edge of a stall at full power, with a ton of ice spread all over the airplane.

Turbulence reporting is not much better off, with those involved letting the rest of us know what it's like in terms of their experience. There has been some work done in the development of an accelerometer-type rough-air-measuring device, but though a lot of money was spent, it was still difficult to arrive at "hard air" criteria which would be applicable to more than just the aircraft in which the measurement was taken.

So the best we can do is adhere as closely as possible to the official turbulence-reporting criteria, published as a table in the *Airman's Information Manual*. The intensity you select (light, moderate, severe, extreme) as the label for the rough air you just came through will most likely be further interpreted by the person to whom you're reporting, and will almost always be one notch higher than it actually was—it's human nature. Especially when flying tales are being told around a bar, the stories of severe—nay, even *extreme*—turbulence become so commonplace that one wonders if it's ever safe to wander into the sky. If you ever anticipate such a round of stories coming, at the first mention of turbulence jump right in with the wildest, wing-sheddingest, seat-belt-breakingest fabrication you can concoct; unless the first lie is wrapped in extreme turbulence, it's doomed to failure in one of aviation's favorite "Can You Top This?" categories.

Let's get the criteria straight; you can apply them to your operation as you see fit, keeping in mind that light turbulence to a jetliner is something entirely different to a single-engine four-banger.

Light turbulence:
Turbulence that momentarily causes slight, erratic changes in altitude and/or attitude.

Moderate turbulence:
> Similar to light turbulence, but of greater intensity. Changes in altitude and/or attitude occur but the aircraft remains in positive control at all times. It usually causes variations in indicated airspeed.

(By the way, do you recall our reference to the different kind of reaction when a high-speed airplane encounters turbulence? When you hear that deep-voiced airline captain talking about light chop, he's going through what you would label light turbulence; the big difference being the rate at which he's driving across the railroad ties. Light chop causes slight, rapid and somewhat rhythmic bumpiness without appreciable changes in altitude or attitude. Moderate chop is much the same except for the intensity, and the rhythmic bumpiness changes to "rapid bumps or jolts.")

Severe turbulence:
> Causes large, abrupt changes in altitude and/or attitude. Usually causes large variations in indicated airspeed. *Aircraft may be momentarily out of control.* (Emphasis is the author's—now, how many of those "severe turbulence" stories do you want to retract?)

Extreme turbulence:
> Turbulence in which the aircraft is violently tossed about and is practically impossible to control. It may cause structural damage. (There aren't many pilots who have *flown* in extreme turbulence—they were just along for the ride; you have to hold on to the seat with *both* hands.)

HOW ABOUT THOSE POOR FOLKS
WHO CAME ALONG FOR THE RIDE?

The Turbulence-Reporting Criteria Table provides an alternate method of determining the grade of rough air in which you may find yourself, or, if you want to look at it another way, what to expect when one of the intensities is reported where you intend to fly. The criteria mentioned previously were concerned with the reaction of the aircraft, but the following descriptions are of "Reaction Inside Aircraft." For example, in light turbulence (according to the official description), "occupants may feel a slight strain against seat belts or shoulder straps. Unsecured objects may be displaced slightly. Food service may be conducted and little or no difficulty is encountered in walking."

(What the description *really* means is that when you are in doubt as to the grade of turbulence, turn and ask your passengers if any of them feel a slight strain against his seat belt or shoulder straps. Sleeping children are seen to shift position just a little in light turbulence. Mother may go ahead and serve the basket lunch she packed, and anyone on his way to the lavatory will be observed having no trouble getting there.)

When moderate turbulence comes along, "occupants feel definite strains against seat belts or shoulder straps. Unsecure objects are dislodged. Food service and walking are difficult."

(What the description *really* means is that someone in the airplane taps you on the shoulder and says, "I think I just felt a definite strain against my seat belt or shoulder strap." Two of the children have been thrown to the floor of the airplane, Mother now has a lap full of potato salad and baked beans and people with slightly green faces are noticed banging back and forth against the seats as they fight their way to the bathroom.)

In severe turbulence, "occupants are forced violently against seat belts or shoulder straps. Unsecured objects are tossed about. Food service and walking are impossible."

(What the description *really* means is that the airplane has become a testing laboratory to see how far seat belts or shoulder straps will stretch without breaking; doggedly spooning baked beans and potato salad out of her apron ("I fixed it, by golly they're gonna eat it!"), Mother is alternately occupied with trying to slow down the kids as they ricochet off the cabin walls. The green-faced ones are now barely able to hold up one or two fingers, let alone even *think* about trying to get to the lavatory.)

When (heaven forbid) you get to the top of the line, when you encounter the worst the atmosphere has to offer, there are no criteria listed for "Reaction Inside Aircraft." In extreme turbulence, it probably doesn't matter what you observe in the cabin, because you won't be able to make a report anyway—you'll be speechless. Might as well engage the autopilot and have your hands free to do something meaningful—such as clasping them in front of your chest, and saying to your passengers, "Repeat after me—Our Father . . ."

DON'T GIVE UP

You can't get around it—maintaining a level attitude is the very best thing to do in turbulence, and it's as important psychologically as it is aeronautically. It may be uncomfortable and unpleasant, but you're there—how you got there is of no concern, and you've got to fly out of it—so why not make the best of it, learn something and be better for having come through it? Take the airplane by the horns, say, "Airplane, I'm sorry I brought you here, but we're in it together and I'm going to get us out of it." Saying things like that will bolster your inner self and give you greater strength for the task at hand. If the airplane answers, you've got bigger problems than we can take care of in this book.

10

How to Overcome "Get-Home-Itis"

THE EFFORT THAT'S REQUIRED TO FLY an airplane properly is energy well expended—you couldn't find a better investment to save your neck, which happens to be one of the payoffs. In addition to the obvious safety aspects, the aesthetics of doing it right should be considered; even those pilots who are too haughty to admit it have their emotional strings twanged every now and then by the pleasure that comes from well-disciplined flying. Think back to some of the milestones in your flight training and early hours in the air—the first flight itself, the first solo, your first solo cross-country when you were *really* out there on your own—no matter what the final objective was for you, each flight was a rung on your experience ladder, and the satisfaction grew with the significance of what you accomplished.

Experts in aviation safety have come up with various experience levels that purport to represent the times when a pilot is most vulnerable to misfortune, but these figures are based on the average guy, one of which there isn't in real life. The military and the air carriers can quote accurate figures for their pilots, but the validity of these "Be extra careful!" points is limited to the pilot population for which the numbers were calculated: even then, an occasional accident involving a pilot with an experience level way under or way over the safety experts' theoretical danger zone suggests that flyers can get into trouble just about anytime they want to. The reliability of a "most dangerous time" figure falls apart completely when dealing with general aviation pilots; there are literally thousands of training programs, each a little bit different, accepting candidates from a selection process which does little more than weed out those who are short of cash or who reply "*What* chart?" when the medical examiner asks them to read the eye chart. Add an infinite variety of motivations to these factors, and there's no possibility of coming up with anything but an educated guess as to which rung is most likely to break as a general aviation pilot climbs his own personal experience ladder.

In the final analysis, there is a time for every pilot when his confidence exceeds his skill, and regardless of his background, he is at that moment very accident-prone. While some flyers seem to be able to hold off the problem areas until late in their aeronautical lives, it makes sense to watch for the danger point somewhere in the early stages of experience. Survival of the rigid discipline of training (satisfying even the most lackadaisical flight instructor requires more line-toeing than the average citizen is used to) and the sudden release of restraints when they're turned loose have an insidious way of convincing certain types of pilots that there are wing buds under their shoulder blades, that they are natural aviators, born to fly. Maybe it's true: perhaps they should take up residence in trees and eat worms; but like young birds (who also have operational problems each spring), "young" airmen haven't fallen out of the nest enough to even *know* about all the extraordinary situations out there, let alone have the skill to handle them.

Most of us learn as we go, biting off chewable-size chunks of progressively more demanding situations; accepting a little more crosswind, a little more turbulence, a little less runway, and each time finding out a bit more about the limits of man and machine. The super-smart pilot stays close to a good instructor long after the check ride, and draws on the other's experience to continuously upgrade his "cope-ability." Of course, there aren't many dragons to slay in the Sunday-afternoon traffic pattern, or between here and Grandma's on a bright, calm and cloudless day; if that's as far out as you intend to stick your neck, godspeed—and may you thoroughly enjoy your kind of flying, on your own terms.

But let's assume that your airplane was acquired to provide efficient transportation—not necessarily faster than a speeding bullet, but at least faster than whatever surface transportation is available tomorrow, when you plan to fly from Here to There for an important meeting. Why not invite three friends to go along? Good idea—somebody to talk to, and it costs less when everything is divided by four instead of one. A couple of phone calls and it's all set, but you'll have to be back by three o'clock, because Charlie has an appointment at four, Bill must get to the bank before closing and Clyde's kitchen pass expires at dinnertime. Forecasts look good, so you commit yourself; "No sweat, guys; it's gonna be a beautiful day, and we'll be home by three, guaranteed."

When you're alone, the failure of a "guaranteed prompt return" is just an inconvenience, but the obligation builds in direct proportion to the number of passengers on board. In this case, your promise will result in three people setting schedules, and at least three others will program their day accordingly; Charlie's appointment, Bill's banker and Clyde's wife. Should the weather do a 180 you'll be under the gun, because you've promised to have everyone home at a certain time.

Sonofagun—the weather *did* a 180 at going-home time, and the atmosphere is now in a state of great unrest. Go or no-go? A decision has to be made, and right now. With all the pressures working, you're a pushover for a disease more common than most of us are willing to admit. You won't find it in medical dictionaries, but it's capable of terminating your existence just as effectively as a wing coming off in flight, and its name is get-home-itis.

Once introduced into the system, get-home-itis spreads quickly throughout the entire mental cavity and settles down in the common-sense gland, where it can distort your thinking in either one of two possible directions. At the negative extreme, there's the pilot who will curl up and cancel at the smallest hint of trouble on the way home, while the macho type at the other end of the scale elects to press on regardless—"Nothing can stop me." Most pilots, a little more audacious than Caspar Milquetoast and a bit less intrepid than Superman, operate somewhere between bold and bashful. When you're willing to find out what lies beyond the next cloud (nothing ventured, nothing gained), do it cautiously, carefully and in your own good time—be patient; you'll probably get to joust with all the windmills sooner or later.

You've whipped half of the get-home-itis bad guys as soon as you realize that the weather (or approaching darkness, or rough terrain, or a hangover, or any of a hundred reasons for not wanting to go) is something less than ideal, and that there may be a condition out there you don't want to cope with. The other half of the bad news is your three passengers; filled with confidence in your ability after that flawless outbound flight, they can't see why a little weather is a threat to getting home, and they'll begin to press—their reasons for returning have suddenly become more important than getting home itself.

Especially the first time or two, the decision to go or stay can be a little gut-wrenching, with the thunder of an approaching storm in one ear and the pleas of your passengers in the other; somewhere in between, where your good sense resides, there will be a monumental confrontation. The outcome is difficult to predict, because it's not a two-plus-two situation—a human being is involved, which means that a whole spectrum of emotions, character traits and personality soft spots come into play. One manifestation could be indifference—some pilots just don't care what happens, reasoning that they'll "think of something." Occasionally a radical personality change takes place under stress—Caspar Milquetoast becomes a roaring mouse. Greed, impatience and ambition sometimes act as catalysts while an acute case of get-home-itis is brewing.

These symptoms will usually coalesce in an uncommonly

strong sense of urgency which inflates the importance of getting home—it is accompanied by a noticeable increase in the subject's capacity for rationalization, for pretending that things are not really as bad as they look and that everything will work out somehow. And don't think your pride won't get in a lick or two! Whether you like it or not, or even admit its existence, there's a big, strong, swaggering input that will urge you to go ahead just to save face—after all, you got these people here, why can't you get them back?

The knot in your stomach tightens, the reasons for leaping off become more compelling; "Let's go—that appointment means a hundred grand to my company," pleads Charlie. "If I miss dinner again this week, it's instant divorce," whines Clyde, and Bill will be thrown into debtor's prison if the bank closes its doors before he closes his deal. Should you decide that you can't fly safely over, under or around whatever is lurking between here and home, and you've made up your mind that you're not going to leave the ground until things settle down, it's time to make the move—time to chicken out.

With the big decision under your belt, the rest is easy; well, all except breaking the news to your passengers, whose grumblings have escalated to threats of bodily harm. But tell them you must, so you might as well get it over with. There are a thousand ways to get out of a situation like this, and having a selection will help you the first couple of times it happens. Once through the wringer, you'll develop your own techniques; but for starters, here are three classics (in reverse order, starting with the least desirable):

1. After listening patiently to your riders bemoan their respective fates if they don't get home on time, look at the darkening sky and your watch, and allow as how you'd like to wait five minutes for the latest weather reports. Then saunter into the Flight Service Station or the nearest phone booth and waste as much time as you can "studying" weather reports. If you decide on the telephone route, you don't even need to spend your money—go through the dime-in-the-slot motions, and with concern on your face, listen to the dial

tone for ten minutes—your passengers will never know the difference. Timed properly, this technique will allow the squall line to move across the airport, and your drenched friends will have to admit that you've a good head on your shoulders after all. (Suggested special qualification for chicken-out technique No. 1: a touch of theatrical talent.)

2. Get the airplane loaded and everybody strapped in, then pretend that you forgot something on your preflight inspection. While poking around importantly in the engine compartment, yank any handy wire loose, then take your sweet time refastening the access door. (In cases of extreme passenger pressure, remove a section of cowling.) If by this time the storm hasn't struck, reboard and restrap, and after going through a slow, painstaking checklist (you might even consider losing your place and starting over a couple of times), begin cranking the engine. It won't start, of course, but you'll kill a lot of time trying, and you'll kill the battery, too. "Sorry 'bout that, she just won't fire—battery's dead—guess we'll have to call a mechanic." And you know what kind of a delay *that* will cause. (Technique No. 2 will cost you some money—neither batteries nor mechanics come cheap these days.)

3. The best way to chicken out is the easiest, and involves an established theory of communication—KISS—Keep It Simple, Stupid. "Charlie, Bill, Clyde, this weather was unexpected, but it's here. I'm not sure I can handle it, and I don't intend to find out the hard way. We're not going to fly home, at least not right now." (A No. 3 chicken requires more guts than the other two, but it gets easier every time.)

In the chorus of unhappiness, there may be heard a discouraging word, like "chicken pilot." Might as well agree, and save your breath—you'll never make that guy understand the difference between chicken and smart. If you like, there are plenty of clichés to use: live chicken versus dead hero; or that antique about old pilots and bold pilots but no old, bold pilots; if the public relations waters are that troubled, you'll think of some kind of oil to pour on them.

Flying loses some of its superstitions every day as it becomes a more routine way of life, but there is apparently no immunity from the gremlins, those puckish little fellows who take such delight in making fools of pilots; and it's doubtful that you can outwit them. On a day when the weather forecasts are so grim that there's a bearded prophet marching up and down in front of the terminal building proclaiming the imminent end of the world, you elect the chicken-out route. An hour later, only halfway home in a rented car and very much on the wrong side of your three-o'clock promise, you realize you've been diddled—dry road, blue sky, no wind, bum forecast—that's one for the gremlins.

So, go with the information you've got. When you do your best to find out what's happening and act accordingly, you'll come out on top of the situation more often than not. Weather forecasts seem too good to be true?—start checking; they probably aren't. Look at the sequence reports (*reports,* not forecasts) for stations to the west of where you are and where you want to go; in most parts of the country, that's where you'll find the weather that will affect you soon. When you're far away and the home-base forecasts look a bit squirrely, invest in a long-distance phone call to the weatherman back there; he knows local conditions much better than the man where you are.

Weather is the most visible and the most frequently encountered source of get-home-itis, but other situations deserve equal consideration, maybe more—if the weather deteriorates and you're called upon to deliver all you've got in the way of skill and talent and sharp thinking, the weakest link in the performance chain is the one that will give. A fuzzy head, a tired body or pigheaded determination to press on will likely add to the problem.

Aviation seems to have ten *thousand* commandments, of which these three will do a lot for your longevity:

1. Never go anywhere in an airplane unless you're prepared (and willing) to come home by some other means of transportation.

2. Before every flight, take inventory of yourself, your equipment, your "cope-ability," the weather, how current you are: in short, know thyself.

3. This one transcends all else: *never need to get anywhere so badly that you're willing to pay the ultimate price.*

No matter how hard your passengers try to sell you on making like a bird when you don't think it's a good idea, take up the white feather—"Folks, we're not going to fly today!"—simple, direct, gets the point across. The really insistent Charlies and Bills and Clydes are very much a minority, but don't be put down when one of them ruffles your chicken feathers—after all, you're warm and breathing and *able* to be ruffled—what could be more important than that?

11

Basics of ADF Navigation

THERE ARE A LOT OF PILOTS AROUND TODAY whose ears still ring with the static that was part and parcel of low-frequency radio navigation, and their backs still ache a bit from leaning forward in the seat as if moving even a foot closer to the station would help to filter a Morse identifier out of all that noise. When a signal was particularly elusive, they'd conjure up a special hell where cockpit designers would have to spend eternity holding their arms overhead twisting tuning cranks on the cabin ceiling. And even after those aviators of an earlier day got the right frequency, they had to locate the null, or no-signal, position of the manual loop that provided the only clue to the whereabouts of the transmitter.

It was known as RDF then, for Radio Direction Finder, and when the R give way to A for Automatic, it did nothing for the static, but a lot for pilots' arms; with ADF, the flick of a switch commanded the loop to move itself and point to the station. So if one of the holes in your instrument panel is filled up with an automatic direction finder, take a moment and pay silent homage to those sore-armed, half-deaf, hunchbacked aviation pioneers who preceded you. Better yet, learn how to use ADF, so that their ears and arms and backs will not have been bent in vain.

It's a lot better than it used to be, but ADF hasn't changed much over the years. The avionics mills turn out new-generation black boxes almost daily, but the automatic direction finder you buy off the shelf today does no more and really doesn't do it any better than the one you might inherit with the purchase of a thirty-year-old airplane. A machine of that vintage may even have a loop antenna on its belly or back; guaranteed ice collectors, they were later enclosed in streamlined bubbles which collected only a little bit less ice. Today's electronic loops hide in the skin of the airplane, and don't collect any ice at all—that's progress! But even with flush antennas and digital tuning devices and back-lighted dials and fancy indicators, the ADF can be no more than it was yesteryear—an electronic bird dog which points to a radio station—and unless you know what the dog is trying to tell you, it isn't worth turning on.

Perhaps that is too strong a statement—the ADF does provide another dial and a couple of switches with which you can impress the ground pounders, and since it is basically an AM radio receiver, you can listen to ballgames, news bulletins and the Top Forty, if you can stand it. The ADF could be a backup receiver in a really tight bind where the only rope that potential rescuers can throw to you is the spoken word. On the aeronautical chart, every navigational frequency which is not underlined is capable of carrying voice transmissions, the voice in the wilderness that might be enough to get you out of trouble someday. There are also enough continuous-broadcast beacons around the country to make weather information rather generally available. Most of these medium- to high-powered stations are navigational eunuchs: no longer able to provide that nostalgic aural "beam" which air-mail pilots and movie stars were always coming in on, they are the remnants of the four-course radio ranges. Here's where ADF can make a social contribution—when the rainy-day conversations in the pilots' lounge get overly uninteresting, just mention that you flew over the

XYZ beacon yesterday, and if there is an old pilot in the group worth the patina on his wings, he'll fill the afternoon with tales of earlier days on the XYZ range.

Baseball games and music notwithstanding, there are practical uses for ADF, and because of the transmission characteristics of low-frequency radio waves, it will come in handiest when VOR falls on its line-of-sight face. When you're down low, wandering among the mountains, or out in the boondocks more miles from the nearest omni than its signal can be received, ever-ready ADF will do its job as long as it's within range of a transmitter. The receiver cares not whether you select a navigational beacon or a commercial broadcast station; if you can identify the signal, you can most likely depend on the pointer. Unlike VHF, low-frequency radio waves are distance-limited more by the power output of the transmitter than by line of sight. Altitude obviously doesn't matter much—don't low-frequency AM stations come in just fine on your car radio?

The function selector on a typical contemporary receiver has OFF, COMP (or sometimes ADF) and REC (or maybe ANT) positions. The first one is self-explanatory, but the other two are important if you intend to get the most out of the ADF unit. Whenever you are tuning the set, do it on REC or ANT, for they abbreviate RECeive and ANTenna and, when selected, cut the loop motor (or other means of direction sensing) out of the system. After identifying the station, switch to ADF or COMP (for COMPASS) and let the needle do its job. If you rotate the tuning knob or crank while the function switch is on ADF or COMP, the pointer tries to point to every station you pass on the radio dial.

There are three situations in which ADF can be of considerable help to the fair-weather pilot; cross-checking position with ADF bearings, tracking to a station and tracking from one. Now before you get all tangled up in terminology, let's agree at the outset that fair-weather ADFing will deal only in generalizations; a "bearing" is the number of degrees between nose or tail of airplane ("0" or "180" index on the ADF dial) and nose of needle when the ADF is pointing to a radio station. To "track" means to proceed in a straight line from here to there. That's all you need to know for now, but if you later decide to pursue more exacting direction-finding problems, like looking for an airport in the fog, ADF work under the hood or inside a cloud will be a piece of cake; the principles are the same, you just tighten the tolerance screws a turn or two when you're on instruments.

Take the easy one first: Imagine flying from A to B, two points a number of miles apart which happen to be connected by a straight stretch of railroad. Since you will be dealing with "tracking" to and from radio stations later on, begin right now to associate any desired course with the term "track." You can also call the track a "line of position," or LOP—with no major landmarks around, you'd like to find out just where on that LOP you are. If there's any kind of a low-frequency radio station within range, tune it, identify it, and when the needle settles down, note the *general* direction it points: perhaps it comes to rest halfway between the nose and the right wingtip of the little airplane centered on the ADF dial. No little airplane there?—cut one out of a magazine and paste it on, to help visualize the bearing.

On the chart, imagine an airplane lined up with the track in the direction you're flying, with an ADF needle pointing between the nose and the right wingtip. With a plotter or the folded edge of a chart or a pencil, make the needle long enough to reach the charted position of the radio station (you'll have to move the extended ADF needle back and forth along the track until the pointer crosses the station), and you've got *another* line of position. Where the two LOPs cross is where you are—a "fix." The track could be a highway, a coastline, or an LOP from any other source (maybe a VOR radial) which will cross the ADF line of position. You'll always do better to select a radio station as close as possible to a wingtip bearing; the greater the angle between the heading and ADF bearing, the more accurate the fix. Once the direction finder gets you in the ballpark, there is certain to be a crossroads or a lake or something nearby to confirm your position. *Warning*—choose your "somethings" with great care. A pilot who was completely lost in a strange part

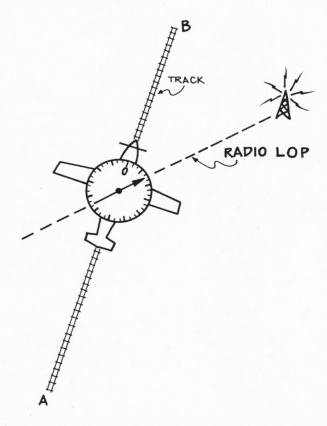

Figure 11–1. Crossing two LOPs (lines of position) to obtain a fix.

of the country felt his orientation hopes soar when he spotted a water tank which appeared to be floating on the top of a thick fog bank. Reasoning that there must be a town underneath, he circled the tank at close range, already speculating on the town name that would surely appear on that round metal signpost. When the six-foot hand-painted letters finally became readable, they announced not the name of the town, but that someone in the CLASS OF '72 had made it to the top of the tank with a can of black paint.

Second situation—tracking *to* a radio station. The objec-

tive is to proceed in a straight line along the track to point
B, which has become endowed with a low-frequency radio
station. You've tuned and identified it, and when you are
over the railroad headed directly toward point B, the ADF
pointer will be on "0." Your heading at this point is a key
item; it's the heading of the railroad, which is also the desired track and the desired course to the station, and it's
where you want to be from here on.

As long as there is no crosswind, you can maintain that
heading and fly to the station, right on the track, with the
ADF on zero all the way. A crosswind will show up visually
as you drift from the track, and the ADF will also provide a
clue as the pointer moves slowly away from "0." Hang on
to that original heading like a terrier, and if the wind blows
you off course, the ADF will always tell you which way to
turn to get back where you belong—over a river or highway the drift is obvious, but suppose this little exercise is
taking place over a trackless desert?—turn toward the
needle!

When drift is recognized, you know that there is some
heading, some crab angle, that will keep you over the railroad once you get back, and your ADF is about to become
a wind-correction-angle indicator. Let's say it becomes necessary to turn into the wind 20 degrees to stay on track—if
that turn were to the *left,* the ADF needle (always pointing
to the station) would appear to move to the *right* on the
face of the dial, and it would move exactly 20 degrees to the
right of the "0" index.

You have set up the basic ADF on-course situation; with
heading adjusted to stay over the railroad (the desired
track), the ADF pointer will be displaced to the *right* the
same number of degrees that you have had to change heading to the *left.* In other words, you are always on course
when the heading change (i.e., crab angle) and the ADF
indication are in balance, each being displaced the same
number of degrees from where they were at the start. If the
crosswind requires 20 degrees of drift correction to the *left,*
the ADF will show it by pointing 20 degrees to the *right* of
"0." A *right* crosswind that requires 15 degrees of crab will

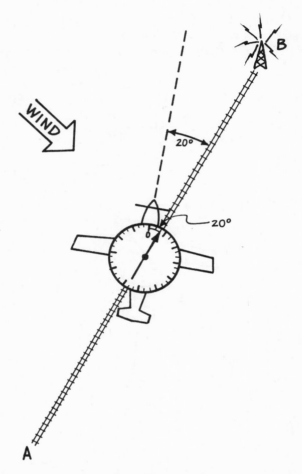

Figure 11–2. A 20-degree correction to the *left* to compensate for wind results in the ADF needle moving 20 degrees to the *right*.

show up as an ADF indication 15 degrees to the *left* of "0." Disregard the numbers which are printed on the face of the ADF dial—your concern is simply how many degrees the needle shows to the left or the right of the zero point.

By the same method, you can always tell when you have

intercepted a desired track by approaching it at a known angle. If your intercept heading is 45 degrees to the *left* of the desired course, you're there when the ADF needle has moved off to the *right* 45 degrees; turn right and fly to the

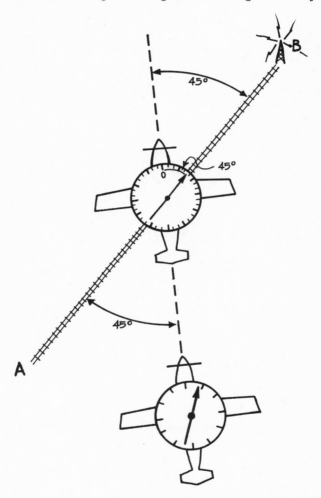

Figure 11–3.   ADF indications when approaching and intercepting a track. Interception angle is 45 degrees.

station. You don't know from this information alone exactly where you might be, but you have an LOP, and that's half of a fix. (By the way, tracking is not to be confused with homing, wherein the ADF needle is kept on the "0" index at all times by turning the airplane. You'll get to the station eventually, but on a curved path across the ground, and at the will of the wind. There's one good feature about homing—in the process of turning to keep the pointer on the nose, you'll arrive finally at a heading which lines you up with the wind, and no further changes will be necessary. Now that you know the wind direction, how does it feel to be flying the world's most expensive weathervane?)

Tracking *from* a station, situation number three, is quite similar—still on course, but now past point *B* and its low-frequency beacon, the ADF pointer has swung around the dial to the 180-degree position (the tail of the airplane), and as long as there is no wind from either side, it will stay there. When drift occurs, the needle will show you which way to turn to get back on course; needle to the right of the tail?—turn right (and the other way round). The balancing act goes on again, with one significant difference: the balance between heading change and ADF indication will be on the *same* side. If you need to crab 20 degrees *right* to stay on course, the ADF needle will also be displaced 20 degrees to the *right* of the "180" point. Consider the "180" as just another zero, and you'll do yourself a big navigational favor —your concern when tracking outbound is not what number lies under the head of the ADF pointer, but how many degrees it has moved from the zero point.

It follows that you can also intercept a given track outbound, if that will help get you where you want to go. Set up a convenient angle between heading and desired track (45 degrees is a good compromise between early interception and making progress downstream), and when the ADF points to that number of degrees from the tail (to the *right* of the tail if your heading is to the *right* of the track and vice versa), you're there.

An ADF needle seldom stays put for very long, even after painstaking efforts to get on course and stay there. This is

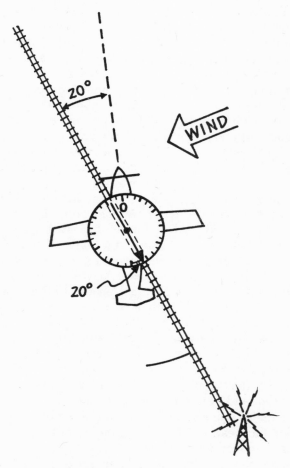

Figure 11–4. Tracking outbound from a radio station. The ADF
needle moves the same number of degrees as the wind correction
angle, and in the same direction.

to be expected, since the wind is probably changing constantly in direction and force. Experiment with five-degree
heading changes; cut and try until you arrive at a heading
that keeps the balance reasonably intact. With practice,

you'll develop a feel for the amount of turn required to make the ADF do what it should. You can always return to the original heading, see which way the needle points and start all over again.

If the needle still seems to misbehave, check your heading discipline. There's no way to do a passable job of ADF navigation without precise heading control, because a low-frequency radio transmitter has no fixed signal pattern. Unlike VOR, where you select a precise electronic course and let the receiver interpret it for you, all courses look alike to your airborne bird dog. You can have heading and ADF needle balanced to a fare-thee-well, but if the track along which you're flying isn't the one you wanted, the entire procedure is worthless. When in doubt, prove the veracity of what you see by turning momentarily to the original heading; if the ADF needle goes to "0," you're on track—but if it settles somewhere else, the track has gotten away from you, and you'll have to start over.

Recall our predecessors who RDFed their way through the air despite static and sore arms? They had one more thing to fight; the aberrations of the magnetic compass, which in anything but perfectly smooth air is far from a steady indication of which way you're headed. When directional gyros came along, the aviation community rejoiced at what they thought was the end of all the wanderings and gyrations of the magnetic compass. Unfortunately, the DG builders didn't advertise the fact that their machine gave out information not one degree better than what the pilot put in—DGs are dumb, senseless things, very much subject to their own errors. Very early in the game, perhaps when some poor soul attempted an ADF approach to Pittsburgh and wound up over Punxsutawney because of the precession in his directional gyro, aviators decided that it would be a good idea to check and reset the DG to agree with magnetic compass readings every fifteen minutes. Unless your airplane carries an inertial navigation system, you'd do well to comply with this four-times-an-hour check.

And even though your success with ADF procedures is

largely dependent on heading control, don't worry about failure of the magnetic compass—if the power source for *that* instrument quits, you've got more to be concerned about than which way is north!

People Seldom Win Arguments
with Propellers

Every once in a while, an overzealous lineman loses his head when he ducks under a just-arrived airplane to render that famous get-you-chocked-before-the-engines-stop service. There's not much you as the pilot can do once he's made his move, but you can form a habit that might prevent such a grim situation.

Since your airplane will roll quite a distance on level ground sans engine, shut it off while you're far enough away from your parking spot to let that airborne guillotine come to a stop and slip silently into the line. Of course, you'll have to judge the distance and the speed, but after a few tries it'll be old-hat. If such a maneuver requires more taxi speed than you care to maintain, use power as long as you need it, but there's never a need to keep the engine running after you've got the chocks "made." Turn off radios and lights and other things while you're taxiing, and as soon as you don't need the motive force any longer, shut 'er down.

Besides, it's a great opportunity to listen to the condition of your brakes.

12

Twelve Ways to Drive Tower Controllers Up Their Glass Walls

THE GUYS AND GALS in Airport Control Towers are as regular a bunch of people as you'll find anywhere. They go to work on schedule, carry their lunches in brown paper bags and bitch about working holidays and weekends, just like the rest of us. When the weather's lousy and nobody's flying, they have a lot of time on their hands and talk about money and fishing and cars and the opposite sex, just like the rest of us. When they're busy they're *really* busy, and a Controller frequently goes home with a shorter nose from having had it against the grindstone all day, just like the rest of us.

But when things get super-hectic around the airport, a Controller is *not* like all the rest of us; he must sometimes feel like a juggler with half a dozen balls in the air at once, and every time he puts one down, another shows up to take its place. When a *foul* ball shows up, a Controller's capacity to endure may be severely tested. If one day you have nothing better to do, here are twelve experience-proven bits of chicanery you can try to see how far a Controller will bend before he breaks.

1. Equip your airplane with at least one very poor quality radio which will transmit nothing but squawks and squeals.

(It's important to use a good receiver so that you can hear the Controller trying to reach you.) The busier the airport the better, because your unintelligible gibberish will block out everyone else, and if you really work at hogging the frequency, the traffic congestion will grow to unbelievable proportions in short order. No fair looking at the Tower cab during all this, since they will no doubt hit you with a flashing white light (return to the ramp) in an effort to unclog the jam-up. When you figure the Controllers have had just about all they can take, switch to your good transmitter and say eagerly, "How do you read *this* transmitter?" You will be cleared for an immediate takeoff, with the Controller's best wishes for an extended cross-country . . . one way.

2. Make your initial call to a busy Tower ". . . ten miles east" when you're really ten miles *west* of the airport. The Controller will schedule your entry and pattern sequence from the east to fit into the flow of traffic around the field, so wait until you're no more than two miles out to let him know your true position, and watch him scramble to readjust things. Besides, this will give other pilots some real-world practice at dodging head-on traffic.

3. This is a variation of the call-in-from-the-wrong-direction trick. Pick a very busy day and wait until you're only two miles from the airport to call the Tower. It doesn't matter a whole lot from which direction you approach when you're in this close, as an unexpected entry in a pattern full of airplanes is in itself enough to set off some frantic controlling. There's a reasonable chance that you'll get a landing clearance ahead of everybody else—the Controller may consider that getting you on the ground in short order is the lesser of two evils.

4. Equally effective on the ground or in the air, this little gem requires a specific set of circumstances; namely, when several airplanes are getting ready to taxi, or when you find yourself at the end of a long line of inbounds to a terminal seething with airborne traffic. On the ramp, for example, you should wait until at least four or five pilots ahead of you have called "ready to taxi," and each one of them has been patiently briefed by the Ground Controller on the runway,

winds and altimeter setting. (Really do it up brown by waiting for a day when the Controller is bound by local policy to advise you of "men and machines working both sides of the parallel taxiway, heavy construction equipment crossing the taxiway two thousand feet from the departure end of the runway, taxi on the right side to avoid fresh paint on the centerline of the taxiway.") Even though you've heard all the good news five times and could repeat it verbatim, don't bother to tell Ground that you "have the numbers"; just call in "ready to taxi," and see if he can do it all over again without losing his cool.

5. Here's one that's a mettle tester for Controllers *and* fellow aviators. It will work only when you're number one for takeoff at an airport logging an arrival or departure every minute or so. When the Tower advises that you're "cleared for *immediate* takeoff," go through your before-takeoff checklist once more just to be sure you haven't missed anything, then ever so slowly start moving toward the runway. There aren't many Controllers who will be able to contain themselves, especially if you amble out to the centerline just in time to make the guy on short final go around.

6. Fly out-of-sight patterns. Turn downwind when the airport is just barely visible on the horizon, extend it to the limit of prevailing visibility, don't turn base until fuel exhaustion becomes a possibility and fly the final approach as slowly as possible. This will test the Controller's vision as well as his sense of fair play, for a sneaky one may try to land several other flights ahead of you. When the Tower asks you to extend your pattern so he can get a couple of long-suffering departures off the ground, *that's* the time to cut 'er close—a sure way to find out if the Controller knows that aircraft on final approach have the right of way.

7. After landing at a completely strange airport (the bigger and more complex the better), don't bother to ask Ground Control how to get where you want to go. Just say "34 Alpha to the ramp" as if you knew the airport like the home 'drome, and drive down the nearest taxiway. More than likely you'll soon be involved nose-to-nose with a DC-10 or something

equally non-turn-aroundable on a taxiway, and then let the Controller unscramble things. A variation of this ploy is to turn onto an active runway, and see if the men in the Tower notice—a great way to find out if they're controlling traffic or playing Chinese checkers.

8. There are two ideal situations that will get the most out of this one, and if you set it up carefully, you might even combine them for twice the effect. In the first case, you should be leading a parade of several aircraft down the final approach to a long, long runway with one taxiway within a thousand feet or so of the approach end, the other one a mile and a half away at the far end. When you're cleared to land, slow up so that all the people behind you have to S-turn and slow-fly and make 360s, then land on the threshold, roll slowly past the first turnoff and go all the way to the other end at no more than twenty miles per hour. Listen carefully to see if the Controller can handle himself with aplomb as he orders three or four missed approaches.

The daily double is yours when there is a gaggle of planes lined up waiting for takeoff—by landing short and rolling long, you will also cause them to be delayed, further complicating the Tower's problems. If this game had points, you'd get a bagful for putting these two together.

9. Here's another one that may blow a Controller's mind when the pattern is bank-full; wait until you're well established on final approach with two or three behind you, then let the Tower know that you've changed your mind, this one will be a full stop. Of course you must have set him up with a long series of touch-and-gos before you drop the bomb. What the heck—those pilots behind you probably needed some go-around practice anyway.

10. "Tower, 34 Alpha ready for takeoff" when you are number ten in line isn't so bad, but you've only begun; as soon as everybody moves up a notch, call the Tower again and repeat every time the line advances. By the time you get to the head of the class, you may have a Controller tearing his hair.

11. Wait for a true fair-weather day when everybody and

his brother are out flying and the airport is the center of attention for a swarm of propeller-driven bees. From ten miles out, call the Tower and identify yourself, making sure to specify your exact position (say "ah-h-h-h" between landmarks while you look over the side to make sure), taking as much time for this transmission as possible. As soon as the Controller has digested all that meaningless information, he'll ask if you're landing at his airport, whereupon you execute the master stroke by informing him that you are just requesting permission to pass through his Control Zone.

You know that Control Zones are of concern only when the airport is reporting less-than-basic-VFR weather, but does he know that? A Controller whose goat is easy to get will ask you to report entering and leaving the "zone," which gives you the opportunity to bug him several more times, but most Tower people figure it's less trouble to clear you on through than to explain that they really don't care— especially when they find out that you're flying 9500 feet above the ground. Want to drive the botherspike a bit deeper? Call the Tower when you're five miles out whether he asks you to or not, hit him again directly overhead and once more at the five-miles point outbound. If you can couple this procedure with Trick No. 1, the unreadable transmitter, you'll have done a bang-up job.

12. Last in the even-dozen lineup of Tower-teasing tricks is another variation of a theme. When you complete your high pass à la No. 11, turn around and come back the other way, but at an altitude of 1000 feet AGL. This time you're right down there with 'em, well under the 3000-foot ceiling of the Airport Traffic Area. If at all possible, push the airplane past the legal speed limit of 156 knots (so they won't be able to put the binocs on your registration number as you smoke by the Tower), fly right over the middle of the field (no sweat, you're all of 200 feet above pattern altitude—if any students or Sunday flyers aren't paying attention to their altimeters and get a little high on downwind that's *their* problem) and of course you're not going to bother the Controller for permission to fly through his back yard. Do keep

your receiver on Tower frequency, though; you'll be the subject of an interesting one-way conversation, and you can eavesdrop the frantic warnings to the student on downwind who's followed by a Sunday flyer, and they're both a little high.

Intersection Takeoffs

When you hang up your helmet and goggles for the last time, chances are better than good that you'll have sweated your way through a couple of takeoffs that turned into "get to the end and pull" exercises. And after one like that, you'll wish you had reverse pitch so you could back up to the threshold to have all the runway available. Don't think it hasn't been done for that extra few feet, even when the pilot has to get out and push the airplane until the rudder is in the bushes. In a situation that's anything less than a three-alarm life-and-death emergency, you've got to wonder whether the risk is really worth all the effort and anxiety.

The "hang the tail over the fence" philosophy is a sound one from several points of view: yours, for example, if the engine quits just after liftoff and there's five thousand feet of beautiful runway straight ahead; or your airport neighbors', who will barely notice the airplanes overhead when full-length departures allow noise-abating climbs; and yours again when you're totin' a heavy barge and trying to lift a max-gross bale and you need every foot of takeoff run you can get.

But, au contraire—there are probably an equal number of situations when time, money and gasoline could be saved and traffic movement enhanced by taking off from a convenient intersection. It's gross inefficency to taxi an airplane a mile and a half to the end of the runway, and then leap into the air after an eight-hundred-foot takeoff roll.

When physical layout, performance altitude, traffic conditions and airport environs favor an intersection takeoff, by all means include such a request in your message to Ground Control. If the man in the minaret feels it would do more harm than good, he'll let you know. Remember that his rules call for a mandatory three-minute delay behind large jets—that's to get *him* off the wingtip-vortices responsibility hook. Terminals with a lot of heavy jet traffic are *not* good places to ask for intersection takeoffs.

On your own at an uncontrolled airport, redouble your sky-scan prior to taking the active runway at an intersection.

The pilot who always uses the full length of every runway

is not to be faulted; he will become quite good at taxiing, will be five minutes behind the guy who makes sensible use of intersections, and probably also wears both suspenders and a belt.

13

Back to Basics: Pilotage and Dead Reckoning

THERE'S A LONG LIST OF WAYS to get from one place to another in an airplane, navigationally speaking. From the bottom up, it all began when airplanes flew so slowly that the pilots were able to relate to familiar objects about the countryside, and though flight gave them a new vista, they could hardly fly fast enough to get lost. The still extant method of following a highway or railroad track helped keep things going the right way, and before long someone figured out how to make a magnetic compass light enough to carry in an airplane, and dead reckoning opened new frontiers for flyers.

Transoceanic flights presented a bit of a problem; granted that if the captain kept the letter E (for Europe) under the lubber line of his magnetic compass he would no doubt make a landfall somewhere on the continent (conversely, W for Wrong was lettered on the reverse side of the compass card to prevent large navigational errors), but airline passengers demanded something more than just getting to the right land mass. Specialists were needed, and seagoing navigators shifted gears and became aerial navigators—the only big difference being that things happened a lot faster.

But celestial navigation, the mainstay of overwater course keeping, had visual limits; and when the airframe industry finally came up with airplanes that would carry the celestial navigator above the clouds, avionics technology had developed navigation systems that made star shooting a dying art. Black boxes have almost totally replaced the proud crew member who carried a flight kit bulging with star charts and the latest copies of the *Navigator's Almanac;* an inertial navigation unit can't find Aldebaran or Betelgeuse or the Chair of Cassiopeia in a star-spattered sky, but its digital readout of latitude and longitude is a thousand times more accurate than even the most artful three-star fix—so long, professional navigator.

Whether you like it or not, even our segment of aviation is going the black-box route; for a price that's not unreasonable now and promises to get more enticing as production builds, you can equip any small airplane with a computer that will fool a VOR/DME station into thinking it's somewhere else, and show you the course and distance to wherever you want to go. But every once in a while it's great fun and even more of a challenge to your total piloting skill to shut off all the switches, send the black boxes out to lunch and navigate by yourself—no VOR, no ADF or radar vectors, just you and the chart and the system that started it all—basic, simple, self-satisfying pilotage.

HOW BASIC CAN YOU GET?

If you really know the lay of the land, you don't need an aeronautical chart to get to Grandma's any more than you need a road map to go downtown—take off and turn right, over the river and across (not through) the woods, to Grandmother's house we go—flying from one easily recognizable landmark to the next, with no concern about groundspeed or heading. Your only interest is in getting there, you don't care how long it takes and you can't get off course because the next checkpoint is always in sight.

(You can overkill when flight planning. I remember a

classroom full of would-be military pilots getting ready for their first solo night cross-country—no detail was spared, we'd listened to step-by-step briefings about what to do in case we got lost and were advised of the omnipresence of airborne shepherds at each turning point. Armed with pencils, computers, plotters, charts and enough navigational planning to estimate anywhere in the United States within thirty seconds, off we went . . . and almost as soon as the gear was up, there were the rotating beacons at both corners of the triangle, like sore thumbs among the ground lights of North Carolina. The purpose was training, of course, and that kind of navigational discipline pays off under less ideal conditions, but I'm not sure those instructors weren't trying to tell us something.)

A strange landscape underneath changes things, but only slightly. Instead of familiar landmarks, you'll be flying from one to the next with reference to a chart; and it doesn't have to be an aeronautical publication either. One of the funniest things one pilot ever did was to let an incredulous passenger think he was navigating down the Bahamian chain with a crumpled, coffee-stained place mat which showed the islands as they were depicted in a centuries-old engraving. If all you're concerned about is highways, rivers and towns, use whatever's handy; but don't expect the Standard Oil Company to help you much when it comes to tower frequencies and VOR locations.

KEEP IT SIMPLE

Put some kind of a course line on your chart so you'll know which way to fly and which landmarks to look for. Over relatively flat land that doesn't require detours around mountain peaks, make it a straight line and use whatever landmarks lie close by; in the mountains you may have to dog-leg it to accommodate your altitude limitations, all the while wending your way in general toward the target.

No straightedge?—just pinch the chart at departure and destination, fold between the pinches and run a pencil along the fold. Even if your pencil falls down between the rudder pedals, a couple of passes along the fold with thumb and forefinger will crease it enough to suffice.

Okay, take off and turn toward your first landmark. A general heading will do; remember this is an exercise in *pilotage,* flying from one visual checkpoint to the next. When you get the airplane squared away and are ready to start looking, turn the chart so that it is headed the same way you're going—don't complicate things by trying to read a chart upside down and backwards at the same time. As landmarks appear, they'll look the same on the ground as on the chart, and vice versa.

Which brings up a bone of contention on which VFR navigators have been gnawing since '03—should you look for features on the ground and then try to find them on the chart, or the other way round? The most sensible method is probably a combination of the two, with the emphasis on *confirmation.* If you're looking in vain for a yellow water tower and in the process spot a lake with a distinctive shape, for heaven's sake look on the chart for a lake with a distinctive shape. On the other hand, when the chart shows a yellow water tower just to the left of the intended course, look for the water tower while you're looking for the lake. When you nail down one or the other, confirm it with a cross-check of what you actually see versus what you should see—the mind tends to lock on to first impressions and throw out other clues. When it does, you can bet that there are two distinctively shaped lakes and two yellow water towers in that area, and you'll pick the wrong one every time.

By the way, don't forget that an elusive landmark might be right underneath. There's nothing that says you can't roll the airplane up on a wing to see what the floorboards are hiding. The same goes for lakes and towns and things directly behind; push a little on a rudder—you may uncover just what you're looking for.

As soon as you're over the middle of the lake put your index finger right there on the chart, and *leave* it there until you are over the next checkpoint downstream. The fastest way to get into trouble on a pilotage trip is to forget where you've been. Watch a veteran navigator at work; whenever he establishes a fix, he'll make some kind of a mark on his chart—it might be a penciled circle or just a smudged fingerprint.

And so it goes, eyeballing and index-fingering your way from one landmark to another, until the next landmark is the airport you're looking for. Of course, the higher you fly, the more features you'll be able to see, but this exercise is just for fun, so try it at a thousand feet—you'll rediscover the world of flight from a seldom used vantage point.

NEXT STOP—DEAD RECKONING

Or DR, as the navigators and over-forty pilots call it. The term comes from marine literature, having to do with the calculation of a ship's position based on how far one had sailed at a known speed while heading in a given direction. "Dead" seems to imply that something is missing, and it is—visual sighting of landmarks (seamarks?) along the way.

It probably wasn't labeled, but you used dead reckoning throughout your cross-country training by estimating and correcting for the effect of wind, and expecting certain towns or railroad tracks to show up on schedule if you and the wind forecaster had both done your homework. When a town was late coming over the horizon, or the tracks ran the wrong way, you made an inflight correction and began anew, DRing to the next checkpoint on a different course or estimating arrival at a different time.

Just like pilotage, dead reckoning is gradually slipping into aviation's less-instrumented past—almost every airplane has a VOR or ADF receiver, and there aren't many destinations which don't underlie a matrix of radio signals these sets can use. So once again, for challenge, for fun and for practice in case it ever becomes a necessity, navigate with the old masters—try dead reckoning.

You need to know a little more than where you've come from and where you intend to go, but those are prime items for planning a DR flight. Draw the course line on the chart again, and measure its angle from north; put that into your computer along with true airspeed and the wind numbers, and you've got the most important number of them all: estimated groundspeed. Barring some really significant change in wind direction or force, your objective should be somewhere very close by when the ETA comes up. It's much like flying across a wide lake; you can't really be sure of your position without visual clues, but you know that if you hold the heading and keep flying, the other shore will show up sooner or later. Then you can start looking for precise landmarks.

So dead reckoning is certainly useful for flying across big lakes, as well as extensive forest areas and deserts—any place where terrain and cultural features are few and far between—at least it imparts some direction and discipline to your navigation. DR can be especially helpful at night, when all towns look alike—fly out your ETA before giving up on a checkpoint.

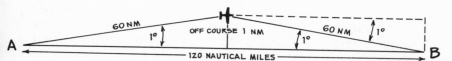

Figure 13-1. The 1-in-60 rule of thumb for off-course corrections.

When you finally spot something on the ground and it appears that you're to the left or right of where you want to be, there's an easy way to get back on course at your next checkpoint with the smallest possible heading change, thereby saving time (the old "shortest distance between two points" trick). It's called the "1 in 60" rule, and here's how it works: whenever you have flown 60 miles and find yourself one mile off course, you will also be one *degree* off course; by correcting your heading one degree, you'll fly parallel to the intended track and will theoretically arrive at the next checkpoint one mile off course. But if you know how far away that next checkpoint is, the rule will provide an additional correction that will get you there directly overhead—if the distance to fly is also 60 miles, when you're off course one mile the additional correction will be another degree, for a total heading change of *two* degrees.

That's fine for the theorists, but there aren't many times in the real world when you'll fly exactly 120 miles with an off-course check at the mid-point. By visualizing the length of any leg as an increment of 60 miles, you can apply the rule in increments of heading correction as well. For example: after a 30-mile flight, that same one-mile error represents *two* degrees off course; after 120 miles, you're only *half* a degree away from centerline for each mile. The "1 in 60" rule will never bring home the bacon for navigational accuracy, but it gives you something to work with.

WHEN NOTHING SEEMS TO WORK

Of the myriad ways that pilots have devised over the years to get lost, one of the most insidious is to let the aircraft heading wander. Without benefit of an autopilot to stand guard over which way the machine is pointed, it's not at all difficult to let the nose swing ten or fifteen degrees while you're consulting a chart, or putting mustard on a ham sandwich. Just as soon as the new heading takes you significantly off the track, cities and lakes, shorelines and highways begin to mysteriously shift their positions on the face of the earth. There's always a town that looks enough like Anytown to fool you, and the first thing you know you're hopelessly lost—all of a sudden there are no more railroad tracks, no lake where a lake should be—what now?

If you catch the error early enough, stretch your vision to the limit in all directions, hoping to catch sight of one of the significant landmarks on your chart. It won't hurt a bit to climb and expand your visual parameters; you'll also be able to broadcast your plight farther and wider if it comes to that. Don't fly in circles; you no doubt realized which way you let the heading slip, so turn back toward your intended course—continuing on the wrong heading isn't going to help at all.

There's a last-ditch procedure you might as well try when all else fails; fly to the nearest river and follow it downstream until you come to a town. If the community isn't big enough to have an airport, remember that as streams get wider, towns get larger, so fly on until you find an air-minded city or until you run out of gas, whichever comes first.

Airplanes Fly by the Minute

Even if you never go outside the traffic pattern, read on—there may come a day when you'll be thankful for every minute of flying time you can squeeze out of the tanks.

Some day in the far-distant future, there won't be selective fuel systems on any general-aviation airplanes except the antiques. New types (that is, new designs) will shortly have to comply with a rule that says fuel shall be either ON or OFF—no selection of right or left or center or wingtip or auxiliary—if you can get the engine running, it should run until the gas is gone.

That's a good deal, even though it's a sop to poor aerial discipline, because it will undoubtedly keep some people from coming to an untimely end through selecting an empty tank. In the meantime, you probably have a fuel selector in your airplane, giving you the choice of left, right or both. You might be amazed to find out that there can be a big difference between the amount of fuel actually in those tanks and what you have always *thought* was there when the needles point to F.

Rather than just bore holes in the sky on your next trip, make a fuel-consumption check. Fill both tanks (or all four, or whatever you've got) and start, taxi, run up, take off and climb on one or the other—whatever you like, but arrive at your normal cruise altitude with an untapped supply. As soon as you have the machine fully set up at the power setting you prefer for cruise, note the time and switch to the full tanks.

If your trip isn't long enough, or your bladder strong enough, fly for as long as practical (at least an hour to get a good check) and before changing anything else, switch back to the original fuel supply. When you get on the ground, note carefully how much the lineman pumps aboard, and you can compute a rather accurate fuel-consumption rate for your airplane at that particular cruise power setting. When you have time, do it again with a different number of horses pulling you through the sky—it will furnish some useful figures for detailed long-range flight planning, and if you get a figure for the maximum-endurance power setting (that's the one where you're literally hanging on the props, getting as much time as possible out of each drop of gasoline), you'll know how long you can stay in the air if you ever have to.

To dope out the absolute number of minutes the airplane will fly on each tank at a fixed power setting, go through the same routine, but after you switch to the full tanks, leave the selector alone until the engine quits—depending on the type of airplane, you may want an airport several thousand feet directly below.

Time it carefully, and on some later flight do the same with the other side—you'll probably start flying by your watch and not by those Mickey Mouse fuel-quantity gauges in most of our airplanes. Having an accurate endurance figure lets you run to within ten minutes or so of fuel exhaustion before switching tanks; knowledge begets confidence and utility.

14

And Then There Were Two . . . Multi-engine Flying

WHAT WAS IT YOU WANTED MOST when you decided to fly a twin? Speed, space, economy, reliability, prestige? All those benefits are part and parcel of the operation of a multi-motored airplane, and in varying amounts, depending on whom you're talking to. Some pilots count speed and economy together, as well they might, for the ability to get from here to there faster often means less money spent in the long run. Others fly with twin powerplants because they need more space inside the cabin than a single can provide. There's the occasional well-to-do flyer whose life style demands something more than just one engine, and he's the guy you'll see stepping from a Mercedes or some other appropriate chariot into his twin. But when you peel away the outer layers of justification, it's a sure bet that somewhere underneath lies a solid core of reliability—the very fact that there's an engine left to bring you home if something goes wrong in the other powerplant.

The pilot operating VFR over hostile terrain or on long water crossings will probably talk about reliability in rather narrow terms—he'd like something more to come in on than a wing and a prayer, and considers the extra engine his salvation from mountain peaks, sharks, alligators and forced

198

marches across burning desert sands. In addition to his concern for those natural hazards, the *instrument* pilot may treat his second engine as nothing more than power for a spare generator—in his all-electronic world, what could be more important than a backup source of electricity?

The reasons you're flying a twin (or thinking about it) may be outside this brief list, but "why" is of little importance when placed beside "how." It's important to operate any airplane as efficiently as possible, but with the additional capabilities and potential of a light twin, everything you do to make that operation more effective will repay your efforts many times over. There's money to be saved, passengers to be made more comfortable and performance to be improved by putting some of these techniques and procedures to work.

TAXIING A TWIN

When was the last time you heard someone call Ground Control requesting "taxi instructions"? Probably no more recently than the last time you were in an airplane, and the Controller's answer should have been, "Release the brakes, add power and steer"—those are taxi *instructions*. What the pilot really wanted was taxi *clearance;* not how to do it, but where to go on the airport. Regardless of the content of the verbal exchange, the immediate objective is to get the airplane under way and arrive expeditiously at the takeoff end of the runway. Unless your tie-down is grassy, snowy, soft, or all three, you may be surprised to discover how little power is required to get most twins moving. On a hard level surface, an idle speed of 1000 RPM or so often provides enough thrust to overcome inertia. Oh, it'll take a few seconds longer, but there's no wind-tunnel blast to kick up dust and gravel and chocks, no sudden gale that makes things uncomfortable for anyone who happens to be walking behind your airplane. Use only the power you need to start rolling, and start rolling slowly, since you're probably in a crowded area anyway.

Contemporary twins offer at least three methods by which

you can drive the machine about on the ground: nose-wheel steering, brakes and differential power. You'll find those used singly and in combination, depending on the amount of maneuvering involved and the guy doing the driving—mostly, it's the latter. Only when an extremely sharp turn is required should you need to stiff-leg the rudder pedal, stand on the brake and roar with the outside engine; some advance planning might have precluded such a tight turn. Pivoting on the inside wheel will get you turned in the shortest possible radius, and will also scrub huge flat spots on the tire and perhaps overstress the nose-gear strut with the additional side loads imposed.

To begin with, it's best to have at least a little forward speed before attempting to turn. Light twins have no need for power steering, and so it takes a strong man to rudder the nose wheel right or left when the airplane is standing still. A rule develops which will make all your twin turning a lot easier—maintain some movement for positive control whenever a turn is required. In addition to cutting down on the muscle strain, you'll find that nose-wheel tires last longer and more hours elapse between adjustments and repairs to the turning mechanism. An abused nose-wheel system soon develops an inordinate amount of loose travel in the rudder pedals—you can flap them back and forth from stop to stop and the airplane doesn't change direction. Keep moving when you're turning—nose-wheel tires and steering linkages cost money.

As long as the wheels are rolling the three means of steering should be used in a definite sequence; always try nose-wheel steering first, then a touch of brake on the inboard wheel and finally power on the outboard engine; but only if it's absolutely necessary. This goes a bit against the previously established grain of never using the brakes unless you're approaching a complete stop; the qualifier here is the type of turning situation. When you're still in the ramp area, having to make relatively sharp turns at low speed, brake pressure is more judicious than throttle jockeying. Each situation has slightly different demands, and, as always, use whatever you have at your command to make the airplane do what you want it to.

Once off the ramp and away from tight quarters, the sequence of steering methods is less flexible. The objective is to stay in the center of the taxiway, and in that respect it's a lot like flying a precise heading—if you'll take care of an errant compass just as soon as you see it move from the desired reading, there won't be much of a correction to be made, and a bit of rudder pressure will do the trick. Nose-wheel steering via the rudder pedals doesn't usually result in a direction change as rapidly as using brakes, but in a straight-ahead situation, there should be no *need* for fast corrections if you start back for the centerline as soon as you leave it. When there's a crosswind strong enough to weathervane the airplane (to make it try to turn upwind), hold some rudder pressure to keep things straight.

The faster you taxi, the less pressure you'll need because the aerodynamic properties of the rudder and the vertical fin are beginning to manifest themselves. This doesn't make a case for fast taxiing, but suggests that there's a compromise speed somewhere between leg cramps and liftoff. It also leads very nicely into the alternate method of heading control on the ground: non-symmetrical power. Given the relatively short distance from ramp to runup at most general-aviation airports (use nearby intersections whenever possible and safe), you won't be taxiing long enough to get much concerned about crosswind-correcting rudder pressure. But if you need to drive a long way and get tired holding a pedal against the wind, there's a simple way to relieve the pressure; add just enough power on the upwind engine to maintain the centerline (or you might *reduce* power a bit on the downwind engine, thereby getting the desired effect without building up taxi speed). It won't take much, so squeeze the throttle until you feel the pedal pressure disappear, remembering that if the taxiway takes a turn, you'll have to readjust. Don't be a throttle jockey; it's hard on engines, passengers and everything else on the airplane, and doesn't say much for your ability at the controls. "Power" steering is a good deal because it saves brakes and leg muscles—the same asymmetrical thrust that overcomes a crosswind taxi works for crosswind takeoffs and landings, and we'll talk about that later.

BRAKES ARE MEANT FOR STOPPING—PERIOD

With regard to taxi speed, there's precious little difference between single-engines and many-motors, but pilot technique varies all over the lot. There are sensible taxiers, and there are cowboys. In the interest of spending the least time on the ground once you've decided to fly, you can hardly be faulted for getting to the takeoff area as rapidly as practicable—the "cowboys" are the ones who taxi just a few knots under takeoff speed, take the turns with tires squealing, then stand on the brakes to stop. Brakes, like nose wheels, don't come cheap. Carry only enough power to keep the airplane moving at a sensible speed; if you must move faster, plan ahead—ease the throttles back to idle and let the airplane slow down of its own accord, using brakes only when you intend to come to a complete stop.

Since you'll usually be taxiing downwind to the takeoff end of the runway, the following wind may push you along faster than you want to go, even with the engines at idle. In that now-and-then situation where there's no way to taxi at a contant reasonable speed, let the velocity build up and then apply firm, smooth brake pressure until the airplane slows to somewhat below the desired speed. By the time taxi speed builds again, the brakes have had a break—they'll cool somewhat during that brief respite, and you'll arrive at the runup pad with cooler wheels. Riding the brakes to control taxi speed will probably overheat them, with the possibility of a wheel fire and serious brake "fade" just when you need them most.

TWIN-ENGINE RUNUP

More will be said about the engine runup in Chapter 16, which deals with checklists, but a touch of additional emphasis on the feathering systems would not be amiss here. Unless you are certain that the propellers will go to the full feather position if it becomes necessary, don't fly! Simple and straight-forward, because a windmilling prop will make it awfully tough to keep on flying in most light twins. If the prop con-tinues to turn after the engine has quit producing power, you will be asking the remaining engine to supply the thrust to maintain flight *and* operate a windmill working against the compression of the dead engine. That's not even mentioning the terrific additional drag of the powerless prop—it's like sticking up a round flat plate in front of the nacelle, and that doesn't do much for the performance characteristics of the airplane. Check your owner's manual, check the checklist in Chapter 16 of this book and, above all, check the props before you commit yourself to takeoff.

NORMAL TAKEOFF

The subtitle for this section could just as well be "From Brake Release to All-Engine Best-Rate-of-Climb Speed in as Little Time as Possible," but there's not enough room across the page. That's the anatomy of a normal takeoff in a light twin, barring the failure of either or both engines along the way—if one quits, there's an out; if both give up at the same time, it'll be *down* and out. The power loading (horsepower per pound) of your airplane and the density altitude will have the most noticeable effect on the time re-quired to achieve the best-rate-of-climb airspeed target—some of the very high-powered twins at light weights get there ahead of their pilots, but load them up on a high-density alti-tude day and you'll think the sweep second hand is running in glue.

A normal twin takeoff is one in which you've no concern about either runway length or obstacles immediately after liftoff, one in which all systems work as advertised and one which is a progression of building-block airspeeds, smoothed at the joints by good pilot technique. As each number is attained and passed, you move into another regime of flight; the more you understand about the capabilities and limitations of each one, the more efficient and safe you'll be. When something *does* go wrong in a properly planned takeoff, the right things to do and not to do will fall into place—a take-off emergency is just another procedure when you're pre-pared for it.

You'll always save time with a rolling takeoff. As soon as you're cleared to go, start moving while still on the taxiway —the knots you put in the acceleration bank with a rolling takeoff might translate into the few feet of altitude you need at the other end to clear a tree, or to get stopped short of the mud if you have to abort. Make the radius of turn as wide as possible, bearing in mind that a crosswind from the inside of the turn will really make tires squeal and push passengers against the side of the cabin. DON'T execute a rolling takeoff on anything but full tanks—the resultant cen-trifugal force may be enough to uncover the supply lines from tank to engine, with obvious and alarming results.

Scratch start or rolling takeoff, throttle management on the runway is pretty important. The name of the game is to apply maximum power to the engines as rapidly as possible without blowing anything apart. Supercharged powerplants are most susceptible to overboosting, but it doesn't really make much difference to the engine innards whether the pressure comes from normal aspiration or a turbine-driven air pump. Advance "regular" throttles smoothly, and as rap-idly as the engines will take the pressure without com-plaint—probably something on the order of three to four seconds from idle to full throttle is reasonable. With most turbos, there is a delay while the turbines spool up to op-erating speed. Once they get moving, the pressure increase is rapid, and with your attention drawn to other matters, you may not notice a ridiculous manifold-pressure reading for a few seconds; it might be enough to cause engine prob-lems if the overboost is large enough, or is repeated enough times to fatigue engine parts.

Full power for every takeoff?—absolutely. The engines will actually turn fewer times when you use all the horses to get off the runway, then reduce to climb power as soon as you're safely airborne; engines are worn out by RPMs, not manifold pressures. Full power will get you to safe single-engine climb speed much faster, so there's a safety factor involved too. Make a final engine-condition check as soon as the power is stabilized; you know what the gauges should look like when all is well, and any errant needles or pointers will stand out as you scan the panel.

In a crosswind, lead a bit with the upwind throttle. As the rudder takes effect, bring in the other engine so that both are at takeoff power just as soon as possible. This technique is much smoother, and easier on passenger ears, than opening both throttles all the way, backing off the downwind engine and running it up again. In addition to the comfort factor, leading with the upwind engine contributes positively to your image as a pilot who knows what he's doing—most people wonder about throttle jockeys.

With the takeoff roll well under way, you'll soon feel the yoke come alive in your left hand as airflow across the tail surfaces picks up. (Always keep the power hand where it belongs—on the power levers, ready for an instant abort if an engine coughs or a moose runs across the runway in front of you.) Just as soon as you get elevator control, put it to use by lightening the load on the nose wheel. There are two reasons for this; first, you're probably close to V_{mc} (minimum control speed) and nearly committed to fly, so might as well get started; second, the nose wheel is the weakest link in the undercarriage of most airplanes—why subject it to any more stress than necessary?

You can also use these few seconds to attune your fingers and hand and arm to the responses of flight by "feeling" the airplane through the yoke. The "keep the nose wheel on the ground until takeoff speed and then pull 'er off" people play their game in earnest with twins—they also buy more nose-wheel repairs, and find themselves surprised on every takeoff by the sudden sensations of flight. Airplanes are meant to be *flown* off the ground, not pulled off.

By easing the pressure off the nose wheel as soon as you can, an attitude is established which will result in liftoff when the machine is ready—with a little practice, you will unstick at just a few knots above V_{mc}, and that's a good safe target. A very heavy airplane won't part company with Mother Earth for a while longer, but when it's ready, it'll fly. Some of the laminar-flow airfoils (those with flatter cross-sections and noticeably less upper curvature) must be rotated to a very positive angle of attack for the most efficient production of lift—if that's your airplane, know what it takes to do the job, and do it, smoothly and positively. (You don't have to guess how much to lift the nose; find a visual reference—most likely the top of the instrument panel or the aircraft nose itself—which allows you to set the same pitch attitude for every takeoff. You may have to cut and try a bit to find it, but when you do, it's as good as gold from then on.)

You've accelerated through V_{mc} (or Decision Speed, depending on the no-go nomenclature in your *Pilot's Operating Handbook*) by this time, and unless you are operating from a super-long runway, you are committed to fly, and there's a short period of tightrope walking on the way to normal climb airspeed. It's important to begin gaining altitude at this point, but it's *more* important to allow the airplane to accelerate rapidly toward normal climb airspeed. A positive pitch attitude is the secret; as airspeed increases, there's a very definite tendency for the nose to pitch up (the elevator deflection that placed the nose in the takeoff attitude is becoming more and more effective) and control pressure *must* be adjusted to keep the nose solidly on the horizon, or whatever visual reference you have determined does the job. Keeping the nose planted right where it belongs will *guarantee* the proper acceleration through the various critical airspeeds, but you can't let the airplane have its head . . . it'll nose up every time.

More than likely, most pilots have a lot to unlearn at this point; you were taught (and properly so) that when taking off in a single-engine airplane, it was very important to put as much vertical distance between you and the runway as soon as possible. Flying a one-motor machine, that's the way it should be done, because a power failure makes you the pilot of a glider, and altitude is the name of that game.

But with a twin, airspeed is the critical item—you've *got* to change your thinking to recognize that when an engine on a light twin fails on takeoff at an airspeed below V_{yse}, there likely will not be enough power in the remaining engine to accelerate the airplane to that speed.

The next milestone in the light-twin normal-takeoff schedule is engine-out best-*angle*-of-climb airspeed (V_{xse}), and it should come hot on the heels of V_{mc}; this should be considered a very transient situation—to be used only if there is an obstacle directly off the end of the runway—and consequently you should accelerate right on through V_{xse} on the way to the next important airspeed.

Once safely airborne and beyond the point where there's any chance for a safe landing on the runway remaining, raise the gear. (CAUTION: On hot days at high-altitude airports and/or with heavy loads, be certain you're really *flying*, not riding on that fickle bubble of air known as ground effect . . . it'll let you down every time.) Since most light twins don't require flaps for normal takeoffs, it makes good sense to get rid of anything hanging out that needn't be— like landing gear. Unless you are very heavy or at a very high density altitude, chances are extremely good that you'll continue flying, even if an engine quits, so what good can the wheels do in the air? The answer is absolutely nothing except slow down the time required to accelerate from liftoff to that all-important safe single-engine speed.

As a rule of thumb, retract the landing gear just as soon as you reach the point where wheels would no longer be useful for landing. In addition to the improvement in performance (without the wheel drag you'll climb faster; be able to reduce power sooner), there's a safety consideration; suppose one of the engines stops right after liftoff. Can't put it back down on the runway, so you elect to continue around the field and make a normal engine-out landing. If you have formed the habit of leaving the wheels down after takeoff until 500 feet, you will probably do the same thing now, and when you reach the downwind leg and come to GEAR on the before-landing checklist, don't think for a minute that you can't reach over and *raise* the wheels, say "gear down," and proceed to a very spectacular arrival . . . it's been done! Get 'em up just as soon and as safely as possible.

The next airspeed in the acceleration schedule is the biggie: V_{yse}, or engine-out best-*rate*-of-climb airspeed. The speed at which the wing is doing its best work with regard to altitude gain, it's the *only* airspeed that is going to save your neck if a powerplant fails during the initial climb. It's the "blueline" speed on the indicator (if yours is an older model and doesn't have such a marking, nothing wrong with painting one there), and you must resolve to attain and maintain that airspeed if you lose an engine. Remember, this number is predicated on the airplane being flown at maximum gross weight, and so a really proficient pilot can experiment a bit with slightly lower speeds *after the engine-out situation is completely under control and a safe altitude has been achieved.* In any case, V_{yse} is the rule until you're high enough to maneuver safely and comfortably back to the airport for landing.

And finally, assuming that both powerplants have managed to remain in operation throughout the takeoff and initial climb, allow the airplane to accelerate to the normal climb airspeed, if you choose to use a number higher than the all-engines best-rate-of-climb speed. For most light twins, you'll be able to see more over the nose, and will cover considerably more ground in the climb if you fly at a higher airspeed while climbing to cruise altitude.

The bottom line of an efficient, normal, twin-engine takeoff procedure ("normal" is when neither of the engines gives you grief), is a well-planned and properly executed profile; a schedule of attitudes and airspeeds that takes you from brake release to enroute climb in the least amount of time, with due consideration given to the trade-offs of safety and performance. The secret is *deliberate acceleration*, which is achieved by maintaining a nearly constant pitch attitude; and for most light twins, that attitude is the same one that served to lighten the weight on the nose gear way back in the pre-liftoff phase of the procedure. Keep in mind that when flying a light twin, airspeed (up to the engine-out best-rate-of-climb airspeed) is more important than altitude should you encounter engine failure, because it's likely that the remaining engine cannot accelerate the airplane to V_{yse} without some loss of altitude—a commodity in very short supply at this juncture.

The schedule below is typical, and needs only the real numbers and attitudes for the airplane you're flying in order to work every time:

1. Brake release, followed by rapid, smooth application of full power.

2. Increase pitch to a predetermined attitude, one that will lighten the weight on the nose gear and put the wings at a positive angle of attack.

3. Make sure the airplane accelerates beyond V_{mc} before liftoff, then maintain the liftoff attitude to permit further acceleration.

4. Monitor pitch attitude to insure that acceleration continues through V_{xse} and V_{yse}, raise the landing gear when safely airborne and beyond the point of possible landing on the runway.

5. Continue acceleration to normal climb speed if desired, reduce power to climb setting (some pilots prefer to leave the handles all the way forward to 1000 AGL . . . no quarrel there).

6. Continue the climbout secure in the knowledge that, if an engine quits, you won't have to sweat a near-impossible single-engine acceleration to V_{yse}.

Light twin all-engines-operating climb rates are usually somewhat greater than the singles can generate, and you will have to monitor the manifold-pressure gauges more closely to maintain climb power; the one-inch-per-thousand-feet lapse rate will continue while you're busy with other chores, and ere long you're expecting the airplane to climb at its normal airspeed, only to find it crippled by the loss of two or three inches of manifold pressure.

HOW FAST TO CLIMB?

Most of the good things about flying are up high, and
that's especially true of twins; higher true airspeed and the
better range that goes with it, smoother air, less traffic,
cooler temperatures, better visibility and so on. There's
hardly a situation when the higher altitudes aren't the better
altitudes. This may be tempered occasionally by very strong
headwinds, but even then you may want to take a close
look at the relatively small increase in trip time when balanced against beating yourself and your passengers about in
the low-altitude turbulence. At any rate, when you're going
upstairs, you might as well get there as fast as practicable,
which means climbing all the way at the best rate-of-climb
airspeed.

Consider for a moment the very meaning of the term—
this speed has been proven to give you the most altitude
gain per unit of time, and will get you to the advantages of
the upper air more rapidly than any other speed. Use best
angle-of-climb all the way up and you'll get there faster so
it seems, but you'll still be over the airport—well, at least
not very far downstream. Another consideration is engine
cooling, and it's getting more important with each new generation of twins; they're cowled so tightly that any speed
less than best rate-of-climb just doesn't provide sufficient
airflow for cooling while you're on the way up.

Like any rule, there are bound to be variations on the
theme, and climb airspeed is no exception. Suppose that you
are westbound in the winter in nearly any part of the United
States, when the chances of strong headwinds are better
than even. Exposing yourself to the negative effect of the
wind for a longer period of time can do nothing but lengthen
your trip, so you might want to consider climbing at a higher
airspeed, therefore covering more miles over the ground on
your way to altitude. This makes sense as long as there's no
hurry to get upstairs; but throw icing into the picture, a
situation in which you'd better climb through the icing
layer as rapidly as possible, and it's a different ball game.

Reverse course and climb to a strong *tail*wind, and there's a lot to be said for climbing at V_y in order to get up there and take early advantage of the free ride.

ALWAYS OPERATE UNDER PRESSURE

When you make a power change on any airplane, it's usually accompanied by a change in noise level; small ups or downs in manifold pressure are hardly detectable with the ears, but whenever propeller RPM changes, you can tell the difference right away. Your passengers can *really* tell the difference, especially those who are not regular light-plane flyers and who consider anything other than smooth, uninterrupted sounds of flight a herald of impending disaster.

For the sudden change which results when a prop control is moved, substitute the slow, gentle decrease of RPMs that comes from the application of slow, gentle *pressure* on the prop controls. During that first power reduction after take-off, your passengers will appreciate your concern; close to the ground and convinced that they've had it if anything happens to those two nacellesful of horses, passenger reaction is completely understandable when they hear a sudden power change. The twin adds the discomforting sound of unsynchronization, turning a poorly executed power change into a saw-toothed exercise in strange noises that needn't have been produced at all.

When your twin was brand-new, or fresh from its yearly physical, the levers were probably matched when the props themselves were turning at the same speed. But after a while some sag and stretch may develop in the sinews that connect actuator to actuated, and seldom will matched levers mean matched RPMs. They'll be full forward at take-off, and when you ease the props back to climb power, enclose the knobs with as many fingers as you have available. Press the levers together as you press them back, maybe even with one finger between them for a spacer; reasoning that any disparity in lever position at a given RPM setting will also show up when the power's changed, you'll be carrying that difference smoothly to the new setting. Strive to know how much the prop levers on your airplane need to move when you reduce from takeoff to climb, and from climb to cruise. With practice, prop changes can be taken care of so smoothly and slowly (there's no hurry) that your passengers will barely notice.

The same pressing together of the levers works wonders with your throttle technique too.

TWIN-ENGINE CRUISE

Once you've gotten as far as you intend to go vertically, don't throw away the benefits of altitude with an inefficient transition from climb to cruise. The objective should be to accelerate to cruise airspeed just as rapidly as possible; some of the older multis (the *much* older ones like PBYs, Ford Trimotors and such) didn't have this problem, because they climbed, cruised and descended at the same speed—very slowly. But today's twins can move out smartly when the reins are loosed in level flight. The sooner you get to cruise speed, the more efficient the entire operation becomes.

There are two generally accepted ways to level off; stop the climb on the desired altitude and let climb power accelerate the airplane to cruise airspeed, or deliberately climb a hundred feet or so above your altitude and cut down the acceleration time by using gravity to help the speedup. Which is better?—that's a tossup, but a good case for the second method can be made when you're leveling a heavy airplane at a high altitude—the weight-performance-altitude combination will require a relatively high angle of attack throughout the climb and at level-off, resulting in a longer time to build cruise airspeed. The time involved in climbing another hundred feet will hardly be noticed, but going downhill that hundred feet will get you off to a running start, eliminating a long, sluggish acceleration.

The term "aerodynamic step" has been a bone of contention for as long as there have been airplanes, and if you want to start a verbal donnybrook around the pilots' lounge, mention that as your reason for the high level-off; the arguments pro and con about "getting on the step" (and whether a step even exists) may last into the wee hours.

Choose whichever method seems best at the time, but either way, allow cruise airspeed to build up before you reduce power. While the airplane's accelerating, do whatever you can to help. Open cowl flaps are great drag producers, so if they're not needed, close 'em down—recommended climb airspeed should have kept the cylinder-head temperatures in the green, and the increase in airspeed at level-off will keep things cool until you reduce to cruise power. Start trimming as soon as you feel the need for it. Every little bit counts, and trim tabs sticking out into the airstream when they're not needed contribute nothing to efficient flight.

TIME TO SHIFT GEARS

Here's where the wise pilot makes (or saves) some money by referring to the power chart before hauling back on the power levers. There's not a lot on your mind during the last thousand feet or so of the climb, and it's a good time to look up the numbers. You'll come close enough to cruise-altitude temperature if you glance at the outside air temperature gauge now (it won't change more than a couple of degrees in a thousand feet), and you can arrive at a rough power setting—plenty of time to make fine adjustments in a few minutes. When the airspeed needle has gone as far as it's going to go, change power in the time-honored engine-saving fashion—throttles first, then props—to approximately the settings shown on the power chart for the number of horses you want. After everything settles down, recheck the outside air temperature and adjust manifold pressure accordingly; it won't usually be much of a change unless you're flying in very cold or very warm air.

The gear into which you shift is more important in a twin than in most singles (except the high-powered ones, and particularly those with turbos) because of the vast differences in range and/or time that can result. When you're just out boring holes in the sky, use the lowest percentage of power that will keep you comfortably airborne; when you need to get somewhere on schedule, use a power setting that maximizes the airspeed/fuel-burn relationship. A little power planning goes a long way; it makes no sense to charge down the airways hell-bent for election and have to stop somewhere for more fuel. A slight power reduction to favor range over speed will often more than overcome the time spent on a refueling stop (even when you unicom ahead for a quick turn-around, the gas truck is always on the other side of the field when you taxi up to the ramp), especially when you're really making time at altitude. The operational flexibility of your airplane is one of its greatest benefits; don't let it go unused by insisting on just one power setting.

While on the subject of power charts, notice the wide range of power settings available. In addition to the usual 55 percent, 65 percent, and 75 percent columns (some charts have lower settings for bladder-busting trips), there are usually two or three RPM settings for each percentage; pick the one that pleases your ears the most. If there's a rumble or vibration or buzz-saw effect at a certain RPM, look up another and give it a try. When the most comfortable setting falls between two of those published, there's nothing wrong with interpolating a bit to find a manifold pressure to go with it.

And if you have been a devotee of the "squared" power setting (one inch of manifold pressure for each one hundred RPMs, such as 23″–2300, 22″–2200, etc.), the power chart may hold some pleasant surprises for you. There may be a number of MP–RPM combinations which disprove the "squared" concept. The power chart won't let you get into trouble, so long as you observe its restrictions; true, squared power settings won't exceed engine limits, but using that rationale won't give you a dollar's worth of performance for a dollar of flying expense either.

HOW TO CURE PROPELLERUS SYNCHRONITIS

. . . which is an operational disease easily (almost inevitably) contracted by any airplane with more than one

powerplant. Did you think it affects only prop-driven airplanes? Not on your eardrum—sit between the engines on a
twin- or trimotored jet; the dissonance of two or three jet
engines when they're rotating at slightly different speeds is
worse than the Chinese water torture. The big difference
between jet unsynch and two props beating against each
other is the level of the sound and the fact that in most light
twins you can't get up and move away from the sound.

Passengers who don't know any better will put up with it,
a courteous single-engine pilot may ignore it, but the best
indicator of a slight disparity in propeller RPMs is another
multi-engine pilot—it doesn't matter whether he's in the seat
next to you or clear in the back of the airplane—when that
first yammering rowrr-rowrr-rowrr sets his teeth on edge,
he'll let you know. Oh, there'll be a slight pause before he
does anything; after all, you deserve a reasonable amount of
time to recognize and correct the problem, and he'll give
you about two rowrrs before he takes action.

There are as many ways of letting you know the props
are out of synch as there are clever pilots. One of the least
offensive practitioners is the panel tapper, who rests one
hand on the glare shield and moves an index finger up and
down, up and down, in harmony with the rowrr-rowrr-
rowrr. Should you not take the hint right away, he may
move the tapping site to the tachometer itself.

Albeit somewhat erosive to the pilot-in-command position
you occupy, there's a more direct method if the tapping
doesn't work; directing your attention to something outside
the airplane, the clever pilot will move one of the prop controls while you're distracted. If it doesn't settle the beating
the first time, he'll think up some other distraction, and another, until he's satisfied.

The *gentleman* pilot who perceives a lack of synchronization will put up with it until the blurring of his vision every
two seconds is more than he can take, then, "Pardon me,
sir, but can something be done about that horrible thrum-
ming noise?" Or the ungentleman who puts down your
efforts at getting the props together with "Well, ya got one
of 'em running at the right speed, now how about the other

one?"—in a voice calculated to be heard by everyone else in the airplane, of course.

Unsynchronized props can be used as weapons too—I used to go unrecognized unless there was a pipe stuck in my face, and one of my frequent companions just couldn't stand the smoke. Every time I'd light up, he'd unsynch the props to almost the threshold of pain, then make a deal: "I'll put the props where they belong as soon as you put that pipe where it belongs." I didn't quit smoking because of what the Surgeon General said; I quit because it gave me such terrible headaches every time I flew.

When the rowrring is due to faulty or inadequate governors, unsynchronized propellers can best be handled by a visit to the repair shop; but when this truly unnerving phenomenon is caused by the pilot's lack of attention, it's inexcusable. One way to keep it from happening is to use the same fingers-wrapped-around-the-knobs technique discussed earlier—once the props are running at the same speed, keep them that way during a power change by grasping the levers and pressing them equal distances; chances are good that identical movement, maintaining whatever inequality might exist in the actual position of the levers, will produce matched RPMs at the new setting.

At the first hint of dissonance, apply *pressure* to one of the prop levers until the rowrrs slow down and finally stop altogether. The average light twin's tachometers aren't accurate enough to make fine adjustments—your ear is a lot more reliable. It doesn't matter a whole lot which prop you press, but since the throttles are going to stay where they are, perhaps it's better to change to the safe side, meaning an increase in RPM to smooth things out—pulling one of the props back very far could bring that engine to the brink of overboost, especially if you've set the manifold pressure to the limit for that RPM and temperature. *Pressure* on the props is the key—try to move the levers, and you'll probably go too far, resulting in an even worse condition than the one you're trying to correct. Take your time; when the beating slows you're going in the right direction, then keep up the pressure until your ears are satisfied.

A growing number of light twins comes off the assembly line equipped with electronic propeller synchronizers, a super-luxurious option that will maintain precise RPMs on both sides of the airplane for hours on end. In most of these systems, engine speed is determined by sensors in the magnetos, and oil pressure is directed to the pitch-change mechanism in order to keep the props turning at identical RPMs. The left engine is usually the "master," the right engine adjusting its speed to match.

The pilot's role in operating a prop-synch system is rather inelegant, and consists of moving the switch to ON after takeoff, and to OFF just before landing. But an understanding of what's happening out there will help you to make the most of this rather expensive addition to your twin's goodie list. First, it's always best to manually synch the props before engaging the system; there's an actuator in all synchronizers that changes the pitch of the slave-propeller blades to match the RPM of the master. When the actuator reaches the limit of its travel, synchronization is impossible until the switch is turned OFF momentarily, which centers the actuator and makes the full range of travel available again.

Contrary to popular opinion, there's no good reason to switch the system off just because you need to change RPM; if you are careful, and ease the prop controls smoothly to the new setting with slow, deliberate *pressure*, the actuator should remain roughly centered, and synchronization should be retained throughout the change. Pressure wins again.

There's not a prop-synch system around that doesn't have an accompanying operating limitation that says one way or the other that you may not use it during takeoff and landing. The reason bears on safety; remember that one engine is slaved to the other in terms of RPM, and if the master should fail at a critical time (takeoff or landing) and drag down the RPM of the remaining engine, there would obviously be no way you could extract maximum power from the good engine. And with a light twin, you're going to need every horse you can get!

ALL RIGHT, LET'S GET THIS THING
ON THE GROUND!

The actual landing of a twin shouldn't be any different
from that of any other airplane—power completely off just
before touching down at the slowest possible forward speed
will produce a grease job every time. A *crosswind* landing
in a twin will be smoother and more efficient when it's made
into the corner of the runway, removing as much of the
crosswind component as possible. But let's face up to the
fact that a twin's higher landing speed will often preclude
the corner technique, because there just isn't enough diag-
onal runway there. When this is the case, "cross" the runway
as much as you can in combination with the wing-low-land-
on-the-upwind-wheel-first act, and you've got the crosswind
whipped.

There's a lot of steering in those two throttles, and you
shouldn't hesitate to use it when you begin to run out of
rudder (maybe this is really more crosswind than you should
be battling . . . ?), but don't forget that steering power is
also "go" power, and the other end of the runway will show
up a lot sooner.

Directional control with the throttles can be a lifesaver
on an ice-covered runway, when nose-wheel steering produces nothing but a super-interesting slide. If nothing else,
the use of asymmetrical power means you can go off the
end of the runway on the heading of your choice. Propellers
whose thrust can be reversed (they're coming!—like everything else, they'll filter down to general aviation someday
when the price gets right) are a bonus and a half on ice.
Years ago there was a four-engine pilot who landed on an
ice-sheeted runway, and promptly found himself in a box—
sliding uncontrollably toward the far threshold, and not
enough runway remaining to go around. In what has to be
one of the quickest mental draws in aviation history, he
reversed both of the left engines, which slewed the airplane

around 180 degrees, and when he was sliding down the runway *backwards,* he applied full power to all four in forward thrust until the airplane stopped. Why not?—he had nothing to lose by trying.

Sheer weight precludes power-off approaches for twins as a normal procedure; while trying to maintain a safe airspeed with zero thrust, an unholy sink rate can, and probably will, develop. If you get to the bottom of one of these express-elevator descents and wait too long to flare, you may become one of the world's shortest pilots. So some kind of modified "airline"-type approach is in order, beginning with a pattern altitude somewhat higher (at least a couple of hundred feet) than the singles milling around the airport. You're moving faster than they are, so stay out of their hair—your higher pattern altitude will also keep slower folks from backing into you.

You can't expect to safely fly the same tight downwind and base that keeps the singles within power-off gliding distance of the runway, so don't try. Pick a reasonable geardown, partial-flap pattern speed (most manufacturers recommend one, and it usually come out somewhere close to 130–140 percent of the power-off stall speed), and fly the downwind leg wide enough to see and avoid, but not so wide that you need a radar vector to the base leg.

Get the most out of your twin by flying into the pattern as fast as you can—time is money. Especially when you're descending from cruise altitude, plan to reach the airport traffic area (five miles from the field) at the 156-knot limit, then decelerate in stages until you're on final approach. A bit of experimenting will develop a magic number on the power gauge which will compromise engine heat, internal pressures and bearing loads, and deceleration to gear-down airspeed (try 15 inches of manifold pressure as a starter and work from there). A touch of flaps will help the slowing-down process (check the manual; the partial-flap extension speed limit is probably much higher than you realize), and by the time the wheels are down and locked, you'll surely be able to extend more flap, and before long the airspeed needle will be pointing to the right number for final approach. If you've judged your pattern well, you can turn final and continue the descent to the runway with no addition of power. A good power-on approach is one in which the only adjustment with throttles is a slow, continual reduction until they're against the stops just before touchdown. The easiest way to maintain power symmetry when throttling back is the same finger-wrapping technique used on the prop levers—unnoticed asymmetrical power on final can build in a phony crosswind and you'll wind up in an unnecessary crab all the way down the chute.

Flaps deserve special mention when talking twins; it's important to use full flaps for every landing (maybe even more important than with singles because of the much-increased landing roll), but don't be in a hurry to extend them all the way. Make it an unbreakable rule—never extend full flaps until you are willing to say, "I can, and *will,* land the airplane no matter what happens from this point on." Go-arounds are the result of someone's poor judgment (could be either yours or a Controller's) and are rare these days; engine failure on a missed approach is even rarer, but should you decide to go around from a low-altitude, full-flap configuration and an engine quits, consider that you'll probably be skating on very thin ice. There's a performance-altitude-gross-weight-airspeed-total-drag condition for every airplane that makes it impossible to gain altitude, and if you elect a go-around in that configuration, the chances of landing safely are just about zero unless there's a long, long runway underneath.

And there you are—don't want to land, can't climb—a bad place to be. If you aren't aware of a rule-of-thumb commitment altitude on final approach for your airplane under the conditions normally encountered, take a test hop and find out; then add some feet for the wife and kids. When you get to that altitude and things don't look good, uncommit yourself—the cost of a precautionary go-around is pretty small compared to the cost of a busted airplane, or a busted neck, or both.

TWIN-ENGINE SHORT-FIELD LANDINGS

They'll *all be* "short-field" landings if you land slow, leave the flaps down and hold the nose up; brakes will become nice things to have on board, but you'll seldom need them on a runway. When you ask for maximum stopping performance from your twin, you should shift gears accordingly, starting with approach airspeed. Because a body in motion tends to remain in motion, the most critical item under your control is airspeed—the faster the airplane is moving when it touches the earth, the more runway it will eat up in the process of getting stopped—so anything you can do to slow down will have a positive effect on stopping distance.

You can hang a single-engine airplane on its prop, stagger up to the pavement at an airspeed just a shade above stall, and when you're over the runway cut the power and land; very quickly, very firmly, with a near-zero landing roll. Doing the same thing in a twin will work out just fine, as long as you're willing to bet your life that both engines will keep running. If you allow the airspeed to drop down into the near-stall range, you'll be carrying considerable power, and if one of the engines burps you may go for an exciting ride in a direction you didn't intend at all. It's unlikely that the airplane would accelerate to best angle-of-climb speed, to say nothing of the violent stall that could possibly occur. You're on the back side of the power curve, that unhappy set of circumstances where there's not enough power available to overcome the high drag configuration—you'll land all right, but not necessarily where you wanted to, or in the attitude you had in mind.

With the consequences of engine failure always nagging, it's good practice to observe V_{mc} as the absolute minimum airspeed at *any* time in a twin, especially close to the ground. An airstrip that's so short it needs to be approached at speeds below V_{mc} is undoubtedly *too* short—it's a calculated risk, and you must decide whether it's worth it. That's one reason bush pilots are underpaid, no matter how much is in the envelope each month.

When you know that you're going to need all the stopping power that's in the airplane, get the flaps up as soon as wheels meet runway. Part of the effectiveness of heavy, high-speed braking is the amount of friction between tires and surface, which means you need to transfer as much weight as possible from wings to wheels. A footful of brake pressure can slam the front wheel down with enough force to jam it right through the baggage compartment, so make certain the nose wheel has touched down before you press on the pedals. Once you start braking, keep increasing the pressure steadily —don't pump—until you're stopped. It won't help much, but since every little bit may count, keep the yoke all the way back, kill the engines, open the cabin door, throw out an anchor—anything to get stopped.

As important as anything else in a short-field situation is to remain steadfast in your resolve to continue the landing even though it's obvious there isn't enough runway ahead. " 'Tis a far, far better thing I do than I have ever done before—to run off the end of the runway under control, than to suffer an uncontrolled crash in the process of attempting an impossible go-around" . . . or something like that, with appropriate apologies to the author. It's a tough decision, but one that must be made—oh, how you wish you hadn't put yourself there, but there you are; ride it out, steer around the bigger trees and you'll more than likely walk away from it.

TWIN-ENGINE TAKEOFF EMERGENCIES

There are three types of multi-engine takeoffs: those in which you have absolute assurance that neither engine will quit, those in which there's a *possibility* that one engine will fail and those takeoffs during which one engine *does* give up the ghost.

Since the first situation has never existed and never will, forget it; consider the second situation, the one we've got to live with every time we open the throttles. For that matter, the specter of engine failure should occupy a prominent place in your pre-takeoff thinking in any airplane—the big

difference between monos and multis is the options available
to the pilot once the power loss happens. The decision is
built in if there's only one set of cylinders involved; when
the only engine quits, you're going to return to earth—somewhere, somehow, and soon—that's all there is to it. You
may be able to control the "somewhere" within certain small
limits, but there's no chance of continuing the flight in anything but a negative vertical direction. Two engines don't
double your capacity for getting out of trouble, but proper
and consistent preparation, knowledge of procedures which
will milk every ounce of performance out of the machine and
timely application of those procedures give you the advantage
of options; to return home, or fly to another airport with
better facilities.

An airline captain has a lot more to work with (better
equipment, more training and experience, highly qualified
help on the flight deck, etc.), but he's bound legally by a
rule that should be good enough for us if it's good enough
for him. It says that should an engine fail, he will deposit
the airplane on the *nearest suitable* airport (time-wise) at
which a *safe* landing can be made. The rule relaxes slightly
as the number of engines available increases, but that's not
important for us—any takeoff emergency should start the
wheels turning—take care of immediate needs but, mentally,
be on the way to that nearest safe airport. If something has
gone wrong, get back on the ground and find out what the
trouble is; when an engine performs as advertised right up
until it quits, you can bet that something has let go internally.
Whatever has come loose is not going to put itself back together, so *land* before things get worse. What if the same nuts
and bolts are nearly ready to come apart in the other engine?

MAINTAIN YOUR ATTITUDE

Whether you want to admit it or not, you are going to be
as ham-handed during your first actual engine-out experience as you were during your first landing. With no practice
(c'mon now, when was the last time you pulled an engine
right after liftoff?) you are bound to flounder a bit until you

get the feel of the airplane in its crippled configuration. Likely as not, the engine will quit when you are carrying a full load of petrol, people and portmanteaus—the airplane must be handled carefully if you intend to fly out of trouble. "Carefully" means doing all the right things and not doing any of the wrong things. You've got to settle down, slow down and do things properly—in a phrase, "Don't just do something, sit there!"

Emergency actions must be deliberate, planned and timely, but not so rushed that they're the wrong ones. When an emergency has been considered in terms of "What do I do when it happens?" it is just another procedure—and the first thing to do is go to a checklist so you don't forget a single lever or switch, and so that you'll pull or push or reset in the proper order. There's only one twin-engine power-failure situation that requires immediate, almost unthinking action, and that's the subject coming up next.

ENGINE FAILURE ON THE RUNWAY

Sellers of modern twins have every right to holler "short-field capability" and "engine reliability" when they're doing their thing. These two attributes of multi-engine operations go a long way toward making them the useful machines they are; but capability and reliability have wrapped too many pilots in super security blankets—although they firmly believe that the airplane will carry them to safety if an engine quits in the air (and it probably will), little thought is given to what happens when one of the fans stops turning on the runway. Putting all your worry eggs in one basket won't do a damn bit of good if the eggs break before you can get them there. Engine failure during the takeoff roll presents a decision that is undoubtedly the most important one you'll have to make on any multi-engine flight; it may be superseded only by the decision that this runway is too short to begin with!

At this point, you've got to take a closer look at a speed that was purposely omitted from the discussion of a normal takeoff with both engines operating. It's no-go speed, and it has no reason for being except for that once-in-a-million situation when an engine packs up before you leave the ground. You'll know right away when something significant has gone wrong—the message may be conveyed via visual, auditory or olfactory senses, but it's just as likely that the engine failure will manifest itself in more subtle ways. From here on, consider an aborted (or "balked") takeoff one which results from either a complete and sudden loss of power or your decision to call off the ball game because you don't like the sights or sounds or smells.

The importance of no-go speed can best be understood by defining it: the speed to which you can accelerate the airplane with both engines operating at full power, suffer the loss of an engine and bring the airplane to a full stop. At no-go speed, your airplane has developed a certain amount of kinetic energy, the energy of motion. One way or the other, that energy must be dissipated to bring the airplane to a stop—in the form of heat soaked up in the brake linings, or the work required to plow an airplane-sized furrow through the grass off the end of the runway or, on the macabre side, whatever energy is required to tear off wings and wheels and roll the airplane up into a ball of aluminum. Most pilots prefer the first method, so it's advisable to figure out well in advance of the engine failure just what speed will represent no more energy than the brakes on your airplane are capable of soaking up.

Figure 14–1 is a hypothetical chart illustrating a very simplified way to present the accelerate/stop requirement. Notice carefully the conditions; any difference in weight, type of takeoff surface (grass, mud, snow, etc.), temperature, atmospheric pressure, or wind would change the numbers. Take a 3000-foot runway for example; under the stated conditions, you could allow the airplane to accelerate to 90 mph and, at least theoretically, decide to call it off and get stopped before you reached the far end of the pavement. Of course, if you went all the way to 90 mph you'd be lifting off, but it's nice to know that 3000 feet provides considerable room

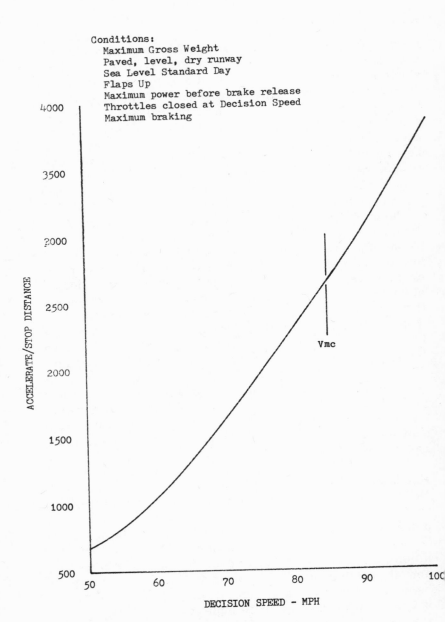

Figure 14-1. Simplified accelerate/stop chart.

in which to make a go/no-go decision. On shorter runways—say, a 2000-foot strip—you would be committed to running off the end should you decide to abort after achieving 76 mph, and there's no guarantee that you'd be able to fly out of trouble if one of the engines packed up immediately thereafter. Keep in mind that a chart such as this one has nothing to do with engine-out *takeoff* performance . . . its sole purpose is to let you know how much runway is required to stop, having accelerated to certain velocities.

Figure 14–2 (another hypothetical chart) presents the accelerate/stop problem in much more detail. Obviously intended for a more complicated airplane, this chart provides data for density altitude (temperature and pressure altitude), aircraft weight, and wind. The dashed line follows the solution of a typical problem, but the result is remarkably different from the earlier chart. In this case, notice that engine failure is assumed to take place at *takeoff speed,* a value that changes with gross weight (takeoff speeds are listed for each weight in the upper-left-hand corner). Since takeoff speed is always higher than V_{mc}, there's a built-in safety factor; if the runway available is enough to contain the accelerate-stop distance as calculated on this chart, you can be assured of having plenty of runway for stopping if you make up your mind to abort at V_{mc}. (By the way, an airplane with a chart like this in the *Pilot's Operating Handbook* will quite likely also have a chart to show the accelerate-go distance. In other words, the number of feet required for the airplane to build up enough airspeed to keep on flying when an engine quits *after* takeoff.)

Like all performance charts, the numbers represent the best effort of a professional test pilot working with an airplane in top condition. Are your brakes that effective? Do you know just how much pressure to apply to obtain maximum stopping power? Will you always react with a split-second decision to abort when you recognize that all is not well in the engine room? If the answer to any of those questions is negative, you'd best figure out your own accelerate-stop distance.

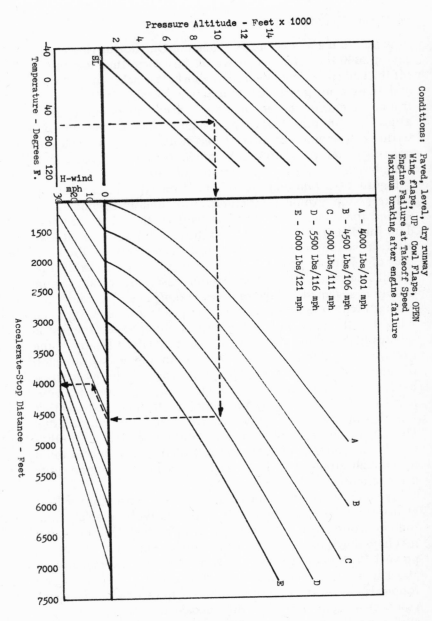

Figure 14–2. Accelerate/stop distance chart with provisions for density altitude, aircraft weight, and wind.

START WITH A STANDARD

"Everybody's gotta be somewhere," so why not begin at home? The familiar markings of the runway you use most will help you develop a performance standard, to be adjusted up or down for future conditions at other airports or for seasonal changes at home. If you operate your light twin from a 10,000-foot runway, remember that it was designed for the big smokers—you'd probably have to hold your airplane on the ground in order to reach a speed that would use up all that concrete in the stopping. On the other hand, such a runway gives you a comfortable safety factor for your tests, since you can start by finding out how many feet are required to stop after attaining V_{mc}, your all-time, long-runway no-go speed.

The more likely environment, and the one that will produce more realistic numbers, is the average-length general-aviation runway, one in the 3000-to-5000-foot class. On a day as close to standard as possible (a sea-level airport when the altimeter setting is 29.92″ and the temperature is 59° F and there's no wind), load your airplane to its maximum gross weight (or your usual load, whichever comes first) and get ready for the test. If you don't line up at the very end of the runway on the first run, you probably will in successive tests! Let the Tower know what you intend, and open the throttles; time being an important ingredient in this stew, unleash the horses rapidly but smoothly, remembering that the few seconds wasted in a too slow application might become precious feet at the other end of the runway.

Runway lights are quite likely the handiest yardstick for your accelerate-stop test. They're going to be right there for every takeoff from the home airport, and the distance can be converted to total run for application at other fields. Most runway lights are planted 200 feet apart; sometimes less, seldom more—the airport manager knows the numbers. Perhaps even more important is their presence during a night takeoff, when your perceptions of distance suffer strange aberrations.

The first test must be strictly cut-and-try. Let the airplane accelerate until engine power has stabilized, and when you reach the third or fourth row of lights (or some other runway marking, taxiway or intersection), close the throttles very smoothly but very quickly and start pressing on the brakes. (Pumping the pedals won't do you a bit of good, since the airplane is not decelerating whenever you're not pushing—smooth, firm pressure is the name of the game, constantly increasing up to just short of skidding the tires. In a for-real maximum-performance stop, you should remember that the greatest braking action occurs with a 15 percent "rolling skid" —which leaves some rubber on the runway but uses up a lot of heat in the process.) Your first effort at accelerate-stop-distance testing must be a very conservative one, to make sure you don't run past the other end of the runway, so set your reject point not very far from the start.

Surprised at the number of feet required to stop, even when you hollered "abort" much earlier than you thought you should have? Give the brakes a chance to cool, go back and try it again, and you'll find that as you wait longer to abort the takeoff, the stopping distance begins to increase remarkably. Time is getting into the act; for each second the decision is delayed, the airplane has moved farther toward the end of the runway, and it moves farther at a constantly increasing rate. The energy level, a direct indicator of re-quired stopping distance, increases as the *square* of the speed increase. In plain language, if you elect to begin stopping at a speed of 60 knots instead of 30, you will somehow have to come up with *four* times the stopping power you needed at 30 knots.

And while you're contemplating the advisability of getting on the binders at the instant you decide that you're not going to fly, consider this: it takes as much runway to slow an airplane from 85 knots to 65 knots as it does to reduce its speed from 55 knots to 7 knots. The message is clear—when you make up your mind, press on the pedals . . . firmly.

ADJUSTING THE STANDARD

When you find that elusive standard day and make a couple of test runs, you'll have something to work with, a number that will keep you safe. Bear in mind that a headwind will shorten the distance, as will a drop in temperature or humidity. Anything that increases the density of the air in which you're operating will provide more power, therefore less time to accelerate to takeoff speed; less time, less distance used up and more runway available in which to get stopped. Whenever accelerate-stop distance is significantly less than runway available, you have the happy options of carrying more weight, or taking an extra second or two to confirm which engine belched, or the assurance that you can stop safely with distance to spare.

Some *unhappy* options show up when you move to the negative adjustment of your standard accelerate-stop distance. It's a seasonal thing, difficult to measure and dangerous to play with. Density altitude is more often than not the culprit, but there are other thieves in the night—crosswinds, tailwinds, heavy loads, weak brakes and sorry engines, to name a few. When you run out of runway before you run out of energy, you'll go off the end, that's for sure—the only thing open to question is how *fast* you'll go off the end.

Faced with a runway that isn't long enough to accommodate an aborted takeoff, you've a choice: either leave somebody and his suitcase behind or wait for improved conditions —a drier, higher-pressure day or the normal morning-evening temperature drop. Or you can accept the calculated risk that a pre-liftoff engine failure would present. In the latter situation, accelerating the airplane to even a bare minimum takeoff speed puts you past the point where you can abort and get stopped if an engine quits. Take everything into consideration, and if you need to fly that badly, have at it. But remember that a power loss prior to staggering into the air will have an inevitable result—you haven't enough speed to fly but you have too much speed to stop—hello, overrun. Hope that whatever terrain lies on the other side of the threshold is hospitable, and that you can convince the investigators of the wisdom of your decision to go; *that's* gonna be tough to do. Unacceptable risk?—easy decision; don't go.

ENGINE FAILURE IMMEDIATELY AFTER TAKEOFF

It's a safe bet that one of the first numbers you learned when you started jumping through the twin-engine checkout hoops was V_{mc}—minimum control speed. Stated simply, V_{mc} is the airspeed at which there's enough air flowing over the control surfaces (the rudder, primarily) to keep the airplane from turning toward the failed engine when the other one is operating at full power. Or looking at the grim side, it's the speed *below* which you can't keep the airplane from turning. This doesn't mean that you'll go into "automatic crash" if you try to fly on one engine at less than V_{mc}, but it *does* mean that even with the rudder pedal all the way to the floorboard, the airplane will turn toward the dead engine until you (1) allow the airspeed to increase or (2) reduce power somewhat on the engine that's still running.

Those are two rather compromising choices, and it should be obvious that anyone who lifts a twin from the runway at a speed less than V_{mc} is laying himself wide open for a first-class disaster. How'd you like to be faced with the prospect of either flying through the hangar beside the runway or settling into the trees off the end as you reduce power on the good engine? Most pilots would find it difficult, if not impossible, to make themselves pull back the throttle of the engine that's keeping them aloft. There's an easy way out of the dilemma; never, never take a twin off the ground until you're past V_{mc}—it's the most magic of the multi-engine numbers. Oh, the airplane will fly at lower speeds, and you can really impress the airport crowd with an astounding short-field takeoff, but what if an engine quits?—you'll probably perform an equally outstanding short-field *crash*, that's what!

There is probably no more critical time in a twin-engine takeoff than the seconds between liftoff and the attainment of the best all-engine rate-of-climb airspeed. It's a critical time because of the enormous loss of go power when half of your powerplant lies down and dies. If the airplane is heavy enough, or the density altitude adverse enough, or the piloting sloppy enough, or all three, it's quite possible that the remaining engine can't provide enough thrust to accelerate the airplane from V_{mc} to the best single-engine *angle*-of-climb speed, let alone its best rate-of-climb speed— when you lose half your power, you lose a heck of a lot more than half your climb capability. Richard Aarons has calculated the climb-performance loss for some twins when they are suddenly singles. Are you ready for a shock? Sit down, and find your airplane . . .

PERFORMANCE LOSS OF REPRESENTATIVE TWINS WITH ONE ENGINE OUT

Pistons	All-engine climb rate (fpm)	One-engine climb rate (fpm)	Percent loss
Beech Baron 58	1694	382	80.70
Beech Duke	1601	307	80.82
Beech Queen Air	1275	210	83.53
Cessna 310	1495	327	78.13
Cessna 340	1500	250	83.33
Cessna 402B	1610	225	86.02
Cessna 421B	1850	305	83.51
Piper Aztec	1490	240	83.89
Piper Navajo Chieftain	1390	230	83.45
Piper Pressurized Navajo	1740	240	86.21
Piper Seneca	1860	190	89.78

Turboprops	All-engine climb rate (fpm)	One-engine climb rate (fpm)	Percent loss
Beech King Air E90	1870	470	74.87

(Table continued on next page.)

PERFORMANCE LOSS OF REPRESENTATIVE TWINS
WITH ONE ENGINE OUT

Turboprops	All-engine climb rate (fpm)	One-engine climb rate (fpm)	Percent loss
Mitsubishi MU2-J	2690	845	68.59
Rockwell Commander 690A	2849	893	68.66
Swearingen Merlin III	2530	620	75.49

(Reprinted by permission from the July 1973 issue of *Business and Commercial Aviation*.)

Now how do you feel about that Twin Tornado you've been squiring about the sky? If you have absolute faith in both engines, ignore the numbers—but if you're a bold pilot who wishes also to become an *old* pilot, you'd best make some advance preparation for the day which will hopefully never come round—an engine failure immediately after take-off. Considering the terribly significant loss of climb capability in *all* the light-medium twins, your initial reaction to a power loss will probably be the most important move you'll ever make.

WHAT TO DO FIRST?

In *any* twin, you're not going anywhere but down until you can somehow reach a speed at which there's enough air flowing over the wings to provide more lift than the weight of the airplane. An equal lift-weight relationship may help you hold your own for a while, but the terrain around most airports doesn't offer much in the way of continued clearance—if you can't climb, it doesn't take much of a rise in the terrain to bring your level-flight excursion to a rapid and firm conclusion. So you *must* accelerate to at least best single-engine angle-of-climb speed (V_{xse}) as soon as possible, followed by best single-engine rate-of-climb. The lower V_{xse} may soon have the good engine's tongue hanging out—there's not much cooling airflow at that speed.

Here's a generalized, safe sequence of events to work with in setting up an engine-failure-after-takeoff checklist— it isn't so complicated that you can't remember the cardinal items. When you're all alone (the only pilot) on the flight deck, your hands will be mighty full; get the procedure firmly in mind, review it before every takeoff and by all means consult the *Pilot's Operating Handbook* for the variations applicable to your airplane.

1. CONTROL THE AIRPLANE
   What could be more important than this? You're above V_{mc}, so use whatever rudder you need to maintain heading. In that rare situation where it seems advisable to turn a few degrees to steer toward a less-obstructed flight path, do it the same way porcupines make love—very carefully. Be even more gentle with pitch attitude, as airspeed control is paramount. You *must* accelerate to climb speed and maintain it.

2. REDUCE DRAG
   If the landing gear isn't tucked away in its streamlined place, put it there. This assumes that the engine came un-glued above a runway which offers absolutely no chance of a normal landing—you're committed to fly. If circumstances are such that you're going to touch down whether you want to or not, might as well leave the wheels down; they'll dissipate some energy as they separate from the airframe. While you're in the drag-reducing department, check the wing-flap position; most light twins are designed to lift off and climb out most efficiently with a zero flap setting, but make sure you know what's proper for *your* airplane.

3. IDENTIFY THE FAILED ENGINE
   This is the easiest thing on the checklist; it can also be the final item if your determination is wrong. When an engine quits, the airplane will turn toward the failed-engine side, and you'll need rudder pressure to maintain heading. (If you're not going very fast, you'll need some rudder *movement!*) Here's the place to force yourself to slow down, slap the knee that isn't working and say to yourself, "dead

leg, dead engine." Don't trust anything or anyone else—
engine gauges are too easily misread, a gusty crosswind
could possibly swing the nose a bit in the opposite direction, another pilot with you could shout the wrong thing—
your dead leg will be your best friend. The idea is to not
shut down the good engine. A light twin becomes a
seriously crippled single in an engine-out situation, and a
nonpowered glider (brick type) if you err by closing the
throttle of the remaining powerplant. You'll know right
away if you grab the wrong lever.

4. SHUT DOWN THE FAILED ENGINE
   If the power problem at hand has been caused by a massive
   internal hemorrhage in the oil system, the engine may take
   care of the shutdown all by itself, with no inputs from the
   pilot. On some twins, the feather system is held in abey-
   ance, so to speak, by engine oil pressure. When something
   lets go and oil pressure drops below a preset value, feathering occurs automatically—your first indication of trouble
   may be a severe yaw followed by a good view of the back
   side of a stopped propeller. In addition to a leak causing
   the pressure drop, a common everyday power failure (fuel
   starvation, ignition breakdown, mechanical failure, whatever) may allow engine RPM to drop so low that the engine-
   driven oil pump can't produce; when the pressure falls
   below a certain point, wham—the prop will feather.

   An auto-feather system is great, but don't count on it;
   shut down a failed engine by closing the throttle (carefully, while confirming that you did indeed choose the
   dead leg), actuating the feather system (by pulling the prop
   lever to its most rearward position on most light twins)
   and finally, moving the mixture lever to OFF.

5. LAND AS SOON AS POSSIBLE
   With only 20 to 30 percent of your two-engine climb capability remaining, you've no choice but to get on the ground
   right away. This is where judgment shows up—you've got
   to climb above whatever obstacles lie between you and
   wherever you intend to touch down, allow enough time
   to extend the landing gear (you may have to pump or
   crank it down) and be cognizant of temperature limits on

the good engine, especially on hot days at high altitudes. Most light-twin engines will run wide open all day long . . . if nothing else goes wrong.

In extreme cases, "land as soon as possible" may mean somewhere out there in the boondocks—there's just no argument in favor of a stall-spin disaster while trying to reach an unreachable airport when a controlled crash would have been a better choice. If you're going to land on an unairport, do so while you still have complete control of the airplane—your chances of surviving are quite high. A cartwheel or inverted landing can ruin your whole day.

The engine-failure-immediately-after-takeoff checklist summarized:

1. CONTROL THE AIRPLANE
   Rudder and aileron as needed (up to 5° bank away from the failed engine to aid directional control and reduce drag), pitch altitude as required to maintain V_{yse}.
2. REDUCE DRAG
   Gear up, flaps up (or as specified).
3. IDENTIFY THE FAILED ENGINE
   Dead leg, dead engine.
4. SHUT DOWN THE FAILED ENGINE
   Throttle closed.
   Feather prop.
   Mixture OFF.
5. LAND AS SOON AS POSSIBLE
   Do what you think is best, if you are afforded the luxury of a choice.

ENGINE FAILURE IN FLIGHT

There's a big difference between the first two power-loss situations (failure on the runway and failure immediately after takeoff) and an engine failure in flight. "In flight" is a rather loose description; for procedural purposes, it covers the time from attainment of best all-engine rate-of-climb speed (V_y) to the point at which you are committed to land. Agreed that the loss of an engine at the same instant you get to V_y will tighten you up a bit more than a failure at 10,000 feet—aviators have a natural aversion to the ground unless they planned it that way, as in a normal landing. But, at least academically, once you've struggled to best rate-of-climb airspeed you're past the danger point, and unless the airplane is loaded above its allowable weight or the density altitude is very adverse or the terrain rises so steeply that you can't out-climb it on one engine, you should be able to extract yourself handily from an engine-out predicament. If the motor goes when you're cruising, you've got not only a comfortable air-speed pad, you've also got some altitude at your disposal. *Caution:* Spend airspeed and altitude as if your life depended on them—the implication is obvious.

The procedure for an in-flight engine failure is only slightly different from its right-after-takeoff counterpart, since you will certainly be operating at something less than maximum power.

1. CONTROL THE AIRPLANE
   This once again heads the list of things to do. Maintaining heading and attitude helps to keep you oriented through-out whatever may follow, and forces a certain amount of slow-down and mental discipline. It's a place from which to proceed, and that's important in an emergency situation.

2. ADJUST POWER
   An optional second step which can be judged only in the light of the circumstances that prevail. If you are in a condition of flight that requires all the single-engine power you can muster, pour it on. Go to the next higher power setting; mixtures first, then props, finally throttles. If you've a long way to go on that remaining engine, have plenty of altitude and want to do anything you can to keep it running, power down a bit.

3. REDUCE DRAG
   Just as before, check gear up and flaps up—it takes only a couple of seconds to reassure yourself that these two are where they should be. When do you suppose gear and flap systems spring small internal leaks or short circuits and allow those components to slowly creep out into the

slipstream?—you guessed it; when you're trying desperately to get home on one engine and your attention is diverted.

4. IDENTIFY THE FAILED ENGINE

Same dead-leg, dead-engine trick. Higher airspeed at cruise and lower power settings on the engines will make the yaw less noticeable, but it'll be there.

5. SHUT DOWN THE FAILED ENGINE

When you're absolutely certain you know which one has quit (you'll have a lot more time to make this decision than you did right above the runway), shut it down the same way as before—throttle, feather, mixture. You'll see a marked increase in efficiency as the prop paddles to a stop.

6. CLEAN UP THE AIRPLANE

Close the cowl flaps on both engines if temperatures allow, but certainly on the dead engine. They're of no use to those stone-cold-dead cylinders, so get rid of the drag and pick up a couple of knots or pull the good engine back a horse or two. You should also give consideration to *completely* shutting down the dead engine by turning off the fuel valve (don't want any of that precious stuff siphoning or leaking—you may need it later), and switching off the magnetos and generator on the failed engine.

7. LAND AS SOON AS POSSIBLE

Just as before, your situation is not going to get any better; when everything is under control and you're settled down, head for the *nearest suitable airport*. Decide what is suitable in light of what's available and what's safe, but make up your mind and stick to your plan. Just because the good engine is ticking away and shows no signs of trouble, don't be led down the garden path and press on to some far distant airport when you can land safely and not too inconveniently on the one directly under you.

The engine failure-in-flight checklist summarized:

1. CONTROL THE AIRPLANE

Rudder and aileron as needed (5-degree bank away from the failed engine will aid directional control and reduce drag).

2. ADJUST POWER

   Mixture full rich. Props to next higher power setting. Throttles as required. (Increase the settings on *both* engines, with the remote hope that you may get part of the lost power back. If it isn't needed, you can reduce power a bit on the good engine after the checklist is complete.)

3. REDUCE DRAG

   Gear up, flaps up.

4. IDENTIFY THE FAILED ENGINE

   Dead leg, dead engine.

5. SHUT DOWN THE FAILED ENGINE

   Throttle closed. Prop feathered. Mixture OFF.

6. CLEAN UP THE AIRPLANE

   Cowl flaps closed (both engines if temperatures permit, on the failed engine for sure). Shut off fuel to the dead engine. Switch off magnetos and generators on the dead engine.

7. LAND AS SOON AS POSSIBLE

   Plenty of latitude for good judgment here. Don't overfly a safe, convenient field.

ENGINE FIRE IN FLIGHT

You can always get out and run when an engine catches fire on the ground, but let one flame in flight and you have a real problem on your hands. Most light twins don't have built-in fire extinguishers, which means that unless you can somehow cause the fire to cease and desist, you'd better start for the ground pronto, so that you *can* get out and run! There's the outside chance that a very rapid descent will blow out the fire, but don't count on it—once the flames get their teeth into the wing structure, they'll burn right on through until there's nothing left to burn. If you can't get the airplane on the ground before the wing burns off, you won't have any problem to solve; it'll take care of itself.

The possibility of an engine fire in flight can be somewhat lessened by taking a good look at the powerplants during preflight and never letting engine temperatures get higher than normal. Inside the nacelles of today's tightly cowled aircraft engines are numerous fuel and oil lines designed to hold up under normal heat conditions. When things get super-hot in there, the hoses may spring leaks and spray everything around with liquids that immediately burst into flame. Sometimes a small leak will build a pool of gasoline or oil and nothing happens until the vapors get to the hot parts of the engine—then the trouble starts.

No matter how the fire begins, when you know it's there, do something about it, and do it right now. The quickest way to shut off the most probable source of combustibles to an engine fire is via the mixture—move the control to OFF *right now* and get rid of the fuel. If you do this before the fire has ignited the metal parts of the engine and wing, you stand a good chance of completing the flight with nothing worse than a blackened engine and a big repair bill . . . which is a lot better than trying to fly the airplane with one wing burned off. After the mixture control is closed, clean up the airplane using the engine-failure-in-flight checklist, and do whatever appears best at the time.

Suppose by the time you recognize an engine fire it has progressed to the point where shutting off the fuel doesn't help? With no fire-extinguishing agent available in the nacelle, you've no choice but to begin an immediate and very rapid descent—if you continue flying you'll do little more than fan the flames and cause the fire to burn brighter. Pick the softest spot you can see (at night, might as well head for a dark area and hope nobody is living there with the lights out) and plan for an off-airport landing. If you can put the airplane down while you still have control, you'll probably survive—on the other hand, very few pilots walk away from a one-wing landing.

The engine-restarting-in-flight checklist that's in your owner's manual is put there strictly as a practice procedure, for those times when you are familiarizing yourself with your airplane's foibles with an engine out. Whenever you shut one down for real, the circumstances that would warrant a restart would have to be rather dire. When you shut down because of an engine fire, read those circumstances as completely unattainable—you can't get so bad off that you're willing to rekindle the flames. Whatever was burning before will burn just as readily again, so when you kill a burning engine, don't resurrect it—ever.

DEPARTURES FROM ROUTINE
AND OTHER ENGINE-OUT TIPS

Given the marginal engine-out performance of light twins, and the fact that each situation will be slightly different, the checklist must serve only as a guide; there will be times when other courses of action are better for reasons of safety. For example, if your twin is one that has only one hydraulic pump to operate gear and flaps, and it's powered by the engine that quits, it may be best to forget the wheels until the failed engine is feathered—imagine yourself with a badly incapacitated airplane in one hand and a pump handle in the other. When a prop windmills, the drag it creates will probably do you in faster than the drag of the wheels; you may want to feather first. Now, if you're able to continue climbing on one engine even with the wheels down and locked, for heaven's sake *leave* them down and land, soon. Having a secure set of rollers underneath is a big chunk of engine-out happiness.

It may be possible and advisable to reduce power on the remaining engine when you reach a safe maneuvering altitude, one from which you can miss most of the obstacles on the way back to the airport. That good engine is all you've got left, so treat it right. Don't ever allow the airspeed to fall below best single-engine rate-of-climb, and keep it as far above that figure as practical. Remember that if you let the airspeed sag, you're not likely to get it back without spending altitude, a lot of which you may not have.

Cowl flaps, becoming commonplace on today's tightly cowled twins, are usually open at takeoff and produce their share of drag during flight. As soon as the failed engine is secured, make sure the cowl flaps for that engine are closed —what a shame to execute an otherwise perfect single-engine procedure, only to wind up short of the runway because the

drag-producing and airflow-disturbing cowl flaps were for-
gotten.

A single-engine landing shouldn't be any different from
a normal one, but don't kid yourself—you'll be on the edge
of your seat with the old adrenaline pump running full tilt.
That's not all bad, because all your senses will be height-
ened; if you were asleep when the engine quit, you'll be
wide awake now! Recognize the situation for what it is, plan
ahead, and chances are it will be the smoothest landing
you've ever made—there *is* a sense of urgency about it, a
realization that everything has got to go right the first time.
If you don't know how long it takes for the wheels to come
down and lock, find out; you'll need this information to set
up your pattern (time the gear extension with both normal
and emergency systems).

Remember that the wings don't know or care how many
motors are furnishing the motive power; all they have to
work with is the number of molecules of air moving around
them. Airspeed control is almost as important in the engine-out landing phase as it was back there when the engine
stopped. Single-engine approach airspeeds should be very
close to normal approach speeds, with a major limit—if you
let the airspeed fall below the best single-engine rate-of-
climb speed, you have probably committed yourself to landing. Once below the altitude where you *know* a go-around
is impossible, or even questionable, don't try—put the airplane down while you're still in control. Flaps shouldn't be
extended at all until they're needed, and only partially
until you're willing to land—another point of commitment.

Most pilots tend to add a few knots for the wife and kids
when the chips are down, and if mother never heard of the
pill, the additional speed may turn into non-stoppable energy
at the other end of the runway, to say nothing of the wheelbarrowing tendency of a hot landing. If there's anything not
needed at this point, it's a hard-to-control airplane. Add to
this the zero thrust and zero drag of the feathered prop, and
your extra knots may do you in. A single-engine approach,
once begun, should be completed with a normal landing unless something truly dangerous gets in your way. When

you've decided to touch down, reduce power on the good engine and make as normal a landing as you can—the only real problem may be taxiing back to the ramp on one engine.

Multi-engine airplanes are designed so that all the fuel can be used by the remaining engine when the other is shut down. If you are not intimately familiar with the fuel system of your airplane, take some time and get that way; in a tight situation where you need every gallon of gasoline, your recollection of which valves and switches to move may evaporate. Since the fuel-transfer procedure is one you won't practice every time you fly, make sure there is a description of the process (a fuel-management checklist) stored permanently in the airplane, and don't change a thing without referring to it. In a really critical single-engine performance situation, the one thing you don't want to do is to stop the good engine. Don't rely on memory—have a checklist and use it to accomplish any change in the fuel source to the engine that will get you home safely.

Flying high in a twin is one of the best ways to maximize the investment in those two powerplants and the speed they can provide; but when one of them expires, you will probably have to give up your lofty perch. The loss of an engine is going to mean a compromise of airspeed and altitude; if you need to maintain airspeed you'll have to descend, to stay at cruise altitude will cost you some knots—there's no way around that trade-off. Here's where altitude is money in the bank, because it gives you more time to solve the problem. There can't be a checklist for what to do now, not with all the different situations that can exist; the nearest airport is a hundred miles away over the mountains at night, or you're in the middle of the Gulf of Mexico when the engine gives up, or the only difference between maximum gross weight and what you weigh now is the fuel you burned during climb, or any one of a thousand combinations of bad news.

In the worst possible box—higher than single-engine ceiling, heavy, a long way to go to a suitable landing spot—you'll be faced with an unavoidable loss of altitude. (If you must cross terrain that pokes more feet into the sky than your airplane can clear on one engine, you've accepted the risk of a possible forced landing. You should have considered this before launch, and now you must give serious thought not to *whether* you'll spend the night in the boonies, but to *where*. Give thanks for small favors—at least you have the option of picking your landing spot, so start looking for the softest one you can find.) How many of those precious feet you lose depends in great measure on how you handle the airplane following an engine failure.

Airspeed is the key item, as it is whenever you're trying to get the most out of the machine. After a power loss, go through the engine-failure-in-flight checklist and get everything cleaned up, but don't give up a foot of altitude until the airspeed bleeds off to single-engine best-rate-of-climb, where the wings provide the most efficient lifting force; even though it may be a negative result, you'll be "unclimbing" at the lowest possible number of feet per minute—this technique is called "driftdown." Things get better with every foot you descend into more dense air, and sooner or later you'll find an altitude where the negative rate of climb ceases and the airplane can hold its own. As long as this altitude is above whatever stands between you and an acceptable place to land, you're home free.

Now you've a happy choice—when the altimeter stops unwinding, you can either reduce power and continue at V_y (a particularly useful airspeed if you've still many miles to travel) or leave the good-engine go handles where they are and get home faster. Your problems are not completely solved, but it's comforting to know that once again you're the master of your own destiny—you're not being forced to accept whatever comes along.

Wouldn't it be a cryin' shame to slog your way successfully through an engine-failure situation and close your performance with a gear-up landing? When the runway is in sight and you've "got it made," don't give up—force yourself to check and double-check everything that you can think of. And one of the most important is the before-landing checklist, GUMPS. The other items are of lesser interest, but remember the wheels—in a time of stress, the human mind tends to lock on to that which represents salvation, in this case the airport and the runway. If you've habitualized the GUMPS checks into an unforgettable portion of your before-landing preparations, it won't fail when you need it most.

WHEN IS AN ENGINE FAILURE
NOT AN ENGINE FAILURE?

All of the procedures and techniques up to this point have been based on a sudden and complete loss of power, with no consideration given to a partial failure. There's a very strong possibility of salvaging some power from a sick engine (as opposed to a dead one), unless the stoppage is due to fuel starvation or a major internal failure. *Any* power available will improve the performance of the airplane, and may be just what you need to climb over the tall trees or fly safely to the next airport. You'll have to judge the merits of con-tinuing at partial power or shutting the engine down com-pletely. The decision will be an easy one if you can't possibly climb out of trouble or maintain a safe altitude on the thrust from one engine—in this bind, might as well let 'er run; what have you got to lose?

It's possible that the problem may be caused by the engine's sudden inability to operate at the high pressures and tem-peratures of takeoff power; or at the cruise setting, one small link in the power chain has broken down. When you start to close the throttle in the shutdown sequence, do it slowly and carefully. You may find a partial-power situation that you can live with, at least until you reach a safe altitude or turn the corner toward home. Unless the engine is about to shake itself off the mounts or is burning, any thrust you can get out of it is good thrust when it means the difference between flying and not flying; to heck with trying to save the engine—it's probably ruined anyway.

YOU CAN'T BEAT THE NUMBERS

In one of the most expensive compromises in a compro-mise-filled business, the engine-out capabilities of a light twin (or the lack thereof) can lead even an experienced pilot down the primrose path. There are going to be situations in which your twin will *not* do what must be done—the numbers prove it. Whenever you release the brakes at a weight that can't be stopped on the runway available after accelerating to at least V_{mc}, or when there are obstacles in your path that can't be cleared even at best single-engine *angle*-of-climb speed, you have forged the first link in a chain of events that may have an unhappy ending if an engine quits—disaster at worst, expensive embarrassment at best.

Runway behind and altitude above are useless aeronautical commodities for any pilot; their uselessness comes through in spades when you're in control of a twin. But in that fourth word back—"control"—is the key to success in multi-engine flying; *you* have complete *control* over whatever happens every time you fly. If you've planned and figured and your computations come up with a set of numbers that will allow you to stop on the pavement if you have to, or climb to a safe altitude on one engine if that becomes necessary, you have exercised *control* over the situation.

When the numbers—weight, runway length, density altitude, climb capability—are ignored, look out; you're asking for trouble, and the fates of aviation being what they are, if ye ask long enough ye shall certainly receive—double.

15

. . . On Getting Stopped

THERE'S AN OLD SAW IN OUR BUSINESS that refers to a couple of aeronautical commodities useless to a pilot: "altitude above, and runway behind." While the author is lost to the ages (I may hear from a dozen aviators claiming they thought of it!), the basic truth of that famous statement remains intact, and we're most concerned here with the latter portion thereof . . . runway behind, or "Some Thoughts on Bringing Your Airplane to a Stop This Side of the Other End of the Concrete." We all get spoiled when most of our landings are on long-enough, level, paved runways, situations in which the only need for anything more than normal braking is to let us turn off at a more convenient taxiway. But when approaching a strip that promises to test the short-field capability of both plane and pilot, it's good to have a reservoir of maximum-performance knowledge. Here are some principles and techniques dealing with rapid deceleration.

Getting an airplane stopped in the shortest possible distance is simply a matter of energy management, but the problem goes beyond "simple" when all the variables are considered, not the least of which is the pilot technique involved. In the final analysis, however, the distance required for a landing roll will be related to the speed at touchdown, which is nothing more than an expression of the energy of motion. That statement is not going to make front pages anywhere, but the effect of each nonessential knot may get your attention; energy level (and, therefore, stopping distance) increases as the *square* of an increase in speed.

Consider a skid-equipped helicopter making running landings on a dry runway at groundspeeds of 5, 10, and 15 knots; square those speeds (25, 100, 225), divide by 25 to simplify the numbers—1, 4, 9—and you have an easily digestible relationship of the energy levels involved. Since stopping distance is directly proportional to the amount of energy in the vehicle, the touchdown at ten knots requires *four* times the runway used up in the five-knot landing, and when the skids make contact at fifteen knots, *nine* times the distance is needed. Immutable laws of physics these, and the relationships apply just as precisely to fixed-wing operators as to those Frisbee-flyers who grind off several centimeters of skid during running landings.

With wind left out of the picture for the moment, it appears that the largest single factor in a minimum-run landing is the speed at touchdown. But even with the slowest possible approach speed, questions come up about braking: When should you stomp on the binders; early in the landing roll? or later on, when the machine has slowed a bit and there's less chance of blowing a tire or two? The myth of "late braking" is very effectively shattered by another translation of the energy levels associated with touchdown speeds: It takes as much energy to slow an airplane from 85 to 65 knots as it does to reduce its speed from 55 to 7 knots. Since the airplane will move down the runway a lot farther while decelerating from 85 to 65, the answer is clear—apply maximum braking (but not enough to lock the wheels and blow out the tires!) as soon as the rubber is on the runway.

Now let's put wind back into the equation, because it is undoubtedly the pilot's best friend in a short-field situation . . . *if* the wind can be landed into, not with. The effects of a strong headwind on shrinking the landing roll are dramatic and commonplace, but what about those *light* zephyrs wafting up and down the runway? Run the numbers out again, and you'll find that an aircraft that touches down at 50 knots will require 23 percent more runway to get stopped when landing *with* a three-knot tailwind than it does when landing *into* the same wind. For touchdown speeds of 60 and 70 knots, the tailwind penalties amount to 22 and 19 percent, respectively. When you have a choice in a critical runway-length situation, *land into the wind,* no matter how light. For a rule of thumb, when wind velocity is 10 percent of the aircraft's touchdown speed, a downwind landing will require 50 percent more ground roll than a landing into the same wind.

When there's plenty of favorable wind, when you've planted the airplane right smack on the end of the runway at the lowest possible speed, all that's left to complete a successful short-field landing is optimum use of the brakes. Maximum braking is a function of the amount of friction between tires and surface, and the weight pressing down on the tires. There's little to be done about the coefficient of friction (be sure you keep well-treaded tires on the airplane, that'll help), but the pilot has complete control over seeing that aircraft weight is transferred from wings to wheels as soon as possible after touchdown. Holding the nose wheel off the ground until elevator power disappears guarantees that *all* the weight not being borne by the wings will be expressed at the main wheels, and flap retraction immediately after contact will dump whatever lift is still being generated at low speed. Absent the spoilers, reversers, and anti-skid devices that are part and parcel of most turbine designs because of their high landing speeds, the length of the landing roll now depends on maximum braking—another matter of pilot technique. When the optimum coefficient of friction is reached, the tires will actually be turning about 20 percent slower than the airplane is traveling—a "rolling skid." This technique will leave some rubber on the pavement, but not nearly as much as when a wheel is locked; then, the tire may actually hydroplane on its own melted rubber, and *all* braking action is lost.

In any configuration, aerodynamic drag increases as the

square of the aircraft's velocity, so in those wet or icy situations where brakes cannot be used (or where a combination of wheel brakes and aerodynamic braking seems best), a similar rule applies—start stopping as early as possible in the landing roll. Remember that as speed drops, so does total drag, once again by a factor of the square of speed; as a result, aerodynamic braking—while it looks spectacular from the sidelines—is of little help at speeds less than 60 to 70 percent of the touchdown speed.

Rainy Days and Runways

Without belaboring the physical principles involved, it's not difficult to imagine a slippery runway's adverse effect on braking action; the coefficient of friction (a measure of how much runway the tires will grab when the brakes are applied) drops alarmingly when the surface gets wet. Transport aircraft crews figure an additional 15 percent of normal stopping distance on wet runways, and most of them have anti-skid devices and reverse thrust. If you are in the habit of saving something for a rainy day, make it runway length; you never know when you might need to withdraw a few hundred feet from your account.

When there's enough rain on the runway to let the tires slide along on top of a film of water, hyproplaning may develop. You can count on zero braking action until the tires once again come in contact with the pavement. Speed is usually the villain, since hydroplaning starts when water can't get out of the way fast enough; the tires climb up on the wave they have created, and off you go on a free ride that you neither want nor need, eating up runway at an alarming rate. Since you have no control over which way the airplane is sliding, any crosswind will show up as a definite tendency to move sideways despite your best efforts with rudder and power.

Hydroplaning will continue until speed it reduced to the point where the tires can push water out of the way and grab the ground, or until they can muscle their way through the film of water with increased weight as the wings gradually lose lift. As the mysteries of hydroplaning were explored, researchers found an interesting relationship between tire pressure and the onset of hydroplaning. Given runway conditions which would induce this super-slipperiness, the minimum speed for hydroplaning (in knots) can be calculated by multiplying the square root of the main-gear tire pressure by nine. It won't take place until and unless this speed is reached, and it will stop when you slow down below that number. This is in no way intended to influence your choice of tire pressure, but to make you very aware of the dangerous situation that can develop at speeds approaching the magic number for hydroplaning—once it starts, you've lost control of the airplane for at least a little while.

16

CIFFTRS and GUMPS . . . The Universal Checklists

You've seen them both perform—the puddle-jumper pilot who spends an hour on his preflight inspection, and his four-stripe counterpart who boards his airplane through a jetway and never even sees the tires, let alone kicks them. To all appearances, they are exercises in absurdity; preflight overkill on the one hand and a complete lack of concern on the other. But that hour spent fooling around with the airplane is a big part of the total aviation experience for a lot of people; and the four-engine flyer sees a lot more in a quick glance than you realize, for his experience and training help him spot discrepancies that the average pilot wouldn't see if he walked right up next to the airplane; besides, it has already been checked nearly rivet by rivet by several others—that's part of the crew concept.

The length of a preflight notwithstanding, there are certain essentials that must operate if you're going to aviate—if you can get the engine(s) started and manage to arrive at the end of the runway without anything falling off the airplane, it will probably fly. The duration of the flight is not guaranteed, but you'll likely get it off the ground. With a modern, properly maintained airplane, the presumption that everything will work right is a reasonable one; when you leap in and leap off, using the time saved for what you consider more worthwhile pursuits, your faith will be justified more often than not.

But when some component that's absolutely necessary for flight *doesn't* work, and you don't find it out until after you've left the ground, the result can be either inconvenience or disaster—it takes only one little error or omission to do you in. Running the car out of gas on a freeway doesn't do much for your disposition, and is usually accompanied by a great deal of self-deprecation, but the solution is at worst a hike away. In an airplane, the stupidity that creates an out-of-gas situation deserves the severe penalty that might be imposed —like waking up in some other world.

Methodists in aviation (not necessarily the churchgoing variety) came up with a list of items that should be looked into before attempting flight, and when the items were put together on a sheet, it became a checkoff list, since shortened to "checklist." Intended originally as a reminder of things that had to be done for safety's sake, checklists today are procedural guides, and the bigger the airplane, the more important checklists become. The Wright brothers' prop pullers didn't care much at what point Orville opened the fuel valve, but introduce the juice to a jet engine at the wrong time and the whole starting sequence can turn into a bucket of worms flambé—it's got to be done at the proper time, which you'll find on the checklist.

For more years than safety experts like to remember, a big-airplane pilot's ability was measured by how fast he could reel off the lengthy checklists that applied to emergency situations—and then in the air, he was expected to exhibit dazzling speed as he accomplished those items from memory. If, in the quest for speed, he moved levers that shouldn't have been moved or switched things that shouldn't have been switched, it was written off to lack of memory training, and the pilot was sent back to the books to drill some more. It was a long time and many unfortunate accidents later that someone finally broke the chain of dependence on memory, and realized that the human mind is most fallible when it is undergoing stress; and what, short of an actual emergency situation, is more stressful than when the check pilot lays an engine fire on you under the hood, followed by a hydraulic failure and an explosive decompression?

In time, the requirements for memory were pared down to only those items considered critical to continued flight, but as airplanes got larger and more complicated, it became obvious that no one could possibly remember all the things that had to be done; just as important was the order in which certain moves had to be made. Some aircraft have checklists so long they are wound on scrolls, and there's probably a de luxe model somewhere that has a powered scroll—some people will do anything to sell an airplane. In most cases, the only checklist item the captain needs to commit to memory is the word "checklist," preceded, of course, by a word or phrase which lets the copilot know which one to dig out, such as "before landing" or "engine fire in flight" or "breakfast" or whatever.

Even when it's in charge of the arrangements for getting the smallest of airplanes safely into the air and back again, the human mind is easily boggled. If you forget a really critical item, it won't make any difference to you whether the final flight was in a C-5 (by Lockheed) or a C-3 (by Aeronca). Considering the things that must get done, the parts of the airplane that must be checked, you can develop a pair of memory joggers for those two fraught-with-forget-fulness segments of powered flight—before takeoff and before landing. And when you shake out the absolutely essential items for any airplane that has ever been built, you'll have a before-takeoff checklist that includes controls, instruments, fuel, flaps, trim, runup and seat belts; the universal before-landing checklist must consider gas, undercarriage, mixture, propeller and seat belts. As you hang more goodies on your airplane, each of these major categories on your checklist may have subordinate listings of things to look at and do, and some of the basic items may require more than a glance or a touch to insure that all is well, but the critical items remain. Even when riding herd on nearly a million pounds of jetliner, the flight crew must be concerned with those things somewhere in the pages of checklists they wade through, item by item—all right, so they can forget about props and mixtures, but the rest of the checklist is valid. You can't go too far wrong with these two checklists, and the smaller the airplane, the more practical they become.

Now you need something to remind you of the reminder—so line up the before-takeoff checklist items vertically, and the first letters spell CIFFTRS; the before-landing items work out to GUMPS. They're two nonsense words (the first one sounds like "sifters" and the second is self-pronouncing) but they will stick in your mind, get you started and help you maintain continuity as you check those items vital to safe flight. CIFFTRS and GUMPS are adequate for almost all single-engine airplanes, and many of the light twins; if your airplane has additional systems or modifications that require more detailed checking, expand each of the basic items to accommodate your specific situation. All set? Call for your before-takeoff checklist and we'll CIFFTR a typical lightplane.

CONTROLS

Check for two things here, freedom of movement and proper direction of travel. (How could flight controls get reversed?—don't ever forget Murphy's Law, which says that if anything can be done backwards, someone will do it eventually.) Here's a sequence that will make the control check as efficient and rapid as possible: First move the wheel or stick to the right, look to the right, and the right aileron should be up. While still looking to the right, move the stick or wheel left, and make sure the right aileron moves down. Now swivel your head and the left aileron should be up; stick or wheel back to the right, and the left aileron should move down.

Look back, and pull the wheel all the way to the rearmost stop, whereupon the elevator should be positioned full up. Reverse the process, and to save wear and tear on your neck, check the rudder for proper travel while you're looking in that direction. Can't see the rudder from where you sit?—better include a control check in your outside pre-flight, just to be sure.

When you put your shoulder to the control and nothing happens, the most probable cause is something jammed in the control surfaces, and the most frequent something is a control lock which wasn't removed during the tire-kicking process. That's the real reason for the "Controls" part of the CIFFTRS check, to keep pilots from attempting a takeoff with the flippers immobilized. If you are the pioneer type who likes to do things first, don't expect to acquire im-mortality by being the first one to take off with the controls locked—it's been tried too many times. Most attempts have met with instant failure, but now and then a lucky soul makes it; the odds against you are staggering, because the trim tabs were not designed to fly the airplane. If you use CIFFTRS religiously, there is no excuse for trying to take off with locked controls.

INSTRUMENTS

The IFR pilot about to fling himself into the inside of a bunch of clouds has a lot to do at this point, seeing that he will soon be completely dependent on the accuracy and proper readings of all those clocks, but the Fair-Weather Flyer needn't do much more than make sure everything is in place. Here's where you should recheck the altimeter and DG settings, and check the engine instruments to see that they're in the green or moving that way. Modern en-gines don't require a prolonged warmup, but you'll do that expensive collection of moving parts a big favor by holding the RPMs to a moderate number until the oil temperature needle has at least climbed off the COLD peg. The owner's manual will tell you how warm the horses should be before you ask them to run faster.

When you'll be using VOR for navigation right after takeoff, set up what you want on the appropriate dials; it's something else you don't have to do during climbout, when

your attention is better invested elsewhere, like watching
for other airplanes.

FUEL

Of course you checked the tanks during your preflight, so
this is no time to be concerned about how much. Small
sermon: Don't ever take anybody's word for what's in the
tanks. "Anybody" includes people and instruments; be absolutely certain that *you* know the tanks are full, or half full,
or whatever you want, and that it's the right kind of gas. No
matter how hard it's raining, how cold the wind or how much
the clock is pushing you, make the visual fuel check an unbreakable rule—it's not often you'll find anything amiss, but
when it counts, it really counts! The selector(s) should be
set on the fullest tanks for every takeoff, and this point in
the CIFFTRS check is not too late to make the switch from
FUMES to FULL—the engine runup will use enough gas to
insure liquid continuity between tank and carburetor. Let
reason prevail; the concern is the sloshing about of that
glob of gas in a partly filled tank, and the possible subsequent
engine failure from fuel starvation. When the difference between tanks is only a couple of gallons, who cares?—but
when the level is low, be mindful of sharp turns onto the
runway, and keep things coordinated during takeoff.

Boost pumps should be turned on (if recommended by
the people who put the bird together) as part of the "fuel"
portion of CIFFTRS. Figure out some way to tell whether
the pumps are working—it could be a rise on the fuel-pres-
sure gauge, the whine of the pump motor or increased electrical load. A bum booster on a high-wing airplane presents
no big problem (few of them have boost pumps anyway; if
you lose the source of power in a gravity-feed system, you've
got bigger problems than where the fuel is coming from),
but when the engine's feedbag is lower than the carburetor,
a poor pump should be a no-go item—without the backup
pressure from the booster, an engine-driven-pump failure
leaves you way out on a rather fragile limb.

FLAPS

Before the first flight of the day, move the flaps all the
way down and back up again, checking for freedom of
movement and symmetry. You'll probably make this check
a thousand times and nothing untoward will show up; but
keep it in your checklist. On Complacency Day, when you
elect to pass over the second F in CIFFTRS, one flap will
go down while the other stays put; you won't know about
it until full-flap time on final approach, and the resulting
slow roll will surely be one of the most spectacular things
you've ever done. Also, be sure that both flaps come up together, as a rolling go-around is best left to the professional
aerobats.

Going for maximum performance on this takeoff, with a
partial flap setting?—now's the time to put the flaps where
they should be; don't wait until you're on the runway, because it's so easy to forget. When you've got to get off the
ground within a confined space and you need flaps, don't
count on the special dispensation that was granted to one
of the B-25 pilots who followed Jimmy Doolittle to Tokyo
in 1942—overstressed mentally with the concerns of lifting
an overloaded land-based bomber from the deck of an aircraft carrier, he just plain forgot to put the flaps down for
takeoff, a demonstrated necessity for such a super-maximum
effort. He made it, but you can bet he still looks heaven-
ward and says "thanks" once in a while.

Even if your airplane has no flaps, say "flaps" anyway; it
may inspire you to buy a bigger airplane just to have something meaningful to do at this point. It also makes for better
continuity in the CIFFTRS check.

TRIM

You'll be able to overcome the effects of improper trim
settings when you're airborne, but why fight it? Set the
wheels or cranks or levers or switches where you know

they'll do you some good on takeoff, and in the initial climb-out. Don't arbitrarily put the pointers "in the green" and expect optimum results; experiment with different weights and load distributions, and have some idea of where the trim should be to help you the most (particularly the elevator trim, since it is most noticeably affected by changes in weight or the distribution thereof). Trim tabs should be adjusted to whatever setting takes the pressure off the controls, which means it's impossible to formulate a set of standard, always-on-the-same mark settings—each day, each load, each power setting requires its own trim—but you've got to start somewhere, so put in what you think you'll need when you get to the T in CIFFTRS.

RUNUP

Here's a great opportunity to ruin an engine or two either by ignoring the check altogether and asking the powerplant to do something it can't (supplying the necessary motive force to get you off the ground) or by making such an extensive check of engine condition that it's ruined before it gets a chance to show its stuff. Today's aircraft engines are not designed to be worked hard on the ground—not only from the standpoint of cooling but also because extended high-power operation sucks a lot of indigestible grit and dirt into the engine. The FBO has a whole garageful of expensive runway-sweeping equipment, so leave that chore to him. Next time there are puddles on the taxiway, park for just a moment in the middle of one and observe the tiny tornado that develops just under the prop; you may even dry up the little lake, but remember that whatever is in that water is probably going through your engine, usually to its disadvantage. As a general rule, never use more power than is needed to get the airplane started and to keep it moving (probably much less than you realize), and get the engine check over with in the shortest possible time.

There are two types of propellers in use today, and the

differences are significant enough to require one runup checklist for fixed-pitch, another for controllable-pitch.

Fixed-pitch first: While the engine is *idling,* check carburetor heat. Remember that your selection of HOT opens the door to unfiltered, heated air, which is not particularly good for the engine when it's on the ground. This check is *not* made to determine how hot the air will be, but merely to find out if the levers and arms that operate the carb air doors are working. With that in mind, pull out the knob or move the lever all the way, and just as soon as you notice the effect (obvious change in noise level as the engine slows down because of the power loss from the hot, less dense air), return the control to COLD, and do it just once—that's all—you've proved that you can put hot air into the carburetor if you need it.

On this simple engine, move right on to the power check, to see if the magnetos and spark plugs are doing what they are supposed to. Know what RPM your engine manufacturer recommends for the power check, go to it quickly and check the mags—LEFT, BOTH, RIGHT, BOTH—know what to watch and listen for, and get it over with. Since power problems of enough magnitude to cause concern will show up right now (after all, you're dealing with electricity, and it moves *fast*), there's no good reason for prolonging the mag check: running an aircraft engine at a high power setting on the ground any longer than absolutely necessary is bad procedure.

The only time a full-power static check makes sense is when you're about to take off from a high-altitude airport. The engine doesn't need all the fuel you're feeding it on takeoff with the mixture at full rich, but it does require some additional cooling, which is handled by the extra, non-power-producing gasoline. So you're really operating with an overrich mixture for every liftoff, and when you leave an airport a couple of thousand feet or more above sea level, the mixture is rich enough to reduce power considerably. To get the most out of the engine, open the throttle, then lean slowly until the RPMs begin to fall off; now push the mixture knob back toward RICH a bit to provide a fudge factor, and you'll have the best power available for your takeoff. It goes without saying that you must watch engine temperatures more carefully than you normally do.

But a full-power check at sea-level airports runs against the grain of the engine-preservation philosophy; besides, aren't you going to make a full-power check as soon as the tower clears you for takeoff? A smooth, rapid movement of the go handle will tell you whether your powerplant is sickly or well, and in a matter of just a few seconds; that gives you plenty of time to make a no-go decision and still bring the airplane to a stop. Engine problems on the runway are prettly easily solved—take those same problems into the air, and your troubles multiply.

Now to the checklist for a controllable-pitch prop, which encompasses the same general items but takes a look at the operation of two more systems—normal pitch change and prop feathering. As before, carb heat should be checked at idle; if you have a carburetor air temperature gauge, use it—but only as an indication of the heat system's operation. As soon as the needle moves, return the handle to COLD. Gauge or no, you'll still be able to recognize the changes in RPM and sound level.

The owner's manual suggests an engine speed for the prop check, so set the throttle to produce that RPM (prop levers full forward, of course), then move the propeller control all the way back to the low RPM stops, and do it ONCE. Unless the RPM change is slow due to cold, sluggish oil in the pitch-change mechanism, there's nothing to be gained by doing it again and again—given normal temperatures, all you're looking for is an indication that the pitch change is taking place.

The next item should be a check of the feathering system, again at the manual-suggested RPM; get it over with quickly to ease the strain on the engine, but make it a conclusive check. You don't want the prop to go all the way to full feather because of vibrations, high internal engine pressures and other things that can be harmful to the whole powerplant, but you do need to know for certain that you have feathering capability. Most light twins have the feathering actuator built right into the prop-control levers, so pull them all the way back into the detent until you see (and hear) a decrease in propeller RPM—the instant this is apparent, move the prop levers smartly back to the high-RPM position. Once is almost always enough, but on those days when it's so cold the brass monkeys are heading south, you may have to move the props into feather several times to get warm oil into the system. When you need feathering, you need it *right now*— a slowly feathering prop is almost as big a drag as no feather at all.

Unless your aircraft has an operating limitation which precludes the feather check (and there are a few models so restricted), it is a *must*; if you can't shut down a sick engine in flight, you may wind up with a sorry choice—either an overspeeding prop producing no power and high drag or a nearly feathered fan doing essentially the same thing. Either way, it's no good; climb capability will sag considerably on any airplane when one of the props is windmilling, so if you can't feather the blades on runup, or if the action is very sluggish even after several cycles in cold weather, don't go. You're asking for trouble, and the gremlins are out there eager to answer your request.

Make a magneto and spark-plug check just as outlined for the fixed-pitch types, and you're ready to take the green flag except for one more item common to all airplanes, large or small—recheck your seat belts and shoulder harness (S for SEAT BELT), turn around and tell your passengers to do the same. The law requires the pilot-in-command to notify his riders that their safety belts must be fastened for takeoff and landing—don't get caught short legally if something happens —sound off in a loud, clear voice or ring a bell or hold up a sign; do whatever it takes to make sure everybody on board knows it's time to buckle up.

You'd best leave the engine runup until you're parked, with brakes set, but the rest of the CIFFTRS check can be accomplished as you taxi out to the active runway. Why tie up a line of brother airmen by waiting until you're at the head of the runway to start through the before-takeoff checklist? An airplane on the ground with the engine running costs nothing but money, so do whatever you can on the way out, and accomplish the balance of the checklist in short order—there's nothing wrong with hurrying, but there's a lot wrong with *being* hurried.

Before you commit yourself to flight, make one final check of engine condition during the takeoff roll (the early part, obviously). Let your ears tell you as much as they can about what's going on in front of the firewall, and as soon as full power is set and stablized, scan the engine instruments; if you know what the panel should look like when you let out the reins and kick 'er in the slats, any instrument that's not where it ought to be will flash an unmistakable signal to bring the machine to a stop—it's not ready to fly! On the last of the big prop-driven Boeings, one of the flight engineer's several panels had about two square feet of engine instruments, so small and so closely arranged that there wasn't time to look at, assimilate and interpret each one. The designers rotated each gauge unit in the panel so that when takeoff power was "in the green," each and every needle pointed in the same direction—the engineer could pick out an errant indication right away. You should likewise know what takeoff power looks like in terms of the engine instrument display on your airplane, and when in doubt, abort.

When the airplane involved is a very simple one (i.e., fixed landing gear, one-pitch prop, no flaps or mixture control and a fuel system that's being properly managed anytime the engine's running), a before-landing checklist is good for laughs, because there's little you can do except close the throttle, point the plane at the airport, and land. If you feel compelled to check the status of landing wheels which have been down and locked ever since the airplane came off the assembly line, say "gear" and take a look, but say it to yourself—passengers will laugh otherwise. It's a good habit to form, and later on in a retractable, you'll have the gear-check groove worn so deep you'll never forget.

The universal before-landing checklist—GUMPS—came

about the same way as CIFFTRS, by lining up certain essential items in a vertical column and arranging them so that the first letters formed an easily remembered word. With a more complex airplane, each item may have to be expanded to fit system requirements, but if you check each of these—gas, undercarriage, mixture, props and seat belts—before every landing, you won't miss anything of vital importance. A good place to start is as soon as you turn downwind in the pattern, or a comparable distance from the airport when you're landing straight in. GUMPS also furnishes a quick, organized double-check when you reach the point of commitment, just before touchdown, especially when the landing gear is the type that goes up and down—you can't wear out the gear lights by looking at them. By the numbers, then, GUMPS.

GAS

For the same reasons as the before-takeoff check, select the fullest tank at this time. If the airplane builder thinks it's a good idea to use boost pumps during the landing, turn them on now and check fuel pressure.

UNDERCARRIAGE

An obvious borrow from the British, but it's hard to say the words that result from using "wheels" or "landing gear" —try GWMPS or GLGMPS—let's stick with U for undercarriage. When airspeed is below the maximum for roller dropping, put the wheels down and go no further in the checklist until you have assured yourself that they are down and locked; there must be absolutely no doubt in your mind. Check whatever you have available—lights, hydraulic pressure, visual indicators, feel of the rudder pedals, that comfortable chunking sound on some airplanes as the downlocks work into place—and if you don't have one, consider the few bucks to put a mirror on the nacelle so that you can see the nose wheel sticking down. A little ingenuity and a couple more mirrors will probably bring the mains into your field of vision if you want to be completely sure of the landing-gear situation.

MIXTURE

Should be moved to full rich at this point. With a non-turbo engine, the mixture should be gradually increased throughout the descent from cruise altitude (if you forget, the engine will let you know it's too lean by running progressively rougher as you get lower, and if you still ignore it, will quit altogether—that's bound to get your attention). Regardless of the type of engine, go to full rich when you get to the M in GUMPS.

PROPELLERS

Fixed-pitchers, mouth the word to form a habit for the future, but there's nothing you can do about it. All others, don't do anything yet; you're most likely still on downwind with something less than cruise power required to maintain pattern airspeed with the wheels hanging out. If you jam the prop levers forward, the blades will go to a low-pitch, high-RPM setting which is hard on the engine, the prop mechanism, your ears and the serenity of people on the ground. You shouldn't need more than cruise power to maintain pattern altitude, even with partial flaps, so hold the checklist (and the props) until you're on final approach at a low airspeed and with very little power on the engines. In this condition, without engine power to drive them, the props won't respond to a governor-setting change, but you will have preset low gear if you need it for a missed approach.

SEAT BELTS

Check your personal-restraint system again, and turn to the passengers with a kind word for their safety—forming this habit might just save you a nasty day in court—it's in the book; you've got to remind them to fasten the straps.

That's GUMPS—not a bad idea to run lightly across it once more as you approach your commitment point, especially the U part; it helps prevent the embarrassment that follows a banner headline: LOCAL PILOT LANDS WHEELS-UP. Let's face it, you'll never live it down; visualize your name in the story under that headline, and you'll check the gear indicator more frequently.

Did we forget flaps on the before-landing checklist? It hardly seems necessary to include something that is assumed to be at the full down position for every landing, but add "flaps" to your personal checklist if you like. Where you fit an F into GUMPS is completely up to you.

While on the subject of covering everything that might be included, a word about the preflight checklist. This phase tends to get a little overworked, especially if you fly the same airplane all the time. You're going to check everything that can move, run, pump or make noise later on anyway, but it's important to have some sort of routine walk-around check so that anything out of the ordinary will catch your eye. Airplanes aren't intended for display, they're built to fly, and when they don't for long periods of time, seals dry out and shrink, gaskets begin leaking, and you should pay special attention to the signs of neglect—the longer your plane sits between flights, the closer you should look for oil, fuel and hydraulic leaks.

Control locks and pitot covers are two major problem areas, and in the spring of the year air intakes and engine cowlings become irresistible to nest builders—industrious birds have been known to airlift unbelievable quantities of grass into the nooks and crannies of an unattended airplane in a matter of hours.

Always start your preflight inside the airplane to be certain the mixture, mags and master switch are OFF. There's a suggested route for the walk-around somewhere in the owner's manual, but if you don't like that one, make up your own—the important point is to do it the same way every time, so that when something *is* out of whack, you'll notice it. Before every "new" flight, when the airplane has been serviced prior to your arriving on the scene, you *must* check gas and oil; confirm the quantity and quality of each, and make sure the caps are properly seated. Draining the fuel sumps is a particularly messy chore on some airplanes, but it's got to be done at least now and then, and especially when the machine has been sitting out in rainy or cold weather.

One of the best features of the CIFFTRS/GUMPS system is its simplicity—if you have to break in with something else, like a radio transmission or a change in traffic pattern or a long delay before takeoff, it's easy to go back and pick up the checklist where you left off, or if memory fails you completely, it's not all that difficult to go back to the beginning and start over again. Never continue a checklist with the good intention of coming back to an unaccomplished item later; the road to an aircraft accident is paved with good intentions. Complex airplanes are most susceptible —you enter the pattern well above maximum gear-down speed and go ahead with GUMPS, promising yourself that you'll get the wheels down as soon as airspeed permits. Then you are distracted by other airplanes and tower talk, and you never do get around to lowering the gear . . . crunch —it *can* happen!

The GUMPS check probably grew from the still extant military practice of making acronyms out of everything possible—this is a great communications compressor, but there are dangers involved when the communicatee doesn't understand the jargon. A case in point was a foreign student some years ago whose T-6 instructor had trouble getting him to accomplish checklists at the proper time. On his third ride, the poor student missed the before-landing checklist completely, and the instructor reminded him via interphone from the back seat. Seeing that the message wasn't making any electronic progress between cockpits, the instructor finally hollered "GUMP, GUMP, GUMP!" With the conditioned response of a well-trained cadet, the student jumped— just what he thought he had been ordered to do. Moral? When you speak in checklistese, talk to yourself.

And this chapter wouldn't be complete without some advice for those of you operating larger airplanes on longer routes, involving one or more RONS. At the tail end of a corporate aircraft shutdown checklist, you might well find:

Engine analyzer	OFF
Lights	OFF
Inverter	OFF
APU	OFF
Batteries	OFF
Wedding band	ON

17

Wing Flaps . . . When and How to Use Them

AN AIRPORT DEDICATION is no more a virginal event than the official opening of a superhighway. The local speed freaks have probably been using the road as a drag strip ever since the concrete hardened, and some audacious pilot has surely rolled his wheels on the brand-new runway long before the ceremony. Nevertheless, for the sake of officialdom and political pride, the flashiest airplane that the airport PR man can find will cut a ceremonial ribbon with its landing gear and officially open the field.

Along with bits of ribbon, the "first" landing will leave its rubberized signature on the runway, and if the new airport is a walloping success, those two black tire streaks will grow into a huge inkspot of rubber. Where many-tired airplanes are involved, the landing marks sometimes get so thick they have to be removed—the coefficient of friction of a wet rubber runway is lower than a belly-mounted strobe light after a gear-up landing.

The premise that every landing must leave some expensive tireskin behind hasn't always been accepted, like during the Big War, when our air armadas required huge amounts of rubber. Unfortunately, the people who had cornered the natural-rubber market weren't on our side, so we thought up ways to make aircraft tires last longer. One scheme was to attach rubber vanes to the sidewalls of aircraft tires, so when the pilot hollered "gear down" and the wheels dropped into the slipstream, the vanes would pop out, windmill-like, and start spinning the tire. "With the tire already rolling at touchdown, friction will be considerably reduced, don't you see, and tires will last longer," said the inventor. A great idea, but apparently the vanes cost more than the rubber they saved, and nobody has seen tires like that since.

We have learned to live with a certain amount of rubber reduction at touchdown, although pilots and airplane owners who are concerned with the flow of dollars out of the aviation account would like to see that loss kept to a minimum. The airlines, whose vice-presidents in charge of tires wince at each landing, have worked out operational procedures designed to put the big planes on the ground at the lowest possible speed consistent with safety. A 747 must leave about four bushels of rubber on the runway by the time all eighteen tires have accelerated to the same speed as the airplane, and a lot more goes up in blue smoke when the captain greases it on ten knots faster than he's supposed to.

Unless your brother is in the business and you replace tires as often as possible to keep peace in the family, you've got to vote against hot landings. In addition to tearing up tires, those over-the-fence-at-cruise-speed-and-stand-on-the-pedals-to-get-stopped approaches grind down brake pucks at an alarming rate. They're your tires, and your brakes, and it's your money, even when using a rented airplane; if replacement costs increase, the owner must raise the price, or limit the privilege to pilots he knows will treat the airplane right, or quit renting—whichever he does, you lose. What's to be done? Just make each touchdown as slow as possible, with safety and comfort sharing your concern, and in that order.

Nearly all modern airplanes have a slow-down device built in when they leave the factory. Some are more effective than others, and the names suggest a wide range of technology and intent—plain, split, Fowler, slotted, double-slotted, leading edge and so on—but no matter what else they can do, wing flaps are there to help you slow down: they are, simply and literally, air brakes. For a few bucks buried in the purchase price of the airplane and never noticed again, wing flaps must be one of the best deals in aviation today. Used properly and consistently, flaps earn their keep in the form of longer-wearing tires, extended brake life and the airplane's ability to get into and out of shorter and rougher fields than would be possible with a clean wing. (For those readers whose airplanes have plain, ordinary wings with trailing edges that don't do anything except come to a point, whose cockpits have no levers or handles or switches that say WING FLAPS and whose future plans don't include the operation of such a machine, now is a good time to take the dog for a walk—we'll be finished talking about wing flaps by the time you get back.)

The great controversy, the Flap Flap, was launched on the same day the forward slip was invented. Some clever pilot discovered quite by accident (more likely a series of accidents) that he could shorten the landing roll by proceeding down the final approach sideways—well, partly sideways. The slip was denounced by the stubborn ones as a dangerous maneuver, a nostrum for poorly executed approaches. Their peers' snide comments notwithstanding, the slippers made consistently shorter landings; those with wheel brakes used them less, and pilots who slipped began to see their adroitness at ground looping decay through lack of use. Granted that a ground loop is a very dramatic way to terminate a landing roll, especially before a cheering throng, but it can be uncomfortable when you *have* to do it to keep from getting intimately acquainted with the hedgerow at the end of the field. Better visibility was another plus for slipping; with the front of the airplane out of the way, pilots could actually see the runway on final approach. One good idea deserved another, and the inventive wheels turned until someone came up with a way to create even more drag, and the wing flap was born.

As installed on early airplanes, wing flaps gave rise to two schools of thought; there was the full-flap philosophy and the clean-wing concept, and you had to cast your lot with one or the other—it was an all-or-nothing deal. Today, we're blessed with flap systems that provide up and down and anything you might want in between (some systems are limited to three positions—click, click, click—with an Armstrong Lever). With nigh infinite selectivity, the dispute can now rage on as many fronts as there are flap positions and pilots; not only do we argue the wisdom of using flaps at all, we fight back and forth about *how much* should be used!

The partial-flap people always return the opening salvo with the crosswind argument; to wit, the use of something less than full flaps in a crosswind gives you a better, safer landing because of the increased airspeed and controllability. In rebuttal, the full-flap folks contend that right down to the stall, when there's nothing left, controllability is a function of how far you're willing to move the controls; and they say that even if they increase the airspeed a little bit on a full-flap crosswind approach, they'll still touch down at a lower speed and come to a stop using less runway, rubber and brakes.

Not to be denied, the half-flappers snap right back with their theory that a few extra knots of airspeed by virtue of a partial flap setting puts them in a more nearly level attitude at touchdown, from which it's but a microsecond or two to nose-gear contact and the positive steering which results. "Have it your way," reply 100-percenters, "but remember that, for most pilots, a hot landing is a long landing; we'll concede the advantages of positive directional control in this situation, since you may need it to steer around the threshold lights as you go off the other end of the runway." If the half-flappers still insist that extra airspeed is a good deal even when landing on a super-long runway, their antagonists will say that if the runway's *long* enough to contain a hot landing, it's probably *wide* enough to solve the crosswind problem with another technique. (See Chapter 2, "An Advanced Technique for Crosswind Takeoffs and Landings.")

Getting desperate now, those who preach against full flaps bring up the possibility of a ground loop, claiming that their higher speed at touchdown helps eliminate that embarrassing maneuver. Whereupon the full-flappers point out that, no matter how fast you land, you've got to slow down sooner or later, and if you're really worried about your airplane trying to swap ends, you should be thinking about using another runway, or maybe even another airport.

Taildraggers are in a class unto themselves in the Great Flap Flap, since their stall speeds are so low and crosswinds *do* get strong enough now and then to present control problems. A good three-point landing (the ultimate in taildragging artistry) is always a full-stall landing; in a stiff crosswind with full flaps and the lower stall speed which results, you may find yourself drifting sideways even with stick and rudder against the stops; out of control and out of lift at the same time. Such a dilemma calls for a wheel landing (or the "corner" technique if there's room), which definitely provides more control because it takes more airspeed to keep the tail up; but even a "wheelie" will be a better landing with full flaps and whatever power is required to get the airplane on the runway under complete control at the *lowest possible speed.*

Whatever your preference, when you elect to use flaps, use them with care. Almost all airplanes exhibit a pitch change when the flaps come down, and although the direction the nose tries to move is immaterial, the amount of pitch change can be pretty exciting, especially to that naïve fellow next to you on his first airplane ride. When you turn final approach, the runway appears right in the middle of the windshield, and although still unfamiliar to him, the sight is at least reassuring. The next thing he notices is the blur of motion as your hand goes from flap handle to trim crank, and the windshield that framed the runway a moment ago is suddenly filled with either earth or sky, depending on which way your airplane pitches. You'll get things back where they belong in due time, but it can be a knuckle whitener for someone who neither expects nor understands what has just happened.

First time out in a strange airplane, you're allowed one such excursion while you and the machine get acquainted, but there's no excuse for roller-coastering around the sky after you know what goes on when the flaps are operated. Once you find out, anticipate the trim requirements, and, above all, extend the flaps in increments—never all the way at once, since that just adds to the magnitude of the pitch change. Most flaps produce very little lift but a lot of drag when they pass the halfway-extended mark; so when you add that last notch, there won't be much pitch change, but a lot of slowing down. The higher the performance capabilities of the plane, the more important the limiting speeds become, since you may need the wing flaps to help you slow to pattern airspeed—after all, we agreed a long way back that they are primarily air brakes!

A worthwhile goal is to get the flaps all the way down without your passengers knowing that they were extended at all. Check the manual for your airplane, and you may find progressively lower maximum speeds for the various flap settings; these are structural limits, to keep the flaps from departing the airplane, but they can also serve as a guide for smooth operation. On final approach, when airspeed gets down to the limit for the first normal increment of extension, start 'em down, and as each successive limit speed is reached, push out some more flap. Shoot for the same final approach profile every time, one that will bring you across the fence at the slowest possible safe airspeed, with flaps fully extended, ready to land. The point at which the flaps are all the way down should be regarded as a commitment point, but not an irrevocable one; there's always the possibility of a go-around anytime short of touchdown.

Wing-flap retraction comes in for its share of abuse too. In every flight-training program, students trying to jump through the short-field-landing hoop sometimes lose sight of the objective, as they concentrate on snapping the flaps up the instant rubber meets runway. It's true that effective braking action is hugely dependent on getting weight off the wings and onto the wheels to increase the friction 'twixt tires and runway, so there's no choice when you're faced with a really short landing area. Flaps are the only controls on most light airplanes capable of dumping lift (our big brothers have sophisticated lift-spoiling systems for this purpose), but even when the weight transfer is completed, a maximum-effort stop requires that you apply brake pressure to a point just short of skidding the tires; you'll know you're there (or just a little beyond) when you hear the tires blow. This is a highly developed skill, not normally demanded of the ordinary pilot. And if it is absolutely essential that you get stopped within a confined space, who cares about the tires?—the airplane will stop in an amazingly short distance on the rims.

You may never be faced with landing on a runway short enough to require that kind of braking; but there's a no-strain way to make every ground roll a short one: it builds confidence in yourself and the airplane, and you'll do the people behind you a favor too, by clearing the runway as soon as possible. When a full-flap, low-airspeed approach puts you right on the runway numbers, keep the good work going by leaving the flaps down and hold the nose up in the air (c'mon, hold it *way* up there!) just as long as you can. When you feel the elevator giving up, gently lower the nose, but hold the stick or the wheel all the way back. Now you've got everything working for you; full flaps, full elevator, stick your hand out the window if you think it will help, and you may not even need to touch the brakes in order to turn off at the first taxiway. There's a lot of aerodynamic braking available on any airplane; it's free, and it's most effective during the very first portion of the landing roll when drag is high—as airspeed bleeds away, drag decreases much more rapidly. When you squeeze the last bit of drag from the flaps, be sure to retract them before you open the cabin door and let the people out—if you forget on a low-wing airplane, that first step will be a beaut.

On a wet runway, aerodynamic braking may be your best friend, because the slightest touch of wheel-brake pressure can induce hydroplaning. With most of the weight on the wings and a lot of water on the runway, even a feather-footed pilot might lock the wheels and turn the tires into a pair of giant water skis—and there you go, like a Cypress Gardens Aquamaid, right off the end of the runway. It won't make a bit of difference how careful you are, because hyproplaning depends on the amount of water on the surface, how fast you're moving and the air pressure in the tires—if you're gonna hydroplane, you're gonna hydroplane! So, on a short *slick* runway, get the flaps tucked back into the wings very soon after touchdown. The additional weight on the wheels will help push them through the film of water to get a firm grip on the runway surface, and bring your flight to a more rapid and less exciting conclusion.

Some members of the Hot Landing League finally get converted to full flaps, but they are unable to kick the high-speed habit, and continue to add a few knots for the wife and kids. Pilots with large families will sometimes wind up with approach speeds that would be suitable for an F-111 with the wings swept, and on the day they do this with a lightly loaded airplane, they're prone to discover what "wheelbarrowing" is all about. With the center of gravity a little farther forward than usual, and an abundance of airspeed, the extended flaps may provide just enough extra lift to raise the main wheels off the ground, or at least move them in that direction when the nose gear is lowered to the runway. It makes for difficult steering, to say the least, and the faster you go, the worse it gets—there's only one sure cure for this problem short of getting back into the air for another try, and that's to suck up the flaps and hope you can get stopped on whatever runway remains. But it's so much easier to eliminate the problem in the first place by approaching and touching down at a very low airspeed, lowered even more by virtue of the light weight. Remember that stall speeds in the manual are calculated for maximum gross weight—there may be a lot of knots between the "book" and the "what you actually weigh" stall speed.

On that increasingly rare occasion when you are politely asked to execute a missed approach, you may discover that your hands are full of throttles, props, gear handles, flap levers and microphones at the same time. The first thing you should drop is the mike, since there's no sense talking if you lose control of the airplane in the process; besides, the Controller will be watching, and the change in attitude that shows him you've started the go-around is the best communication he could hope for—seeing is believing. Power, and lots of it, is the most urgently needed ingredient, so it always comes first, and it's considered good technique to leave the wheels down until you're absolutely sure that airplane and runway are not going to meet. Be sure that you know whether to retract landing gear or flaps first—it's not the same for all airplanes, although most procedures call for partial retraction of wing flaps at the outset in order to get rid of all that full-flap drag.

The first lesson in flap-retraction school comes right out of the owner's manual, because some airplanes have interesting reactions to improper flap settings. While one type won't climb well at all with anything but a clean wing, others will fall out of the sky when the flaps are fully retracted on a go-around. The manufacturer's test pilots and design engineers have figured out the best way to do it, so believe, believe. Most light planes will struggle upwards valiantly if not spectacularly with full flaps; there's so much drag involved that it's marginal performance at best. Once you've decided to make the missed-approach move, apply power liberally and then put the flaps where the builder says they should be.

A short-field or soft-field takeoff will get you to the same corner of the performance envelope—low airspeed, high power setting and a commendable desire to get the heck out of there. The partially extended flaps are generating a great deal of lift and very little drag, just the aerodynamic opposite of full flaps. Now when you clean up the wings, they must assume the lifting chore suddenly, entirely, and without the help of the flaps: this can only be accomplished by increasing the angle at which the wings cleave the air. Should this higher angle of attack not be provided in the form of back pressure on the wheel, something will give, and of course the penalty comes out of your altitude account. If you're not as far from the ground as you should be at this point, you may not have to worry about the rest of the climbout. Practice missed approaches at a safe altitude, and discover what gyrations your airplane goes through when the flap setting is changed on a go-around; once you've been there, you're letting the plane fly you if you don't anticipate the trim and pitch changes, and make them behave.

The Great Flap Flap will never be settled, not as long as flying remains an art and pilots are free to land their airplanes pretty much as they want to; but everybody has to take a stand, so here goes: based on the assumption that there's nothing good about landing fast, and nothing bad about landing slow, full flaps should be the rule for every arrival. You'll wind up doing whatever's comfortable for you and your pocketbook (remember those rubber signatures at the end of the runway?), but if you're not a regular user of all the airbrakes on your airplane, the full-flappers would like you to give it an honest try. They'll bet you a new tire and a couple of brake pucks that your operating costs will go down!

Plan the Descent, Save Some Time ($$$)

What goes up must come down, which is not mind-blowing news, but *how* an airplane is ushered from cruise altitude to pattern altitude can made a difference in the air time betwixt *A* and *B*. A nap-of-the-earth trip doesn't warrant much downhill preparation—it's when you fly high that the planned descent takes on economic significance.

The least expensive vertical course is a straight line, beginning at some point while you're still enroute and terminating at pattern altitude a few miles from the airport. On occasion, things get in the way, like turbulence or mountains; but when you can descend in a straight line at a fixed rate, your only likely limits will be airspeed and earspeed—the former is how many knots the airplane can stand, the latter is how many feet per minute your ears can tolerate.

At the heart of the planned-descent philosophy is a resolve to spend most efficiently all the potential energy in the airplane—the higher you climb, the more energy in the bank. It can be withdrawn in a lump sum by staying at cruise altitude until you're directly over the destination airport, then shutting down the engine and proceeding to the ground on potential energy alone. Or you could be stingy about the whole thing by reducing power somewhat just far enough out so that the potential energy of altitude would replace the go-power of the fuel you wouldn't be using. The arrive-overhead-and-glide act is ridiculous, and it would take an IBM computer to know exactly how much to reduce power for the second method—besides, you wouldn't likely save time with either one.

The first step in planning a long-range descent (sometimes called an enroute descent) is to decide what earspeed you want to use. Some people can handle a 1500-fpm descent, most can tolerate 1000 fpm, but for the maximum comfort/time compromise, base your descent planning on 500 feet per minute; that rate can be adjusted a couple hundred feet either way with very little effect on the end result.

Next step, determine how many thousands of feet you'll descend between here and the traffic pattern—use field elevation (nearest thousand feet is close enough) and you'll build in a little pad which usually soaks up the deceleration to pattern airspeed. Suppose you figure the vertical distance is

8000 feet—divide that by 1000 fpm, for an eight-minute descent *if* you go down at 1000 fpm. Since 500 fpm is the planning rate, double the time; sixteen minutes to descend 8000 feet at 500 feet per minute.

Now you must get the airplane out of the barn and do some experimenting. Climb to your normal cruise altitude, set the power at the usual percentage and enter a 500-fpm descent; *leave the power handles alone!* Maintain this condition of flight until the airspeed stabilizes, and notice how much of it increases in the cruise-power descent. Add that number of knots to your groundspeed (boy, does a groundspeed-reading DME come in handy here!) and a simple time-distance calculation will tell you how many miles from destination you should begin the descent.

This is far from an exact procedure, because your groundspeed in the descent will undoubtedly change (winds, you know) and you may have to alter the rate of descent for ear problems or terrain, but it's a lot better than no planning at all.

The only condition that should cause any concern about airspeed is turbulence. Anything more than light bouncing is enough of a signal to slow down a bit—either until you're more comfortable or until the airspeed indicator moves out of the caution range. Most airplanes won't come anywhere close to redline in a 500-fpm descent at cruise power.

Don't neglect your passengers, especially those who have been spoiled by the smooth, slow pressurization systems of airliners. Before commencing the descent, tell them you're starting down, to keep their ears clear and to let you know if they have any trouble. Many folks consider an ear block some kind of unforgivable social sin, and won't say a word—until you're on the ground and it's too late. They spend the rest of the day cussing airplanes . . . and you.

One parting shot: don't let passengers, particularly children, sleep through a prolonged descent. It can be mighty hard on the ears—yours, not theirs, when they wake up on downwind, screaming with pain.

18

Density Altitude and
Aircraft Performance

Altitude comes in enough flavors to make Howard Johnson jealous: pressure, radio, AGL, standard, indicated, MSL, density, true, ASL, absolute, radar and the one you discover just before you whack into the ground, "not enough" altitude.

It would seem that there ought to be a way to eliminate some of these confusing and seemingly unnecessary terms, but in truth each of them has its place and purpose in the flying world. Looking at the list from the simpler side, there's one set of circumstances when they are all the same —flying above the sea in a standard atmosphere, all those types of altitude could be expressed in the same number of feet. (All right, so you wouldn't be Above Ground Level out there, but that's beside the point.)

Radio, radar, absolute and true altitude are most useful to overwater navigators and those executing Category II ILS approaches, and pressure altitude provides a place to start —it tells you how many feet you happen to be above wherever the atmosphere "weighs" 29.92 inches of mercury. Mean Sea Level and Above Sea Level altitudes describe, among other things, most of the regulatory heights you must observe.

When you adjust the instrument so that the current altimeter setting shows up in the little window, you're looking at *indicated* altitude, the one to use for quadrantal separation, traffic patterns and most of the other day-to-day, operational altitudes.

Which leaves density altitude (some performance charts use "standard altitude")—the only one of the group which doesn't define itself very readily. Technically described as pressure altitude corrected for non-standard temperature, it's an *un-altitude;* it doesn't measure feet above anything, but it does tell you something about how well your airplane will perform.

Density altitude is the most important of them all, yet it is the least understood, the only one that is not instrumented in our airplanes, and without a doubt it's the altitude most ignored by pilots. Unfortunately, the airplane can't ignore density altitude. No matter what the regime of flight (or sometimes *attempted* flight!), the poor dumb machine can perform only as well as density altitude will allow. Sometimes, there's no way—the aircraft accident annals overflow with misadventures that were predestined failures because of density altitude.

From a purely physical standpoint, the definition is sound; the density of an air sample can be identified with the density of air at some altitude on a standard day, which happens when the temperature, pressure and moisture content are exactly what the atmospheric scientists say they should be. When sea-level air is less dense than the agreed-upon standard but has the same density as standard-day air at, say, 3000 feet, a "high density altitude" situation prevails. If the air at Sea Shore International Airport is *more* dense than its standard-day counterpart, a "low density altitude" exists.

This is all well and good, but to understand what's likely to happen or not happen when you open the throttle for takeoff, you must invert your thinking and realize that *high* air density means *low* density altitude, and more favorable performance. On the other side of the situation, thin air and the attendant *low* density may create a density altitude so *high* you couldn't get airborne from a ten-mile runway.

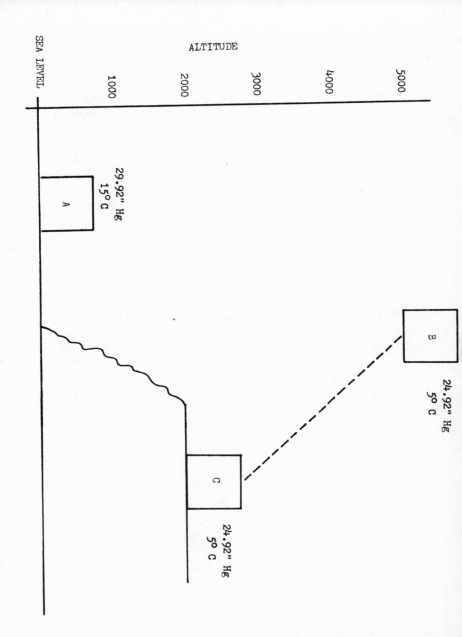

Figure 18–1. Density altitude—the effect of nonstandard temperature and pressure.

Figure 18–1 illustrates the problem. Consider a parcel of air at sea level on a standard day (A in the illustration); it will contain a certain number of molecules of air, and will therefore be of a certain density. The standard atmosphere loses both temperature and pressure with altitude (the lapse rates are one inch of pressure per 1000 feet, and two degrees of temperature), so the air at 5000 feet aloft on a standard day would be much less dense, as in B; and you would expect your airplane to perform with less vigor at that altitude. After all, with fewer molecules of air available there's no way the engine can produce its rated power, which means that the propeller cannot produce as much thrust (to say nothing of the fact that the propeller itself is working with fewer molecules, *further* reducing thrust), with the net result that acceleration to flying speed will require more time and, therefore, more distance.

Now, suppose that on a given day, the temperature/pressure combination at the 2000-foot-elevation airport you're about to use (C in the illustration) is exactly the same as that found on a standard day at 5000 feet MSL. That's a *density altitude* of 5000 feet, and your airplane—poor, dumb machine —will perform as if it were at 5000 feet on a standard day.

DENSITY ALTITUDE NEEDS MORE DEFINITION

Just a suspicion that density altitude is somewhat higher than field elevation isn't good enough, unless the runway is very long and the load is very light. Even then, you're gambling on a guess because density altitude wanders all over the scale as the pressure-temperature combinations vary. (Moisture in the air contributes its frequently-more-than-two-cents'-worth, but try to find an aircraft performance chart with a humidity correction—non-existent, since it's adequately packaged with the other two for light-aircraft purposes.) Your guess may even get you off the ground, the lack of acceleration notwithstanding, only to come a cropper when you try to climb. Most light aircraft are not skyrockets even on a standard day; an adverse density altitude of moderate proportions can make the post-liftoff segment of a flight very, very interesting.

Guessing can cost you airplane utility too. In a situation where it would be advantageous to carry more weight, you should be reluctant unless you *know* what the density altitude is—if it turns out to be a high-performance day, you can add people, fuel or things right up to the maximum gross weight or that weight limited by the length of the runway, whichever comes first. That's using your aviation smarts to get the most out of an expensive flying machine.

Once you've generalized density altitude and determined whether it will help or hurt, find out how much. You might use a standard chart (Figure 18–2) which compares pressure altitude with temperature and reads density altitude to the left of where these two values are plotted. In case you haven't an altimeter handy, there's a correction table in the upper-right-hand corner to provide pressure altitude from an altimeter setting.

Almost all navigational computers can be set up for a density-altitude readout. Look carefully on the slide-rule side for a set of scales that pit pressure altitude against temperature, and a pointer somewhere close by to show you performance altitude. The electronic navigational calculators now available to the pilot community make this determination a piece of cake; enter pressure altitude and temperature, push the COMPUTE button, and there's your answer.

Now, you have a number that by itself, serves no useful purpose—what you really need to know is the *effect* of that density altitude. Don't sweat out a low density-altitude figure, but when it come up *high* (i.e., a density altitude considerably higher than field elevation), start rummaging through the glove box or your flight bag for the airplane's performance charts.

There are as many ways to present takeoff performance and rate of climb as there are chart architects, and of course each one feels that he has built a better mousetrap. Would you like to get next to a rather simple solution to the problem, one that requires a single excursion through the charts

DENSITY ALTITUDE COMPUTATION CHART

SET ALTIMETER TO 29.92 IN. HG.
WHEN READING PRESSURE ALTITUDE

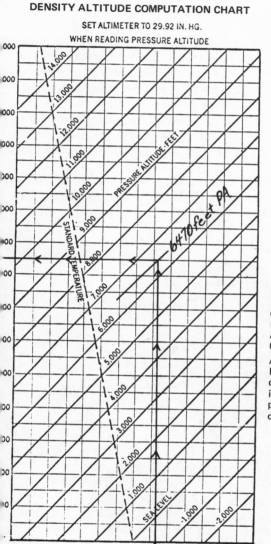

ALTIMETER SETTING IN. HG.	ALTITUDE ADDITION FOR OBTAINING PRESSURE ALTITUDE
28.0	1,825
28.1	1,725
28.2	1,630
28.3	1,535
28.4	1,435
28.5	1,340
28.6	1,245
28.7	1,150
28.8	1,050
28.9	955
29.0	865
29.1	770
29.2	675
29.3	580
29.4	485
29.5	390
29.6	300
29.7	205
29.8	110
29.9	20
29.92	0
30.0	- 75
30.1	-165
30.2	-255
30.3	-350
30.4	-440
30.5	-530
30.6	-620
30.7	-710
30.8	-805
30.9	-895
31.0	-965

EXAMPLE:
Find the density altitude for the following conditions:
Indicated altitude 7000 feet
Altimeter setting 30.50 in.
OAT +70° F

ANSWER:
From table above for altimeter setting of 30.50 subtract 530 feet from indicated altitude to obtain 6470 feet pressure altitude — from chart read density altitude is 8,500 feet.

OUTSIDE AIR TEMPERATURE

Figure 18–2.   Density altitude computation chart.

and provides operational information about as fast as you can say "Denalt Computer"? It hasn't been a runaway best seller, if the number of them you see in pilots' shirt pockets is any indication, but the gadget works, and works well. Produced by the FAA, it may be the most practical thing that august body ever developed for general aviation.

The Denalt (for DENsity ALTitude) takes inputs of temperature and pressure altitude and expresses them in terms of *effect* on takeoff distance and rate of climb; just what you've been looking for.

Figure 18–3 is a Denalt set up with a temperature of 100° F, and it shows that the takeoff distance for an airport at 6000 feet is almost three times the sea-level figure, while

Figure 18–3.   Denalt computer set up with a temperature of 100° F.

the expected rate of climb under the same conditions is only about 25 percent what it would be at sea level. There's the beauty of the Denalt—once you know what your airplane will do under standard-day conditions, one setting and a quick mental calculation provide the *now* numbers. Not terribly accurate, but if you base your figuring on maximum gross weight, you can hardly go wrong when the airplane weighs less. If nothing else, it's a mind energizer; when performance looks to be a little on the scratchy side, you can (and definitely should) go to the detailed airplane charts and figure things right down to the nub. The Denalt is worth its cost if all it does is make you *think* about a marginal situation.

There may be warehouses full of Denalts in Washington, so don't hesitate to order one from the Superintendent of Documents, who lives somewhere in that ancient brick edifice known as the Government Printing Office, Washington, D.C. 20402. Be sure to let him know which you need—there are computers for fixed-pitch and controllable-pitch propelered airplanes. Or be a big spender and get them both.

Looking for a better way to express predicted performance isn't new. The USAF's Strategic Air Command, prone to order its heavy bombers and tankers into the air at nonreducible weights, developed a unique system years ago. "Build longer runways if you have to, but get *all* the bombs and *all* the fuel into the air," said the General. When all the factors that bore on aircraft performance were run through the charts, the number that came out the other end was "equivalent weight." On a standard day, there would be no difference between the airplane's actual weight and the equivalent weight—but when things moved toward a high density altitude, equivalent weight moved upward, with the corresponding longer takeoff roll that a "heavier" airplane would require under standard conditions. Now you know why SAC bases have such super-long runways.

WHERE DOES DENSITY ALTITUDE REALLY COUNT?

In the two instances just discussed, takeoff distance and rate of climb, plus the effect that shows up on landing. Since there are so many different techniques involved in landing an airplane, you'd need a library of Denalt computers for landing distance—takeoff and climb are assumed to be accomplished by the numbers, but you can land fast or slow, flaps or not, and in a host of combinations, not to mention the pilot's ability to brake effectively.

The villain in the landing approach and rollout is *true airspeed;* as pressure altitude and temperature creep up their respective scales, the *real* knots get bigger than the indicated ones. Flying down the chute at your normal approach speed in a low-performance-altitude environment, you are actually moving through the air somewhat faster than you think. The energy of motion will not be denied, and when you touch down, it will manifest itself in more, perhaps *many* more feet of runway under the wings before everything comes to a halt.

Now, let's get very practical about density altitude. Pilots don't get into trouble with it when they operate their light airplanes from paved airports at field elevations of sea level up to a thousand feet or so. It's the short grass strips and the high-altitude airports that generate problems—problems which could be avoided or solved by (a) not being there in the first place or (b) consulting *some* kind of performance indicator to find out if the airplane can rise to the occasion. Even though the rule writers insist that the pilot be aware of all factors bearing on the takeoff distance, climb capability and landing distance before *every* aerial journey, a complete calculation seems, quite frankly, a waste of your valuable time. Let's face it—*most* of the time, you *know* that you can get up and down again with runway to spare.

However, when you aviate to another part of the country that happens to lie many feet above sea level, and/or the temperature is out of sight, you're only fooling yourself if you don't take a look at the numbers. You won't fool the airplane for even a minute—it doesn't know the difference between cement and sagebrush, and will go plowing nonchalantly off the end of the runway if performance altitude dictates that this shall be a non-flying day. The same is true for the short strip when you're loaded to the gills—make two trips, or leave the hunting trophies to the bears, but check the charts and be sure. Here's where the Denalt computer comes through in spades.

Airline operators pay the piper, too, because minimum fuel loads are as firmly regulated as performance requirements. A captain with just enough gas for the trip but with an airplane still too heavy to fit within the rules must take off customers or cargo; ouch—that's *payload!* Density altitude again, but expressed in terms very familiar to the guy in the left seat.

COPING WITH THE PROBLEM

Most pilots who fly regularly in mountainous areas have become accustomed to the differences in sights, sounds, and feels associated with high density-altitude operations. Unfortunately, summertime, when high-altitude airfields are snow-free, accessible, and basking in the warmth of the season, is also the time when the "flatlander" pilots show up in the greatest numbers. And to someone who is trying his hand at high density-altitude flying for the first time, there are some surprising differences in the way the airplane handles.

It may begin with roughness and "galloping" right after engine start, which is not unreasonable, especially if you are asking the engine to run as usual on the super-rich mixture of this high-altitude environment. Remember that when the mixture control is in the FULL RICH position, there's considerably more fuel being delivered than the engine needs, *even at sea level,* let alone way up here. Experience and a few trials may show you that smoother starts are obtained with the mixture control backed off somewhat, and for sure, you'll need to lean the mixture for smooth running at idle power settings.

At takeoff, the power penalty of high density altitude shows up. Since the carburetor (or injector system) is designed to provide a super-rich mixture when both throttle and mixture control are full forward, you can bet that the engine will produce something less than full power. There's not a safe rule of thumb to use in this regard (theoretically, you should lean somewhat whenever you want full power at *any* density altitude above sea level). But the effect will begin to manifest itself at 3000 feet or so, and you will really notice the difference when density altitude approaches and exceeds 5000 feet. So, prior to starting the takeoff roll, adjust the mixture strength for full *available* power by opening the throttle and leaning until maximum RPM is achieved . . . the higher the density altitude, the more you'll have to lean. And, of course, the more you lean the more power you lose, but that's the price of this environment. In any event, this procedure will optimize power production. (Once you know what you're about, leaning for maximum power can be done on the takeoff roll, but only when you *know* there's plenty of runway ahead.)

Few general-aviation propeller-driven airplanes have enough acceleration to slam you back in your seat under the best of conditions, and you should expect even more sluggish takeoff performance as density altitude increases. This is perhaps the first major clue that this takeoff is going to be different. The slow progress of the airspeed needle and the amount of runway used often lull high-altitude beginners into doing one of two things—either of which is bad. Some pilots will horse the airplane off the ground with their usual "run-to-the-takeoff-airspeed-and-pull" technique; others will see the far end of the runway coming up and rotate the nose well in advance of an airspeed that will guarantee flight. Either way, the sorely underpowered machine will usually sink back to the surface (using up precious distance), or stagger along just above the runway, held up by ground effect: the phony bonus of lift that exists because of the compression of air under the wings at altitudes of one half wingspan or so.

The temptation to "pull it off" is very great, and if surrendered to, becomes an even more vicious circumstance because while you *think* you can make the airplane fly (after all, I got it into the air, didn't I?), you may have put yourself between a rock (can fly only in ground effect, not enough power to climb out of it) and a hard place (too late to even think of getting stopped on the runway). Unless the terrain slopes downward off the end of the runway, you've got problems. And how you'll wish that you had decided to abort the takeoff prior to the premature liftoff, while there was still plenty of solid surface on which to get stopped, and not this much airspeed to tear things up when contact is made.

The secrets to success for high-density-altitude takeoffs are first to check the performance charts and be *certain* that there's enough runway to get the job done today; some who have been there recommend that whatever the charts show should be *doubled* to accommodate the unknown factors of engine condition, pilot skill, and so on. Not a bad idea. Second, remember that you are flying a crippled airplane; at least, in terms of the power production you have grown to expect at lower density altitudes, and things are *not* going to be the same. You must allow the airplane to accelerate to the published takeoff airspeed before *any* pitch change, and then you must treat the elevator control with kid gloves; it will be easy (and tempting) to overcontrol in pitch, but with reduced power, every degree of unnecessary pitch attitude adds nothing but drag and will definitely prolong the takeoff roll.

After liftoff, maintain V_x until you are solidly airborne, then hold the airplane in level flight until it accelerates to V_y, which may take considerably longer than you're comfortable with, but *don't try to force the airplane to climb.* Accurate, positive pitch control is the name of the game.

Your high-altitude troubles still aren't over, because even at V_y you'll get a closer look at the terrain surrounding the airport than most of the crop dusters in the area. Some light airplanes taking off in significantly high-density-altitude environments may generate climb rates of only 200–300 feet per minute. At 300 fpm and an airspeed of 90 knots, that's only 200 feet per mile. Pick a landmark exactly one mile from the end of the runway at your airport (be sure it's a *ground-level* landmark), get the tower's permission if applicable, and fly there gaining only 200 feet after liftoff. Unless you get a particular thrill from flying low, you won't want to do that again, but it's the very situation in which

you may well find yourself next summer at some high-
altitude airfield.

The climb to altitude will take considerably longer because you're starting from behind the performance eight ball.
The matter of engine cooling must also be considered, especially with higher-powered airplanes, and an already miser-
able rate of climb may have to be reduced in order to keep
temperatures from going overboard. There are plenty of
costs associated with flying at high density altitudes.

Cruise performance won't suffer much because of density
altitude when you're flying a reciprocating-engine, propeller-
driven airplane (move up to a turbine powerplant, however,
and altitude becomes all-important in terms of specific fuel
consumption, or miles per pound of kerosene). But at the end
of a flight, one of the same problems that gave you fits
during that high-density-altitude takeoff will come back
to haunt you again, whether you're flying a Luscombe or a
LearJet. It's true airspeed, and in a nutshell, here's the
problem: Because of the manner in which the airspeed indicator works (namely, measuring the difference between
static air pressure and ram air pressure, both of which are
reduced with altitude—actual or density), true airspeed will
always be greater than indicated airspeed except at sea level
on a standard day.

But you must fly the approach at the same *indicated* airspeed you'd use down in the flatlands (that's the kind of
airspeed on which the stalling speed is based). So no matter
how you slice it, an approach and touchdown in a high-
density-altitude environment is going to happen at a faster
speed than the same operation performed at some lower
altitude. Higher speed when the rollers meet the runway
means only one thing . . . longer landing distances, and it sometimes stretches to more feet than there is runway. A disap-
pointing number of perfectly good airplanes are rolled up into
balls of aluminum each summer at the far ends of mountain
airports. And a lot of this unhappiness has got to be traceable
to the add-a-few-knots-for-the-wife-and-kids syndrome by
pilots who don't really understand what it's all about.

Fly high-altitude approaches at the same, safe, sane airspeeds you normally use, but before you get to that point, consult the performance charts and be certain that there's enough runway to contain your landing roll. And once again, it's not a bad idea to *double* what the book shows, just to take care of worn brakes, worn tires, and not-often-practiced pilot skills.

In closing, there's not much (if anything) you can do about the conditions that produce the high-density-altitude environment. You can't lower the temperature (although waiting until evening or morning when it's cooler will help), or move the airport to a lower altitude, or crank up the wind to help in your takeoff or landing; but there is one thing over which you have *complete* control, and it is also fortunately one of the most effective factors in the entire situation—aircraft weight. You can *always* leave something or someone behind, and come back to pick them up if need be. *Un*fortunately, the temptation to give it a go with a full load is very strong—how are you gonna tell your buddies that they'll have to wait? Doesn't this airplane have enough seats for all of us? The far end of the runway, when you've given it all you've got and the bloody machine still isn't off the ground, is a very bad place to find out that you're too heavy to fly.

Density altitude. Insidious, ever-present, and hazardous to your health. But it's beatable by knowledge, skill, and understanding. And an occasional journey through the pages of your airplane's performance charts.

IT'S EVERYWHERE

Don't think that the effect of density altitude is limited to those levels of the atmosphere close to the ground: there are a couple Alaskan sheep hunters who found out the hard way that airplane performance is inevitably tied to air density. They took off in a vintage Aeronca from Big Delta one lovely summer morning, and soon spotted a pair of magnificent Dall sheep cavorting about the top of a mountain nearby. The climb rate of an Aeronca being what it is, the hunters used up quite a bit of time climbing high enough to see what they were after, and during that time the temperature had also climbed considerably, as it is wont to do in that part of Alaska in the summertime. The poor old Airknocker carried them faithfully, if slowly, until they were circling near the sheep, looking for a place to land.

The top of that particular mountain is shaped like a bowl, and littered with refrigerator-sized rocks; the pilot wisely decided to vacate the premises and leave the sheep for someone else. But when he opened the throttle, very little came out—the Champ had drifted below the rim of the mountaintop depression, and the altitude-temperature combination had built a density altitude that made it impossible for them to climb out of the bowl.

Talk about being between a rock and a hard place! With no choice but to crash-land, they did; without injury but also without landing gear.

Moral: make sure you can perform before setting out to chase a couple of Dalls.

19

Engine Operation

THE TURBOJET is a marvelous piece of machinery with which to propel an airplane through the skies. It provides plenty of reserve power, high speeds, is reasonably efficient at altitude, costs a lot to purchase but makes up for it in long TBOs and low maintenance, and is extremely easy to operate, that is, there's not much for the pilot to do except push a button to start the engine, then set the thrust lever to the appropriate power setting. All of the adjustments are made by the engine fuel-control system.

But the reciprocating, piston-type powerplant, that's a collection of horses of a much different color. Not only is the pilot required to make nearly all the inflight adjustments himself, he must make them properly if the engine is to perform as advertised—to say nothing of the expense and potential danger that can be caused by improper operation. Unfortunately, the harmful stresses placed on an aircraft engine by not observing the proper techniques and operating limitations may not be manifested until sometime later—when a pilot really needs full power, and the strain is more than the weakest link can bear. Potential disaster, rooted in someone's ham-handedness perhaps many flights ago. In the

interest of your own well-being, as well as that of fellow
pilots who will be flying the same airplane, there's a lot to
be said for understanding what goes on under the hood, and
observing good techniques when managing the horsepower
at your command.

Virtually all of today's general-aviation piston engines are
of the horizontal-opposed variety (there aren't many "round
engines"—the big radials—still flying, and you're not likely
to find yourself behind one unless you get into aerial application or antique-airplane collecting), and they have grown
in both size and complexity over the years as the manufacturers pack more power into engines that have not increased much in physical size; that means more stress, and
the potential for more damage from improper techniques.
The four-cylinder engines in most training aircraft will
accept an incredible amount of abuse and come back for
more, but you can't continue to get away with that kind of
powerplant technique when you move up to the bigger
engines; there are more limitations, more systems, more
operational considerations to be understood.

The almost identical appearance of today's nonturbine
aircraft engines belies some fundamental and very important
differences in how they operate. Some of them are geared
(to accommodate higher engine RPM without turning the
propeller at unacceptably high speed), there are unique
types of electrical systems, and so forth. But these are generally systems over which the pilot has little or no control,
and which don't require specific techniques or knowledge
to operate properly.

Major differences do occur, however, in the "breathing
systems" of modern airplanes, and without knowledge of the
engine type, the pilot will inevitably encounter difficulties
in starting and operating the collection of moving parts that
pulls him through the air. Thinking very generally, reciprocating engines in contemporary aircraft are either normally
aspirated or supercharged, carburetioned, or fuel injected.
"Normally aspirated" means that the engine is totally dependent on ambient air pressure to push the fuel-air charge
into the cylinders when the intake valve opens during the

engine's operating cycle. As altitude increases (this includes a change in density altitude as well as climbing through the atmosphere) and pressure decreases, there will be a corresponding decrease in power production because less fuel-air mixture will be ingested with each "breath." For this reason, a normally aspirated aircraft engine can produce its "rated" power when atmospheric conditions (temperature, pressure, humidity) are the same as those of a standard day at sea level—a relatively inexpensive system, but it has its drawbacks.

The obvious next step is to mount an air pump on the engine so that no matter how high it's flown (within reasonable limits), the fuel-air mixture will be delivered to the intake valve at the same pressure available at sea level; if you consider the fuel-air mixture to be the "charge" for the engine, then such a pumped-up system would represent a "super" (higher) charge, and hence the term "supercharging." On the older, bigger, rounder engines, the air pump was driven by a complicated collection of heavy internal gears; today, all supercharged aircraft engines use the otherwise-wasted energy in the exhaust gases to spin a turbine wheel which is shafted to a centrifugal air pump . . . *turbosupercharging*, or simply "turbocharging," as it's known in the business. These engines don't necessarily make *more* power available (there are still structural considerations that limit the amount of internal pressures an engine can withstand without coming unglued), but they enable you to take sea-level power with you to higher altitudes; and that means higher rates of climb, higher true airspeed at cruise, more muscle to overcome the effects of icing, higher single-engine ceiling for light twins, and, of course, more investment at purchase time and higher maintenance and operating expenses.

Liquid gasoline won't burn (please don't try to prove it!), and the method by which fuel is mixed with incoming air and atomized so that it *will* combust determines the other "major differences" area in aircraft engines; some are carburetored, and some are fitted with fuel-injection systems. In the first situation, air is drawn through a venturi (a smooth, carefully shaped constriction in the intake line), which lowers the pressure and allows liquid fuel to be sucked from the supply line through a small nozzle in the airstream. In doing so, the liquid is broken up into a fine mist that, when mixed with the proper amount of air, will burn and release the heat energy, and which the engine converts into power. Very simple, relatively inexpensive, and making a comeback on a lot of small-aircraft engines as manufacturers seek ways to hold down costs.

The carburetor is not terribly efficient, particularly when you consider that the mixture must be rich enough at the outset to provide a burnable combination of fuel and air at the far end of the intake system; as a result, there are losses due to condensation in the pipes, bends in the tubing, and so forth. The next step upwards in solving this problem was the fuel injector, a sophisticated fuel pump that, geared to engine speed and responsive to throttle setting, provides the precise amount of fuel at the precise instant at the precise spot just outside the intake valve, where carburetion (mixing of fuel and air) takes place very efficiently . . . and rather expensively, because of the precision required in the injection system. You pays yer money, and you takes yer choice.

START WITH THE STARTING

No matter what kind of engine is on your airplane, there are some inescapable facts which apply to the starting procedure. Three elements must be present—fuel, air, ignition— and in the right proportion if there's any hope of getting the fire lighted. And, of course, there must be electrical energy available to power the starter motor, or *nothing's* going to happen! (The venerable Armstrong starter is always available, but hand-propping an airplane engine is very dangerous at best, and almost guaranteed to cause real trouble for the propper who tries to teach himself how to do it.)

The nicest thing you can do for the starter motor and battery is to read the book that prescribes the engine-starting procedure; there's a best way to do it, one that has been researched and tested by the manufacturer. If the engine doesn't fire after several turns, there's something wrong with your interpretation of the procedure, or something wrong within the engine itself.

Fuel-injected engines (those in which the proper amount of liquid gasoline is delivered directly to the individual cylinders by a metering pump instead of being mixed with incoming air in a carburetor) have put the kibosh on the old faithful you-can't-overprime-it starting technique—there's only one way to get such a powerplant running, and if you don't do it the way the book says, you'll probably run out of battery and patience at the same time. Nor will injected-engine procedures work for a "normal" engine, so don't try to mix methods.

The worst situation with any aircraft engine, but particularly with the fuel-injected types, is a "hot" start, when you have shut down only long enough to board passengers or to refuel. Unless engine heat has had a chance to dissipate (it may take a couple of hours or more—depends on outside air temperature), whatever fuel-air charge reaches the cylinders when you turn the engine will be quite warm and ready to burn. Most of the problems pilots experience when trying to start a hot engine stem from their over-priming . . . if a little prime is good, a lot should be better, right? Wrong. And the engine will gasp and sputter, shake and choke, trying to throw off the super-rich mixture of fuel and air that's been forced down its throat.

Consult the *Pilot's Operating Handbook* for the hot-start procedure that applies to your airplane, but when in doubt here's a method that almost always works. Set engine speed to 1000 RPM and shut it down with the mixture control as usual, leaving the throttle where it is. When it's time to crank up again, turn on the mag switches, but don't touch any other engine controls—no fuel boost pump, mixture OFF, throttle where you left it, set for 1000 RPM. When you activate the starter, chances are very good that the engine will start right away, at which time you must, of course, advance the mixture control to keep a good thing going. (Notice that this method *almost* always works; it will fail you under a certain set of conditions, such as when you're late for a business appointment and you crank and crank and crank, and the FBO doesn't have an auxiliary-power unit—*that's* when a fuel-injected engine will defy Messrs. Continental and Lycoming themselves!)

The fuel-air mixture for a hot start is a very touchy thing, and when the engine resists all attempts to make it behave, most handbooks recommend a procedure that takes you back to a known set of conditions—namely, a deliberate flooding —from which point you can proceed. After a few strokes of the primer or a few seconds of boost-pump priming, the engine is literally overloaded with fuel, and you must open the throttle (all the way) and put the mixture control in OFF so that when all that raw fuel ignites, there will be enough air to support combustion. And here's where the fancy hand-work begins; you'll feel (and see) the engine make its first attempts to run, and when it's apparent that a fire is lighted, come back smartly with the throttle (to keep from overturn-ing the airplane parked behind you) and *then* move the mix-ture control to RICH. Wait too long to move the mixture control and the engine will die for lack of gasoline; place the mixture in RICH too soon and you'll kill the engine with liquid fuel. There's a delicate balance required, a bit of tightrope walking on your part, which can only be learned by experience. Unsuccessful hot starts of fuel-injected en-gines have no doubt ruined more aircraft batteries and starter motors (and pilots' egos!) than anything else.

It's tempting at this point to say "Once a reciprocating engine is running smoothly, there's nothing else to do but taxi to the active runway, accomplish the power checks, and take off; there are no adjustments to be made while taxiing." But such is definitely not the case, because this type of aircraft engine doesn't idle at its best with the mixture set at RICH. Even though the carburetion or injection system doesn't pour a lot of extra fuel into the engine for internal cooling until the throttle is opened all the way, the mixture will be super-rich anytime the mixture control is placed to RICH. That's fuel which is not needed for cooling (an econ-omy consideration), it means more antiknock additive—

lead—to foul the spark plugs (a maintenance consideration), and nearly all light-aircraft engines will idle with varying degrees of roughness because the mixture is just too rich for smooth operation.

It's not the same kind of roughness you experience when leaning, because the engine is not protesting a lack of fuel; it rather "gallops" or "lopes," because there's too much gasoline present. You can smooth things out, save fuel, and save spark plugs by adjusting the mixture on the ground. With throttle set to 1000 RPM (a good idle speed for nearly any engine), ease the mixture control toward LEAN and watch the tachometer; it will increase slightly as the mixture strength gets more digestible, and will, of course, drop rapidly when you have leaned the mixture past the point where combustion can be supported. Once you find the mixture setting that lets the engine run smoothly, readjust the throttle to the normal engine-idle speed, leave it there throughout the taxi operation, and enjoy all the benefits. Your engine, your passengers, and your pocketbook will love you for it. (If the RPM changes a great deal—more than a couple hundred RPM—as you lean the mixture at idle, or if it doesn't change at all, there's likely something wrong with the carburetion system. And don't forget to advance the mixture to RICH before attempting a magneto check or a takeoff.)

And one final thing to be considered with regard to starting an aircraft engine: Have you ever stood on a ramp, maybe just looking at the airplanes, or perhaps preflighting your own machine, when the guy in front of you cranked up with a roar that not only would wake the dead, but that also blew dust and dirt and other assorted bits of ramp debris all over you? It's not good airport manners, and it doesn't do the engine any favors either—until the oil is heated and able to move through the tiny passages that facilitate lubrication, the engine is not ready for high-speed operation. If your engine is going to start at all, it will start with the throttle set for a normal, 1000-RPM idle (the hot start described earlier is an obvious exception, but even here you can "catch" the start-up so that engine speed doesn't exceed normal limits). Find out what throttle setting produces a normal idle speed for your engine, and use it for all starts; don't blow away the folks behind you. It's good manners, and it exhibits a professional approach to engine operation.

WHICH HANDLE TO MOVE FIRST?

Next on the list of techniques and procedures that apply to the larger reciprocating engines is the matter of power changes. Granted, there's not much you can do when increasing or decreasing power with a fixed-pitch-propeller installation except change the throttle setting (be smooth, press the throttle in or out, always make power changes as slowly as practical), but a constant-speed-propeller system requires some special considerations.

When you select a specific engine speed with the prop control, you are setting a centrifugal governor that directs changes in propeller-blade angle, thereby maintaining a constant engine speed. Suppose you set the prop lever to obtain 2300 RPM; if the throttle setting is reduced somewhat, the prop would tend to slow down, the governor would sense the change, and the system would automatically decrease the pitch of the blades just enough to bring the governor back to its preset position. Engine RPM won't change noticeably. The opposite takes place when power is increased by opening the throttle; the engine starts to overspeed, the governor notices the change and resets the prop blades to a higher angle (more drag, less speed), so that they hold engine RPM right where you want it. Similar small, unnoticeable changes are taking place almost constantly as you fly, these changes due to loading and unloading of the propeller as aircraft attitude changes.

Now keep in mind that when throttle setting is increased on a *fixed*-pitch installation, the additional air pressure inside the engine (and therefore additional power) is "spread out" over more power pulses because of increased propeller/ engine RPM, which translates to more thrust. But as manifold pressure is increased on a *constant-speed* system (controllable-pitch prop), the added thrust comes from an increase in blade angle, and the additional air pressure must be absorbed by the engine itself, since engine speed will not change. There are structural limits, of course; the engine can only take so much pressure, and when this figure is exceeded, stresses are introduced that shorten the life of the engine; or—if the forces are of sufficient magnitude—may literally blow the engine apart. The term describing this condition of too much pressure is "overboosting," and it is probably more common than you realize. Even though an occasional over-boost may appear to do no immediate harm, the engine structure is inevitably weakened, and on that day when you really need all the horses, it may be more than the engine can tolerate. Limiting combinations of RPM and manifold pressure have been established by the manufacturer, and when power changes are made, it's important that these limits not be violated, for the reasons just mentioned.

There's a rule applicable to power changes, a rule that must become second nature to the pilot flying a constant-speed installation, and it goes like this: When *increasing* power, always increase RPM first, then throttle; when *decreasing* power, always decrease throttle first, then RPM. This is assuming, of course, that when you decide to make a power change the throttle and prop controls are already set to the limiting combination, and any change in the rule would result in an over-boost. For example, when increasing power, if you should open the throttle before changing engine speed, you are asking the engine to absorb more internal pressure without increasing speed—each power stroke must produce more horsepower and the only way that's possible is by increasing pressure. When reducing power, movement of the prop control toward DECREASE RPM without first reducing the throttle setting would also increase the pressure inside the engine. You can prove this point on the ground during the pretakeoff runup by watching the manifold pressure increase as you bring the prop lever back to check its operation. The pressure reduces once again as prop and engine speed up.

Most airplane manufacturers provide a number of suggested manifold-pressure/RPM combinations for takeoff, climb, and cruise; combinations that will keep internal

engine pressure within limits—and you can trust these
charts. The Beech Aircraft Corporation included a much
more comprehensive power-limit chart in the *Pilot's Operating Handbook* for the Duchess, their light-light twin; it

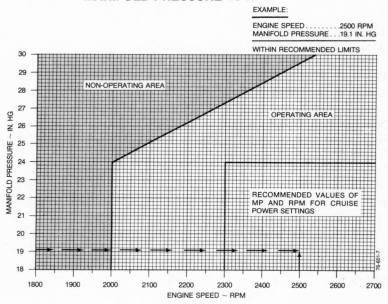

Figure 19–1. Power-setting chart for the Beechcraft Duchess.

shows a vast number of safe combinations of manifold pressure and RPM and gives its pilots great flexibility in selecting power settings. (So who needs flexibility? Well, consider
that flying at the lowest possible RPM and the highest possible manifold pressure will result in fewer turns of the
engine, and, therefore, less wear and tear on all the moving
parts. Also consider that internal friction decreases rather
remarkably with engine speed, and more of the power developed by the engine will find its way to the propeller.
Voila! Something for nothing. You'll also notice that things

get considerably quieter when you pull the props back to the lowest permissible speed . . . ah, that's better, now that you've gotten rid of the buzz-saw vibration of high RPM settings.) The example on the Duchess power chart—19.1 inches of manifold pressure and 2500 RPM—would be noisy and inefficient, but a legal and proper power setting, one which would not exceed internal pressure limits. While Beech chose not to provide percentage-of-power curves on this chart, how much more comfortable you (and your passengers) would be with the go-handles set to something like 2100 RPM and 22 inches, or whatever manifold pressure produces the airspeed you want.

Heresy, you say? In direct contradiction to the old rule about "oversquare," which said that you should *never* set up more inches of manifold pressure than hundreds of RPM (e.g., 22 inches–2200 RPM, 24 inches–2400 RPM, etc.)? That was okay for some of the early radial engines, but it doesn't wash today. *Any* manifold-pressure/RPM combination stated in the airplane charts is permissible.

Most power-change abuse takes place with turbocharged engines; when you open the throttle on a "blown" powerplant, a *lot* of overpressure enters the engine—perhaps 40–50 inches in some cases—and if the engine speed isn't high enough to accommodate this rapid and significant change, damage from overboosting will surely occur. The same thing can happen on a nonturbo engine, with the most likely scenario a go-around, or the procedure following an engine failure on a light twin. In the first case, the pilot who forgets (or who has never been taught) to set the props to FULL INCREASE somewhere on final approach, then slams the throttle to the firewall when he decides to abort the landing, will put a lot of undue stress on the engine structure—to say nothing of the fact that, at a lower-than-maximum RPM, he's operating with considerably less than full power. And in the second situation—when a multi-engine pilot suffers the loss of one powerplant—the everything-forward-right-now adherent will probably overboost the good engine by opening its throttle before increasing engine speed; it takes some conscious effort to do it right, and there aren't that many times when takeoff power is really required to survive on one engine anyway.

POWER MANAGEMENT AT ALTITUDE

When your high-powered turbocharged engine has lofted you to the heights, another factor comes into play, one that was of little concern at the lower altitudes—outside air temperature. Thermometer readings tend to stabilize somewhat in the upper air, but even in the teens, where most turbocharged reciprocating engines do their best work, you should expect air temperature to be affected considerably by seasonal conditions; that is, you'll encounter the problems of overheating in the summer, and underheating in the winter. Cold air doesn't present much in the way of power-management woes; you can close up the cowl flaps, lean the mixture to a fare-thee-well, and enjoy the benefits of operating in a denser-air environment. If anything, you'll need to be very careful not to overboost, even at cruise-power settings.

When the air aloft is much warmer than normal, however, engine-cooling problems begin to show up. Reciprocating powerplants are roughly 30 to 40 percent efficient from a thermal standpoint, which means that a great deal of the heat energy stored in gasoline finds its way to the propeller, but the remainder must be disposed of in the air through which the airplane is moving. When that air is already at a relatively high temperature, much less cooling takes place; and if something isn't done to take up the slack, engine overheating is the inevitable result.

With the turbos providing whatever power you call for, certain adjustments must be made. If you have leaned the fuel-air mixture to the recommended setting, much of the internal engine cooling is handled by excess air; when that cooling air is hot going in, engine temperatures will certainly go up, and one solution is to richen the mixture until there's enough extra fuel to take care of the cooling process. Of course, range and endurance will suffer. Another way to help solve the heat-dissipation problem in hot weather is to open the cowl flaps (most turbocharged installations are so equipped; if your airplane is not "flapped," you've no choice but to fly with a richer mixture and pay the piper at the gas pump), which will exact the price of cooling in terms of reduced speed. There ain't no such thing as a free lunch!

Cruise-power charts for even the largest light-airplane powerplants are simplified, but keep in mind that when you establish a power setting according to the numbers (manifold pressure and RPM) for a particular altitude, the chart figures are based on *standard temperatures,* and reflect the maximum allowable internal pressure based on the density of the air in that altitude/temperature condition. For example, a power setting of 33 inches and 2300 RPM on a certain popular engine produces 73 percent power at 16,000 feet when the temperature is minus 17 degrees Celsius, standard for that level in the atmosphere; but on a day when the temperature at 16,000 feet is 20 degrees *colder* than standard (minus 37 degrees Celsius), the same 33 inches/2300 RPM produces *78 percent* power. The engine is running at the same speed as on the warmer day, so the pilot who opens the throttle to the same manifold pressure reading he used all summer is asking the engine to absorb the increased power internally, and overheating will probably occur if fuel flow is adjusted to the familiar summertime rate. (Of course, airspeed will also increase, and when proper leaning is accomplished, so will fuel flow, but if the objective is to fly at a 73-percent-power setting, an adjustment must be made for air temperature.) Some manufacturers arrange their cruise-performance charts to indicate "the numbers" (percent of rated power, true airspeed, fuel flow, range, endurance, etc.) for standard temperature and convenient variations on either side, say, plus and minus 20 degrees. Others specify a manifold-pressure adjustment which, when applied, will produce the stated percentage of power at the specified conditions of altitude and temperature. Every day and every set of flight conditions will be a little bit (sometimes, a *lot*) different; safe, efficient, predictable engine operation requires more attention to power-management technique. Get familiar with the power limitations of the engine, and apply corrections and adjustments where they are required. Longer engine life and lower maintenance bills are bound to result.

LET'S HEAD FOR THE BARN

Cold air aloft, as mentioned earlier, doesn't present much of a problem for the piston-engine/propeller combination (unless it's *really* cold air, in which case you may have trouble keeping the engine warm enough to run smoothly and efficiently, especially a normally aspirated powerplant), but when the time comes to begin the descent, the pilot who retards the throttle rapidly and heads for terra firma is subjecting his engine to some thermal shock on each such occasion. After the engine has gotten accustomed to the diet of cold air, and all the parts have settled into their operating-temperature routines, a sudden reduction in throttle setting takes away a great deal of the heat that was being produced. It's bad enough to handle the throttle roughly at any time, but particularly when incoming air is very cold, the heat shock is likely to be significant; just like overboosting, the problems may not show up until some future time; a repeated series of thermal shocks takes a little bit out of the engine each time it happens. There's a better way.

Unless the air is more turbulent than you can tolerate at a higher airspeed, one of the most efficient types of descents results from leaving the power settings at the cruise numbers, and trading altitude for airspeed. Power management during such a descent takes several forms, depending on the type of engine installation in your airplane, and the altitude at which you're flying. A fixed-pitch prop will require frequent throttle adjustments to prevent its going past the RPM redline or a selected maximum RPM, whichever comes first. Above 6000 or 7000 feet MSL, you'll have "run out of throttle" with nonturbo powerplants, and the manifold pressure that was lost on the way up will gradually be regained on the way down; so you must include the manifold-pressure gauge in your panel check. As the pressure starts to increase, make small, frequent throttle adjustments so that manifold-pressure/RPM limits are not exceeded. You will also need to make small adjustments to maintain the fuel-air mixture at the proper strength. (Since the nonturbocharged machines will not likely be flying at very high altitudes, the power adjustments to accommodate the changes in the descent are not large ones; nevertheless, it's wise to know what the limiting manifold pressure is for the RPM you carry throughout the letdown, and the approximate fuel flow or EGT readings that go along with that power setting. It's not good practice to automatically set the mixture at RICH when beginning a descent; that's a shameful waste of fuel, and the sudden change in mixture strength also introduces some thermal shock.)

The same problem of increasing manifold pressure with decreasing altitude is present with some of the older turbos and the smaller engines. And the potential for a damaging increase in pressure because of the turbo means that the throttle setting must be given even closer attention during a descent. But the larger engines will have automatic pressure controllers, so that manifold pressure stays put almost no matter what you do with the airplane; mixture strength requires occasional adjustment on the way down to compensate for increasing air temperature.

When the air is rough and you don't care to subject yourself, your passengers, or your airplane to the lumps associated with a high-speed descent (or when you've gotten too close to destination to effect a long, low-rate letdown), a power reduction should be accomplished slowly and smoothly to minimize thermal shock to the engine. And since you have decided to descend at reduced power, why not make the change to a lower RPM? It's a lot quieter, and unless the cruise manifold pressure was right up against the limit, each 100-RPM reduction will account for approximately five percent of the power; check the book to see what the numbers are for your airplane. Your ears and your passengers will be better off for this procedure.

POWER MANAGEMENT IN THE PATTERN

The same slow, smooth, throttle adjustments that worked so well at altitude will be just as beneficial when you're lining up for landing; and the approach during which you make only very small reductions in power all the way down final will mark you as a pilot who exercises good judgment and manages speed, altitude, and power like a pro. Those sudden bursts of throttle, the last-minute addition of full power to salvage a bad approach, are valid only when you're learning—to say nothing of the unhappiness that kind of flying generates among the airport neighbors.

Once again, the fixed-pitch-propeller crowd has little to do in this regard; a properly planned traffic pattern will result in a near-noiseless glide over the heads of the folks who live next to the airport. But on the before-landing checklist of every constant-speed-prop installation, you'll find PROPELLER—HIGH RPM, or PROP CONTROL—FULL FORWARD, or words to that effect. There may also be an expanded checklist section in the handbook, which explains that this change in RPM setting is necessary to guarantee full power (and prevent overboosting) in the event of a go-around. That's good, but it doesn't say that the prop control has to be set at high RPM on *downwind!*

There are two problems associated with such a procedure: Unnecessary noise in the cockpit and on the ground, and engine abuse. Because of the pattern airspeed and the relatively low manifold pressure in use at the time, moving the prop control to its full-forward position will surely mean that the prop blades will twist to the "flat pitch" position— right up against the stops—and you are now, in effect, operating a fixed-pitch propeller. When you move the lever, RPM will increase noticeably and from then on, every change in airspeed or throttle setting will probably result in a change in RPM, and there you go, snarling your way through the rest of the pattern and down final, much to the consternation of the folks on the ground. Perhaps even more annoying to the ground-grippers (landlocked folk) is the situation in which a pilot comes whistling down final approach with a bundle of airspeed, and shifts to high RPM a couple of hundred of feet above the ground. There's no doubt what the propeller will do, and the sudden and significant roar "out of nowhere" will bring the neighbors right up out of their seats, wake babies, start dogs barking, and, in general, do a very negative job of general-aviation public relations.

So how about engine abuse? There are three conditions of flight which come into play here, and the airspeed/power combination is the key: First, when the engine is "driving" the airplane (e.g., whenever positive thrust is needed to accomplish the task at hand—climbing, normal cruise, slow flight); second, a "zero-thrust" situation (essentially, no load on the propulsion system, as in partial-power glide); third, when the airplane is driving the engine, or a "negative-thrust" condition, achieved when airspeed is relatively high and power setting is very low. The prop control does a pretty good job of keeping engine RPM where it belongs in the first and second situations, but when you ask for full high RPM at a "high" airspeed (perhaps as little as 100 knots in some airplanes), the governor has no choice but to set the blades at "flat pitch," and RPM goes to the limit. At the very least, there's a noticeable increase in engine speed. It's very much the same as downshifting your five-speed sports car to second or third gear at 50 mph and then letting out the clutch. Lots of wear and tear on bearings, unbalanced centrifugal loads, and, in general, such a procedure turns your engine from a powerplant into an air compressor . . . a *very noisy* air compressor.

The solution requires some conscious effort on your part, and consists of holding off on the prop control until short final, when airspeed and power setting are low enough to accommodate the change without driving the engine (you'll need to experiment to find the airspeed/power setting for your airplane). It means getting away from the thoughtless, automatonish procedure of shoving the control forward on downwind just so you won't forget it on final. Since go-arounds are so very few and far between, an acceptable procedure is to include the prop control in your final re-check of landing-gear position just prior to touchdown—GEAR DOWN, PROP FORWARD, READY TO LAND. And of course if a go-around does become necessary, you must remind yourself to advance the propeller control before opening the throttle. Train yourself to think ahead *whenever* you make a power change.

Self-administered Proficiency Checks

The biennial flight review is going to be a way of life for general-aviation pilots from now on, and it's about time. No matter how strongly you feel about laying your certificate on the line every once in a while, you've got to admit that there's some good in getting an expert opinion of your proficiency. If you practice your mistakes every time you fly, you'll get very good at doing some things very badly—and that's hardly what you'd call progress.

It's unlikely that the regulations will ever require a flight review for GA pilots more frequently than every other year—remember that it's taken more than seventy years to legislate even a biennial checkup—but the objective won't be attained if pilots go through a quick brushup session for the BFR, sneak by and continue with the same mistakes they've been making all along. A serious pilot will make every flight a proficiency check by never being satisfied with anything but better-than-the-last-time.

There are countless opportunities to improve. In addition to smoothing out the everyday flying tasks, you can on occasion see how much you can shorten a takeoff roll; or touch down right on the numbers and turn off on the first taxiway; or really make the airplane work in a maximum-effort climb for a couple of hundred feet at its best angle-of-climb speed. If you're not good at crosswind takeoffs and landings, pick a day when there's a slight breeze across the strip, get a good instructor to show you the right way and from then on work at it every chance you get. Ask for the crosswind runway every now and then to stay sharp.

Your most recent forced landing was hopefully the *last* one, but you might ask yourself when will the *next* one happen? When it does, will you fly into a panic, or will you merely go through a well-practiced procedure, confident that you *know* what to do? No emergency need be anything but the opening-night performance of a thoroughly dress-rehearsed procedure. Someday when you're just boring holes in the sky, simulate an engine failure over an airport with an empty pattern, and carry the "forced" landing all the way through to touchdown. Prove to yourself that you can do it, then be super-critical—"How could I have done that *better?*"

Although the very fact that you're going to do it to yourself undoes some of the "emergency," pull an engine on takeoff once in a while so you'll know what it's like to abort a departure. Having been there before is a big help when you suddenly find yourself in unfamiliar surroundings, such as a complete power loss just after you break ground. The same is true of a missed approach, when maximum performance of both pilot and airplane is often required—there are few go-around situations that aren't generated by a need to move out in a hurry.

Even if you don't believe in power-off approaches, use them to sharpen your proficiency—after all, the completely throttled 180-degree landing is really another emergency procedure, so you can justify your practice on that basis. You'll find that the power-off techniques will make you a better lander no matter how you choose to approach the runway. And if the flight reviewer elects to have you show him you can do it, you can.

Pilot proficiency extends into the world of weather too. Whenever you're flying, notice changes in the weather and what they tend to presage in your area. When the meteorologists predict significant worsening conditions, keep your eye on things so you'll know what to look for next time. A pilot who knows how and when and why weather happens where he flies is the pilot who will probably never be "caught" by conditions beyond his capability.

By striving to get a little bit better on every flight, you will accomplish two major objectives: first, you'll get more out of your airplane and the dollars you spend for flying; second, you will have built up confidence in your own abilities, a proficiency bank from which you can borrow when the need arises. No pilot can look himself in the eye and say, "I'm as good as I can be," unless he is constantly pushing himself to get better. When that once-in-an-aeronautical-lifetime situation comes around, when you're painted into a corner of the sky and it's going to take all the smarts you can muster to fly out, the proficiency and confidence that comes from making every flight a self-administered check ride will come booming through.

20

Glide Path Control . . . Using the Bugs on Your Windshield

Just about every military flying unit has had a C-45 (that's a Twin Beech in uniform) dripping oil on its hangar floors at one time or another. When it was a "modern" machine it was the latest word in administrative transportation; but in the waning years of its military life, the "Expediter" lost out to bigger, faster and more comfortable airplanes. Especially in the single-engine-jet set, the Twin Beech was denied as an airplane, but grudgingly accepted as a way to move more people and baggage than could be stuffed into a fighter. Noisy, hot and/or cold (depended on where you were sitting), the "twin T-6" stooged around the insect-infested lower levels, and ere long some clever military nicknamer was inspired by the flattened flies and wiped-out wasps which often covered a C-45 windshield—the "Bug Smasher" was born.

If your sympathies lie with the bugs, if you really feel badly when a butterfly buys the farm on the glass in front of your face, take heart—that creature need not have died in vain, because you can use what's left as a target to improve the quality, consistency and safety of your approaches to any runway. Even if you fly in a bug-free atmosphere, there's bound to be a spot of some kind that can be used to put the airplane on the glide path, and keep it there.

The objective of the spot-on-the-windshield technique is to provide a constant-angle glide from some point on final approach right down to the roundout; it will do the same thing for you that the glide-slope needle of an ILS or the lights of a VASI installation do, but a lot less expensively. With the runway in sight and a spot on the windshield, you've got a visual approach system that you can use anywhere, anytime.

Successful employment of the spot technique requires that you subscribe to a pair of propositions: first, that there is something worthwhile about a constant-angle glide path; second, that precise airspeed control will do wonders for consistency and safety as you proceed down final approach. The constant angle means that every approach will look the same to you, there will be no more guesswork concerning where you're going to touch down and you'll undoubtedly find your landings improving in the bargain. By maintaining the same airspeed for all normal approaches, the margin above stall is automatically built in, the corrections for a headwind, no wind or a tailwind will be made with power, as they should be. If you're not a believer in elevators-control-airspeed and throttle-controls-altitude, you might as well go on to another chapter; the spots on your windshield are only spots on the windshield.

IN THE BEGINNING . . .

First thing to do is determine what airspeed works best for you and your airplane; a good-enough number is power-off stall speed (full flaps, of course) times 1.3, or, if it makes more sense to you, 130 percent of that stall speed. It's a pleasant compromise between a comfortable attitude on final approach (over-the-nose visibility is a key item here) and a reasonable roundout when you reach the runway. Any faster than that and you'll float too long, any slower and the airplane may quit flying much sooner than you'd like. A too slow final approach also gets you closer to that unhappy area known as the back side of the power curve. Experiment, and find an airspeed that looks and feels good for you.

By lining up a spot on the runway with a spot on the windshield, you will be effectively aiming the whole airplane toward that point. The ultimate result of continuing the line of flight along this line of sight would be impact with the runway—hopefully softened with a roundout at the appropriate time, but nonetheless at a predetermined location. The beauty of this procedure is that you have decided where you will land, and have controlled the flight of the airplane to make it happen.

FIRST, YOU'VE GOT TO FIND THE SPOT

A normal rectangular traffic pattern won't give you enough time on final approach to really figure out what this bug business is all about, so your experiments should start at a thousand feet or so above the runway and a couple of miles out on final. Set up the airplane in its landing configuration; gear down, full flaps, and airspeed at 1.3 V_{so}. You'll probably wind up with a nose-down attitude and will need some power to maintain altitude. Continue flying level until the numbers of the landing runway appear through the windshield as you look straight ahead; imagine looking through a gunsight lined up with the longitudinal axis of the airplane. This is the key point of the experiment—as soon as the numbers appear in the gunsight, find the spot on the windshield that is directly in your line of sight to the runway. As long as you can hold the spot on the numbers and keep the airspeed precisely under control, that's where you're gonna land!

Since airspeed is determined by pitch attitude, and rate of descent is controlled with throttle, the only way you can stay on that glide path is to ease back on the power. (Oh, you *must* believe that elevators are speed controls and throttles are altitude levers—it's the only way, and if this doesn't prove it, nothing will.) When the numbers come into view through the spot, reduce power and start down. How much? —there's no fixed value, because wind and weight and den-

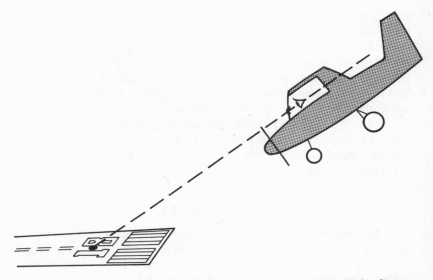

Figure 20-1. Finding the proper spot on the windshield by lining up eyeballs, bug, and runway numbers.

sity altitude will almost never be the same on two consecutive approaches today, let alone tomorrow.

To experience the extremes, reduce power all the way as soon as the spot crosses the numbers, and more than likely the power-off approach path will fall convincingly short of the runway. You'll see it as a definite movement of the spot from the numbers back across the threshold, out onto the grass short of the runway, and if you don't do something, it will continue to move backward until it comes to rest at some point far short of the airport. There is an equally undesirable situation which results from carrying too much power after the spot hits the numbers, and in this case your bug will move down the runway until it stops at the first intersection, or perhaps moves off the runway at the opposite end—*that* would be an interesting landing!

Somewhere in between is the glide path (controlled by power) that you're after—it's the one that keeps the spot on the numbers. Up until now, you've had to guess whether your approach path would lead to the desired touchdown point, but with the spot on the windshield, you've developed a very precise method of nailing it down. Airspeed control is all-important, since the only way it can be changed is to change the pitch attitude, which means the spot on the windshield will also move, and there goes the whole procedure down the drain.

From your experimental vantage point of a thousand feet or so, there will be plenty of time to observe movement of the spot. Fly the practice approach all the way down, and notice carefully the attitude required to maintain the airspeed you've chosen. From now on, if you'll set up all final approaches with this picture (attitude) in the windshield, you can look for the bug and make it do its thing. If the spot appears to move backward, away from the numbers, it means that the airplane is progressing down a glide path that will land you short of where you want to be; stated another way, the rate of descent is too great for existing conditions. This could be the result of a headwind, or your

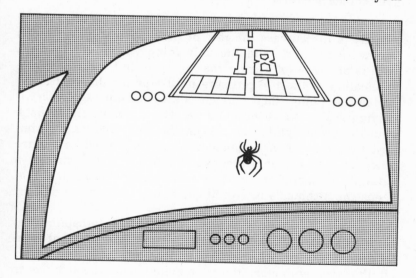

Figure 20–2. This bug indicates a glide path aimed short of the runway threshold.

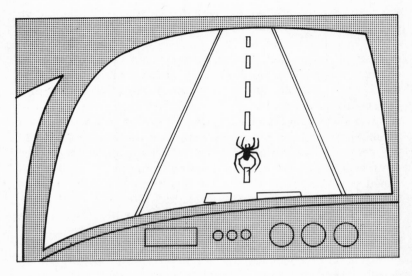

Figure 20–3. This airplane will land long—the bug has already overshot the numbers.

starting downhill too soon, or a combination of these. The remedy is to decrease the rate of descent to stop the spot's backward progress, and the only thing you've got to work with is *power*—not a great roaring blast, but a small, gentle application of throttle pressure until you see the spot slowing and stopping, then enough additional power to start it moving back toward the numbers. When you've flown back onto the proper glide path again, the spot will be superimposed on the runway numbers, and you'll need to reduce power a bit to keep from overshooting. This is strictly a cut-and-try operation until you find a power setting that keeps the airplane's line of flight right down the middle of your line of sight.

Suppose you don't notice the glide-path interception until the spot is well past the intended touchdown point—unless the misjudgment has been a gross one, reducing power all the way will start things moving back toward where they belong. When the spot covers up the numbers, press the throttle forward until the spot stops, and play the minor-adjustment game to keep it there.

MAKE THE BUGS WORK FOR YOU EVERY DAY

Now that you know what to look for, ask for closed traffic the next time around and watch for the bug when you roll out on the final approach leg of the pattern. Depending on how wide you placed your base leg and the amount of altitude lost before turning final, you've got to be in one of three positions; on glide path, above it or below it. By using the bug, you can tell at a glance and can use whatever power you need to maintain or remedy the situation.

Most landings will follow a normal rectangular pattern, so continue your fact finding until you discover a standard place to reduce power on downwind (why not directly opposite the numbers?—every runway has them, or at least some kind of marking to aim at), an airspeed and power setting and flap setting for the base leg and, most important, the airspeed and attitude you intend to maintain on the final approach. Just like the footer for a brick wall, there's got to be something solid on which to build, so be sure you begin every approach from the same altitude and airspeed up there on the downwind leg. If your airplane slips through the air a bit faster than some, you'll want to fly a little farther after the initial power reduction before turning base. But sooner or later a comfortable, efficient pattern procedure will emerge from your experimentation. Now you've something to work with.

Having noticed the altitude above the ground when you turn from base to final, it's a simple matter to remember that number for use when approaching *any* airport; all you've got to do is plan your approach so that you will reach that point at that altitude, and follow the bug to a perfect landing. Normal rectangular patterns are just great, and really the only way to handle a bunch of airplanes making touch-and-go landings, but if you fly to other airports, you'll find that transient traffic is frequently asked to enter on base

leg, or as often as not cleared straight in to the landing runway. With the bug to back you up, a base-leg entry is a
matter of arriving at the glide-path-intercept altitude just
before it's time to turn final; from there on it's a normal approach. Cleared straight in?—just set up your airplane at
pattern altitude the same you you did when experimenting,
and when the line of sight matches the line of flight, start
down.

VARIATIONS ON A THEME

At this point, you've just about worn the numbers off the
runway (bet you never thought you could be so consistently
accurate!), so give them a rest while you explore some other
dirty-windshield tricks.

Suppose you are cleared to land, but with "caution for
wake turbulence from the 747 that just landed." The captain
of that Boeing behemoth has been flying a bug too; it's on
his airspeed indicator, has been painstakingly precomputed
and is designed to plant the main wheels on a spot one
thousand feet from the threshold of the runway; big-airplane
pilots being the "numbers" people they are, he won't miss
it by much. Knowing what you do about wake turbulence
and wingtip vortices, you want to stay well clear of the
airspace below where that monster has just been, and that
means planning an approach path that will keep you above
the 747's. Voila!—bugs to the rescue! If the runway is long
enough to handle the deceleration of a 747, it's got to be long
enough to handle a long landing in your smaller airplane, so
pick a target well down the runway and bug your way to
it, knowing and not guessing that you're safely above the
danger area.

Conversely, there will be times when you'll want to use
every foot of the runway (or the "landing area" at some
boondocky strip next to a trout stream in the mountains)—
a for-real short-field landing. Play with the numbers a bit
on a normal-length runway before you head for the hills,
find a speed which is as slow as possible, yet safe and com-

fortable. Maybe slow down to 1.2 V_{so}, or even 1.1 V_{so} if you really need the performance—the slower you are moving at touchdown, the fewer feet will be required to come to a stop.

When you discover a final-approach airspeed that's as low as you care to go, find the corresponding bug on the windshield and fly some maximum-performance approaches. You may well be amazed what the airplane will do when it's flown by the numbers with the help of the bugs. In addition to slowing your final-approach airspeed, try aiming at a point slightly short of the threshold, remembering that some floating will occur during the flare, no matter how brief a period of time that may be. *Caution!*—sneak up on this ultimately-low-final-airspeed technique a few knots at a time—when you get down to the nitty-gritty airspeed, you'll need quite a bit of power to stay on the bugged glide path. In this configuration, power is most of what's holding you up, and when you reduce the throttle even a little, things will happen right now. If carried to extreme, the *maximum* maximum-performance landing would find the airplane just a few feet above the ground at 1.0 V_{so} with no visible means of support except power—literally hanging on the prop at stall speed, and when power is removed . . . well, you'd better be directly over a suitable landing spot. You can flatten the glide path to further reduce the flare-float problem, but only if the approaches are clear; and remember you're depending on power, so calculate the risk carefully before undertaking such a maneuver. You may also have to select a new bug, because pitch attitude will change for high-power–low-airspeed configurations.

MOUNTAIN AND VALLEY AIRSTRIPS
CAN BE BUGGED TOO

Your average airport is where it is because someone had the foresight to save a bit of land on level ground, and either planned or excavated so that the approaches are over relatively flat terrain. Dyed-in-the-wool flat-landers are now excused, but if you ever intend to operate your airplane into an airstrip which is the carved-off top of a mountain or the only level piece of ground in a canyon, there might be something here for you.

"A funny thing happened to me on the way to the runway"—it sure did, because your eyes are accustomed to a final approach over a broad, flat area; when you turn final to an airport that sits on top of a hill, the old eyeballs can't always adjust to the marked change in perspective. There you are on final at a reasonable altitude, but because of the terrain that slopes up sharply to the runway, there's a lot more air between you and the ground than usual. The conditioned response is to descend to make things look right again, and unless the climb capability of your machine can match the rise of the land, you're in trouble. Keep from landing short (especially if "short" is the vertical face of the mountain) by going back to the bugs—line up the spots and use your eyes to stay on what you *know* is a safe glide path.

Approaching for a landing over terrain that slopes *downward* to the runway can be just as optically confusing, but fortunately the result of not compensating is less disastrous— it usually winds up with a go-around, because you'll probably fly too high on final. There's a built-in human reaction to the realization that you're closer to the ground than you think you ought to be, and that reaction is a strong urge to climb when, in fact, you should be descending to match the slope of the ground. However, the pilot using his bugs can turn final at what he *knows* to be the proper height, line up the spots, and land . . . the first time.

THERE'S ONE MORE SURPRISE
IN THE OPTICAL BAG OF TRICKS

If you elect to approach at some higher airspeed, or don't use full flaps (wow—does *that* cost money in tires and brakes!), the glide path will be considerably flatter than the 1.3 V_{so} situation. However, you can still use the spot on the windshield, recognizing that the spot will be somewhat lower on the glass. But for the 1.3ers, the picture that you see through the windshield will contain more ground than in level flight, and probably more of Mother Earth than you're used to seeing on final approach.

An interesting optical phenomenon occurs, and it's the same thing that happens when you're approaching another airplane in the air—while it's at quite a distance, the rate of closure is barely noticeable; but at some point you seem to be rushing toward the other guy at an alarming velocity. It's got something to do with your visual field being filled rapidly with target, and again an instinctive reaction takes over. If the target happens to be the runway, you'll be tempted to haul back on the wheel to fend off the impending collision; that will kill your airspeed and the lift that goes with it, and unless you can somehow manage to elevate the runway a hundred feet or so, you've got problems.

Expect this to happen at about a hundred feet, maybe less, and concentrate on airspeed control—if you keep the speed needle where it belongs, pitch attitude won't change, and everything will work out just right. (It's assumed that your aeronautical senses are developed to the point where you can determine where to start rounding out; if you maintain the bug airspeed all the way to touchdown, better have the FBO lay in a good supply of nose wheels.)

AIRSPEED IS THE KEY

If it hasn't come booming through yet, let's hit it one more time—without strict airspeed control, the spot-on-the-windshield technique won't work. Once you realize that pitch attitude makes all the difference, you should pay more attention to the picture in the windshield (attitude) and less to the airspeed indicator itself. Burn into your mind's eye the amount of ground between the top of the instrument panel and the horizon when you've established the glide-path configuration—as long as you keep that picture in front of you, the airspeed will take care of itself. When you make gliding turns, be careful not to lower the nose and dive through the turn (elevator trim is a wonderful friend here); maintain the glide-speed picture in the windshield while you roll into the turn, and make sure the top of the panel or whatever you're using for a reference slides straight across the horizon. When you roll out, there's your spot—hopefully on the numbers, but if it's not, a small power correction should put it where it belongs.

You're a long way down the proficiency road when you decide to use bugs to improve your approaches, but don't stop there—keep on cutting and trying; experiment with different approach angles to find the one that suits you best. Which bug seems to fall in the middle of all those experimental attitudes? That's the one that represents the best compromise, and there's nothing that says you can't make a mark on the inside of the windshield so you'll never forget it. Just a dot of some kind for a reminder—an ordinary grease pencil will do. After a short while of consistent use, you'll be lining things up without consciously looking at the spot; when you use a constant stream of visual inputs to detect changes and make the necessary corrections, you've arrived. No more wild blasts of power to keep from landing in the pasture, no more go-arounds because you're too high and no more low and slow, high-powered, window-rattling finals.

Go out and smash a few bugs; you'll be a better pilot for it.

21

Sell Aviation on Every Trip

Just about as frequently as the moon comes up blue, you run across an aviator who flies because he has to; for him, an airplane is simply a faster way to get where he's going, or there's no other way to get from here to there, or it's more favorable economically, or some equally unaesthetic motivation. The overwhelming majority of pilots find flying one of their most satisfying experiences (you may want to qualify that somewhat depending on your life style), and assume that everyone in the airplane with them feels the same way.

Unfortunately, this is far from the way things really are, because a lot of people are still convinced that we would have wings had we been intended to fly. You might be surprised to find out how many of your passengers were not really sure they wanted to go in the first place, and weren't thoroughly convinced afterwards that they should ever do it again. It's easy to let passenger apprehensions languish in the deep shadow of your pleasure and familiarity with the world of flight. Aviation has become so much an everyday thing in our society (hooray!) that the occasional guy who is scared stiff finds himself in a most unenviable position; certain that his life is about to come to a horrible smashing climax, he is forced aboard by social pressure—he'll get about as much enjoyment out of this trip as you would from riding on the shoulders of a tightrope walker a hundred feet above the sawdust with no net.

Some folks' fear of flying is apparently genetic—they're the ones who get acrophobia on a stepladder—and there are passengers who like to fly, until they meet up with a pilot who is careless and insensitive. It's a happy circumstance that both situations can be neatly handled the same way—by flying carefully, smoothly, and assuming a manner that bespeaks your concern for the well-being and pleasure of everybody who rides with you.

In addition to applying the techniques that have been discussed throughout this book, there are some more suggestions which will help you sell aviation to the nonbelievers. They'll probably make your flying even more pleasant for you—so how can you lose?

When you start the engine(s), do it so that the horses don't come alive all at once; set up a starting procedure that gets things going smoothly and quietly at the same time. Most people have gotten used to the near-silent automobile engine. It's also easier on the powerplant and the people standing behind you.

On your first radio communication, turn the volume down so that Ground Control doesn't shout into the ears of your passengers—many light airplanes have loudspeakers that are really LOUDspeakers for the FIBs (Folks in Back).

Unless it's a frying-eggs-on-the-sidewalk day, close doors and windows as soon as you're all on board. Besides heightening the sense of security for the uneasy souls, it will prevent taking off with a door unlatched, which is just about guaranteed to drive some people back to ground transportation.

The engine runup is an important part of your procedure and shouldn't be compromised for public relations—make it rapid but thorough, and although it's a convenient time to talk to yourself about the condition of that left mag, and maybe I'd better check it again, any hesitation on your part will surely be construed as a bellwether of disaster by certain passengers. If you are confident of the results of the engine check, go—if you have any doubt, don't. When you mutter something like "I'm not sure about the left mag, but we'll take off anyway; it'll probably work itself out in flight," don't count on the FIBs believing anything else you say. A planeful of pilots is one thing when the RPM drop is a bit lower than it should be; *one* unhappy nonpilot is the same as a planeload when he suspects that you're not really sure.

It's good common sense, saves fuel and tires and brakes, and also puts passengers at ease when you taxi slowly and smoothly. Use only enough power to get the airplane rolling, and then only enough to keep it moving. Don't jazz the throttles around corners, don't come to a stop with the nose bobbing up and down. If you hold constant brake pressure until the airplane stops moving, it will do so with a jerk— ease off the pedals just before a complete stop so you don't rock the people forward and then slam them back against the seats—you can practice in your car.

To the uninitiated, there's no gibberish like the gibberish that flows from Air Traffic Control and other airplanes. Be the interpreter for your passengers—let them know what's coming, and within the limits of your ability to fly the airplane and talk to them at the same time, decode some of the jargon. If things are super-busy in the listening department, a boom mike and an earpiece (or phones) are worth their cost many times over, particularly when you've done such a good job of selling that one of your passengers won't shut up. You can hold up a finger, wrinkle your brows and shake your head with concern, indicating that there's something coming over the radio that may mean life or death for all of us. You may really be listening for your alma mater's football score on the ADF receiver, but with the loudspeaker cut out, your voluble passenger will sit there and shut up, and need never know what he's missing.

Fly your people as high as practical; it's almost always smoother and more comfortable up there, and they'll enjoy the view. Don't go past the first hint of engine roughness when leaning the mixture, because that upsets first-timers.

Running a tank dry is a bad deal unless you have experienced passengers—no matter how much you explain and prepare, the non-flyer automatically starts counting his beads —when an airplane engine quits, can a crash be far behind?

Finally, your flying should be its smoothest when you are the guide for someone's first excursion into the air. Limit banks to something less than usual (people aren't used to looking at the ground through a side window; remember how it felt the first time you were rolled into a bank?) and make pitch changes as small and as smooth as you can. When you extend flaps, you know what the airplane reaction will be and that it will react more violently at higher airspeeds; so slow down and ease the flaps into position. A good flap extension is one that the passengers don't realize has happened.

The takeoff and landing deserve special attention, since these times are the scariest for beginners, even if they've been riding the airlines for years. Lift off smoothly and positively (nothing like a couple of touch-and-gos on the takeoff roll to destroy their confidence in you and the airplane— passengers wonder if *you* are able to get this thing off the ground, and if *it's* capable of being gotten off the ground) and climb away as rapidly as you can. Somebody will inevitably say, "Gee, the people look like ants down there," and the sooner somebody says that, the better. Of course, there may come a time when you'll have to reply, "Those *are* ants; we're not off the ground yet."

No matter what you think is the most dangerous regime of flight, everybody else *knows* that landing takes first prize in the hazard contest. With this in mind, make a special effort toward every-one-a-grease-job when first-timers are on board. If you can't do it every time, try—they won't all be squeakers, but they'll be better landings than the controlled crashes that result from just "letting it happen."

Rest assured that the people who ride with you will talk about the flight; and one of the major points with which they'll bend the ears of others will be the level of your proficiency. Oh, that landing may not have been so bad from where you sat, but the guy who has nothing to compare it with may describe it differently. Get good at landings, and work to stay that way—wouldn't you have doubts about a friend's ability with his cabin cruiser if he ran into the dock at the end of a fishing trip?

Glossary of Aviation Jargon and Terminology

Abeam   The position of an object directly off either wingtip of an airplane.

Abort   Discontinue a takeoff or a flight.

Absolute altitude   The actual number of feet between your airplane and the surface over which you're flying.

ADF   Automatic Direction Finder—a low-frequency radio receiver which indicates the relative bearing of an NDB when properly tuned.

ADIZ   Air Defense Identification Zone. Under certain conditions, you'd best let somebody know when you plan to fly through one of these border barriers. See Part 1, *AIM*, for details.

Advisory circulars   Frequent educational bulletins from the FAA. If you're not on their mailing list, send your address to Washington; the ACs are very worthwhile.

Affirmative   Radio talk for "yes."

AGL   Above Ground Level—an altitude term used to indicate height of cloud layers and obstructions.

AIM   Airman's Information Manual—a government publication which contains procedures, airport listings, facilities and everything that isn't published somewhere else.

AIRMET   A weather advisory about conditions which will affect primarily light-plane operations.

Airport Advisory Area   A five-mile circle around an uncontrolled airport where a Flight Service Station is able to let you know what's going on.

Airport Advisory Service   What an on-airport FSS provides (see above). Includes weather, winds and known traffic in the immediate vicinity.

Airport Traffic Area   A cylinder of airspace 5 miles in radius and 3000 feet deep over an airport with an operating control tower. You must be in radio contact, there's a speed limit of 156 knots and you should be there only if you're landing or taking off.

Airspeed   See various types—e.g., indicated, true, etc.

Airspeed indicator   Measures the difference between static and dynamic air pressure; indicates the velocity of the airplane through the air.

Airway   A designated route between radio navigation aids; unless otherwise indicated, the controlled airspace it represents begins 1200 feet AGL.

Airworthiness directive   AD—bulletin from the FAA to indicate something's wrong with a particular type of airplane. Unless ADs are complied with, the affected aircraft are not considered airworthy.

Alert Area   A part of the airspace in which your activities are not officially restricted, but extra vigilance should be maintained because of a high volume of air traffic or some unusual type of flying, or both.

ALS   Approach Lighting Systems—the conglomeration of lights just off the end of an ILS-equipped runway.

Altimeter setting   Information available from all ATC facilities to update your altimeter reading to the current atmospheric pressure. Always given in inches of mercury ("Hg).

Altitude   See specific types—e.g., pressure, indicated, etc.

A&P   Someone certificated by the FAA to perform repairs on Airframes and Powerplants.

Approach Control   The ATC facility charged with IFR traffic separation in a terminal area, normally a 30-mile circle around an airport.

APU   Auxiliary Power Unit—the "battery cart"; what you often need on a cold morning or when you've flooded the engine trying to get it going.

Area Navigation   A nav system based on electronic displacement of VORTACs. Also known as RNAV.

ARTCC   Air Route Traffic Control Center—shortened to "Center" for communications purposes, these facilities are primarily responsible for IFR separation during the enroute phase of a flight. Also available to fair-weather flyers for advisories when they're not too busy.

ASL   Above Sea Level—means the same thing as MSL.

ASR   Airport Surveillance Radar—provides Controllers with a radar picture of terminal-area traffic, and can be used to line you up with the final approach course to a runway.

ATC   Air Traffic Control—the entire system of facilities involved in the movement of airplanes in controlled airspace.

ATIS   Automatic Terminal Information Service—a continuous-loop taped broadcast of weather conditions and arrival-departure procedures in effect at a specific airport. ATIS is expected to be used by *all* pilots, VFR and IFR.

ATPC   Airline Transport Pilot Certificate—incorrectly referred to as "ATR"—not at all a rating, it's the highest civilian pilot qualification. The PhD of aviation.

Attitude indicator   A gyroscopic device which provides an artificial horizon to enable flight without outside references. The king of the instruments.

Azimuth   A position measured in angular degrees. Used in aviation to specify relation of an aircraft to a radio station or a radar site.

Balanced field length   As generally used, a situation in which the takeoff distance is exactly the same as the number of feet required to accelerate an airplane to a go/no-go speed, decide to abort the takeoff and come to a complete stop. Important only to multi-engine pilots.

Bearing   Position of an object or radio station stated in terms of azimuth. Can be either to or from the object or the aircraft.

BFR   Biennial Flight Review—the every-other-year visit to the FAA or your own CFI to make sure you're not practicing your mistakes. You may not act as pilot-in-command unless you have a documented, satisfactory BFR within the previous two years.

Binders   Aviation jargon for aircraft brakes.

Blip   A return, or spot of light, on a radar screen that indicates a target (aircraft).

Calibrated airspeed   CAS—indicated airspeed corrected for installation and position errors. All performance and limiting airspeeds are quoted in terms of CAS.

CAT   See Clear Air Turbulence.

CAVU   Ceiling And Visibility Unlimited.

CDI   Course Deviation Indicator—the left-right needle of the VOR display.

Ceiling   The lowest cloud layer that covers enough of the sky to be classified broken or overcast. If the observer calls either of these layers "thin," it's not a ceiling.

Cell   The core of a thunderstorm; a single unit of cumulo-nimbus activity. Radar observers will usually call out observed precipitation in terms of cells and their relation to your position.

Celsius   An expression of temperature in degrees; replaces Centigrade.

Center   See ARTCC.

CFI   Certificated Flight Instructor.

CG   Center of Gravity—the apparent balance point of an airplane. Manufacturers specify an allowable range through which the CG may move; it's up to you to be sure the bird is properly balanced.

Clear Air Turbulence   CAT—bumpy flight conditions not associated with cloud formations. Usually in conjunction with a jet stream, but can also occur in the vicinity of large cumulus clouds, and where a strong wind shear exists.

Clearance   Authorization from any ATC facility to proceed through or within or out of the airspace over which control is exercised.

Compass locator   A low-frequency radio station (NDB) placed in conjunction with an outer marker, so that you can *locate* it with a radio *compass*.

Continental Control Area   All the airspace above 14,500 feet MSL over the continental United States. No VFR flight allowed when conditions are less than basic visual minimums.

Control Area   For practical purposes, all federal airways are Control Areas. Don't fly there when the weather won't permit VFR operations.

Controlled Airspace   A catch-all to specify any airspace over which ATC has responsibility for traffic separation when the weather drops below VFR conditions. You may not then be in Controlled Airspace unless you have been issued a clearance.

Control Zone   Shown on the charts by a dashed circle, this is sacred territory when the airport is reporting IFR conditions. When the weather is less than 1000 and 3, you have no business being in a Control Zone without a clearance—besides, it's against the law.

Course   Same as "track," or the imaginary line across the surface that describes the actual path made good by your airplane.

Cruising altitude   The height at which you are flying or intend to fly on a particular trip or segment thereof. Of interest to radar controllers who have offered to provide advisory service. They'll ask for your "cruising altitude," and would appreciate being advised of any changes you make.

Density altitude   Pressure altitude corrected for non-standard temperature.

Departure Control   The ATC facility responsible for separation of IFR traffic leaving a terminal area.

DF   Direction Finder—the means by which an appropriately equipped ATC facility can determine where you are solely on the basis of your radio transmissions. If all else fails, you can be given vectors to an airport based on the DF information.

Directional gyro (DG)   Presents heading information in a much more stable form than the magnetic compass. Senses nothing; must be set initially and periodically corrected to the reading on the magnetic compass.

Displaced threshold   The lines across a runway which reduce the amount of pavement you may use for landing. The threshold will be marked with green lights at night.

DME   Distance-Measuring Equipment—a small computer installed in an airplane which measures the time it takes a radio signal to go from airplane to VORTAC and back, and converts that time into nautical miles. For a few more bucks, it will also figure the rate of change of the time-distance relationship and display an accurate groundspeed in knots. For a few more bucks, it will calculate time-to-station for you.

DVFR   Defense Visual Flight Rules—a non-IFR pilot can use this option when he must operate into or through an ADIZ. Know how and when to use a DVFR flight plan, and prevent a confrontation with the Air Defense Command.

EGT   Exhaust Gas Temperature—when indicated on a panel instrument, EGT is the most accurate means of adjusting the fuel-air ratio. The leaner the mixture, the hotter the flame . . . until it gets so lean the fire starts to go out. This point is referred to as the "peak" EGT.

ELT   Emergency Locator Transmitter—a separately powered radio which is activated in the event of a crash and provides a rescue signal for search aircraft.

ETA   Estimated Time of Arrival—the numbers on the clock that indicate the time you figure you'll be someplace.

ETD   Estimated Time of Departure—same as above, but refers to the time you intend to take off.

ETE   Estimated Time Enroute—not a clock time, but the hours and minutes you expect to be on the way from takeoff to landing. Should include any stops you intend to make, because the government will start looking for you when an officially filed ETE + 30 minutes has elapsed.

FAA   You surely know what this is.

FAR   Federal Aviation Regulations.

FBO   Fixed-Base Operator—the guy who sells gasoline, airplanes and flight services, and who occasionally gives away coffee and green stamps.

Feather   Cause a propeller blade to streamline itself with the airflow and reduce drag when an engine quits.

Field elevation   The height of an airport expressed in feet above mean sea level (MSL). Use this number to calibrate your altimeter—it should read close to the published field elevation when you insert the current altimeter setting.

Final approach   That portion of a landing pattern which is lined up with the runway, and hopefully terminates at touchdown. Also the last segment of an instrument approach procedure, and a good place to stay away from at busy airports.

Fix   The intersection of any two or more lines of position (could be visual, electronic, or celestial lines) that enable you to say, "I am here."

Flight Level   FL—at 18,000 feet and above, all *flight* is conducted at assigned pressure *levels*, hence Flight Level. The last two zeros are always omitted, so 23,000 feet becomes FL230. All altimeters up there are set to 29.92″ Hg.

Flight Service Station   FSS—an ATC facility whose primary job is to provide preflight and inflight weather briefings, transmit flight-plan requests to Center, and whatever else pilots need. Don't ask them to call a cab—that's pushing it a bit.

Flight Watch   Designed to provide us with the civilian version of the Air Force's pilot-to-forecaster service. If you are within radio range of a Flight Watch station (certain well-staffed FSSs), you can get a complete weather briefing from a qualified person. Not to be used for preflight briefings. Available on the standard Flight Watch frequency, 122.0 MHz.

GADO   General Aviation District Office—the FAA's general-aviation branch. The GADO is your contact with the government, so if you've never been there, stop in someday and get acquainted—they work for you; might as well find out what they do.

Glide slope   The vertical path of an airplane as it descends toward a runway. Whether vertical guidance to the landing surface is provided visually, electronically or with bugs, it's what you try to stay on.

GMT   Greenwich Mean (or Meridian) Time—standard time reference used throughout the world for ATC and weather-reporting and forecasting purposes. Someplace had to be picked as the standard, and the Royal Observatory at Greenwich, England, won.

Gremlins   The little people conceived by military pilots during the second period of worldwide unpleasantness, when they needed someone to blame for otherwise unexplainable malfunctions in airplanes. The gremlins are still around.

Ground Control   The ATC facility responsible for traffic movement on the airport. Since the Ground Controller may know of taxiing airplanes you can't see, check with him before you move off the ramp.

Heading   The direction an airplane is pointed; expressed in angular degrees measured from magnetic north. Same as "course" or "track" when there is no wind correction.

Heavy   A call-sign suffix ("United 746 Heavy," for example) for aircraft weighing 300,000 pounds or more. A warning to all other aircraft (particularly light airplanes) of the strong wingtip vortices that such a machine produces.

Hertz   Hz—replaces "cycles" in radio-frequency parlance: kilohertz, megahertz, etc.

HF   High Frequency—a radio-frequency spectrum used for long-distance aerial communication. HF also describes the radio equipment used for this purpose.

Hyperventilation   Literally, "too much air"—physiological condition caused by rapid, deep breathing, particularly during periods of mental stress. You'll get dizzy and lightheaded, and if breathing is not consciously slowed and shallowed, unconsciousness will set in.

Hypoxia   A condition in which the brain receives too little oxygen to function normally. Symptoms are very much like hyperventilation; if you pass out, you can't tell the difference.

Ident   That function of a radar transponder which causes a blip to "bloom," providing positive identification. When you're asked to "squawk ident," don't say a word, just do it.

IFR   Instrument Flight Rules—the regulations covering operations under less-than-visual weather conditions; also a general term applied to all instrument operations.

ILS   Instrument Landing System—a three-dimensional radio landing aid which uses cockpit displays to guide an airplane to the runway.

Indicated airspeed   The number of knots (or mph) at the end of the pointer.

Indicated altitude   The number of feet shown by the instrument when the current altimeter setting is inserted.

In radar contact   Phrase used by a Controller to indicate that he has positively identified you as one of the blips on his radar screen.

Jet routes   High-altitude (above 18,000 feet) airways.

Jet stream   Fast-moving rivers of air imbedded in the normal flow of winds at high altitudes. Just like the "snowbirds" of the midwestern states, jet streams move south in the winter.

Kilohertz   KHz—one thousand cycles per second.

Kilometer   A metric measure of distance; one thousand meters. Just about the time you get accustomed to knots and nautical miles, the system will probably convert to kilos.

Knot   One nautical mile per hour. Also what your stomach gets tied up in just before a check ride.

LF   Low Frequency—the radio spectrum in which NDBs are grouped.

Line of position   LOP—a course to or from any radio station or visually located object. Cross two lines of position and you've got a fix.

Localizer   The course-guidance signal of an ILS. Activates the left-right needle on a VOR receiver display.

LOM   Locator (at the) Outer Marker—an NDB put in the same place as an Outer Marker so you can get to that spot using an ADF receiver.

LOP   See "line of position."

Mach number   A convenient way to express the velocity of a high-speed airplane. Named in honor of Ernst Mach, it's the ratio of true airspeed to the speed of sound. Any speed greater than Mach 1 is supersonic.

Magnetic   Refers to headings, courses and such which are measured in angular degrees from the magnetic north pole.

Marker beacon   A highly directional radio signal (transmitted straight up) which provides the distance dimension for an ILS.

Max Gross   An early-day aviator who always took off with his airplane loaded to the gills (Max was known to be loaded also on occasion). In his honor, any departure with the maximum allowable number of pounds on board is known as a Max Gross takeoff.

MEA Minimum Enroute Altitude—guarantees reception of a good VOR signal along a Victor airway. Also provides terrain clearance.

Megahertz MHz—one million cycles per second.

MOA Military Operations Area—special-use airspace marked on all aeronautical charts to indicate the limits (both vertical and lateral) of certain types of military activity. IFR flights will be routed safely through; VFR flights may proceed, but should exercise a *great deal* of caution.

MOCA Minimum Obstruction Clearance Altitude—guarantees you won't hit anything while on an airway, but isn't necessarily high enough to provide a good navigational signal.

MSL Mean Sea Level—the average between high and low tides, and the standard to which most altitudes are referenced.

Nautical mile One minute of latitude. Always measured vertically on a chart. There are sixty nautical miles in every degree of latitude.

NDB Non-Directional Beacon—a low-frequency radio transmitter whose signal is not aimed in a specific direction—you should be able to receive it from any position around the station.

Negative An easily understood "no."

No joy Means "I don't see the other airplane you just called to my attention" when a radar Controller issues an advisory. A real time saver on the air.

NOTAM NOtice to AirMen—a published advisory of situations and conditions that bear on flight operations.

NPRM Notice of Proposed Rule Making—an FAA proclamation of regulatory changes under consideration. Here's another mailing list you should be on, since the democratic process requires that the aviation public be advised and given adequate opportunity to respond.

OAT Outside Air Temperature.

OBS Omni Bearing Selector.

OM Outer Marker—one of the marker beacons associated with an ILS; usually about five miles from the runway.

Omni The nickname for a VOR transmitter.

Over Used at the end of a radio transmission to indicate that you're finished talking. Most of the time it's quite unnecessary.

Over and out   Strictly World War II lingo.

PATWAS   Pilots' Automatic Telephone Weather Answering Service—a recorded weather briefing which saves you the trouble of going to the FSS, and saves them the time required for a bunch of person-to-person briefings.

PCA   Positive Control Airspace—begins at FL180, extends to FL600, covers the entire country, and may not be used without an IFR clearance.

PIREP   PIlot REPort of inflight weather conditions.

Pressure altitude   The number of feet above the standard datum plane, or wherever the atmospheric pressure is 29.92″ Hg. An altimeter always reads pressure altitude when the adjustment scale is set to 29.92″.

Prevailing visibility   The lowest visibility that covers at least half of an observer's horizon.

Prohibited Area   A section of airspace over and around some object or area so sensitive (usually in terms of national security) that *no one* is permitted to fly through it.

Radar   RAdio Detection And Ranging—on a radar screen, a Controller can determine the range and azimuth and in some cases the altitude of an aircraft.

Radar advisory service   Provided to VFR flights only when Controllers can take the time from their primary IFR separation duties; lets you know when there is traffic in your vicinity which might present a conflict.

Radar beacon   Same as "transponder."

Radar service terminated   Controller language which means "You're on your own again—no more advisories, no more vectors."

Radial   A magnetic course away from any navigation aid. *All* VOR course information is in terms of radials.

Radio compass   The ADF receiver. Provides a line of position after proper interpretation.

Range   Your distance to or from something.

RCO   Remote Communications Outlet—extends the communications capability of a FSS by means of an unmanned transceiver in a more advantageous location. Found principally in mountainous areas.

Relative bearing   The *bearing* (azimuth) of an object or navaid *relative* to the nose of the airplane. Read directly from the ADF indicator.

RMI Radio Magnetic Indicator—in simplest terms, an ADF indicator with a rotating card which also acts as a directional gyro. May have a needle which responds to a VOR signal. In either case, the needle indicates course to the station.

RNAV See Area Navigation.

RON Remain Over Night.

RPM Revolutions Per Minute.

RVR Runway Visual Range—electronically measured and computed visibility directly alongside a runway. Quoted in hundreds of feet; the most accurate visibility report, second only to being there in person.

Say again "Please repeat what you just said."

Say again all after . . . "Please repeat everything you just said after [the word or phrase that precedes what was missed]."

Say again slow "C'mon now, take it easy—you can't expect me to get all that when you talk so fast."

SIGMET SIGnificant METeorological advisory. Of interest to *all* aviators, SIGMETs are warnings of impending hazardous weather conditions.

Special VFR A clearance from ATC to operate into, out of or through a Control Zone as long as you can see a mile and remain clear of clouds. An instrument rating is required for this at night.

Squawk Controller's verb for "activate your transponder"; as in "squawk ident," "squawk one two zero zero," "squawk off," etc.

Standard day When the atmospheric pressure at sea level is 29.92″ Hg and the temperature is 15° Celsius.

Stand by "Please wait a minute."

STOL Short Take Off and Landing—an aircraft with the capability of taking off and landing within a very short distance.

Straight-in approach A clearance (or your decision at an uncontrolled airport) to execute the landing by flying directly to the runway with no turns. Eliminates the traffic pattern and saves time.

Supercharger An air pump mounted on a reciprocating engine to boost the air charge into the cylinders. Effectively enables the engine to put out sea-level power at high altitudes. If it is a gear-driven pump, it's a supercharger; when the extra pressure comes from an exhaust-driven turbine, it's called a *turbo*supercharger.

Surveillance radar See ASR.

TACAN TACtical Air Navigation—a military radio aid to navigation which is usually combined with a VOR to make a VORTAC. Now you can get both range and azimuth information from the same station.

Taildragger Sobriquet for what used to be the "conventional" landing-gear arrangement. Plane has a tail wheel or skid instead of a nose wheel. When you *really* want to learn how to fly, go to a taildragger.

Tally ho When ATC calls out traffic for you, let them know you see it with a simple "Tally ho."

TCA Terminal Control Area—the infamous upside-down wedding cakes of positive control sitting atop the country's busiest airports. There are enough restrictions to warrant your checking into the details of each one before you get there.

Track The actual course across the ground made good by an airplane.

Transition Area Controlled airspace above an airport which has a published instrument approach procedure but which doesn't qualify for a Control Zone. A Transition Area usually takes effect 700 feet above the ground. Watch out when flying in the vicinity of such an airport in scratchy VFR conditions—stay away from the instrument approach area.

TRSA Terminal Radar Service Area—airspace of locally determined dimensions in which Approach and Departure Control radar can give you a hand in traffic separation even though you're not on an IFR clearance. It's a voluntary sort of thing, so let them know if you don't want to play their game. ATIS will have all the details.

True Courses, headings and such measured in angular degrees from the true north pole, the one the chart makers use.

True airspeed TAS—calibrated airspeed corrected for altitude and temperature. Generally, there's an increase of about 2 percent per thousand feet—if you're flying at 10,000 feet, for example, your true airspeed should be very close to 120 percent of calibrated airspeed.

Transponder An airborne black box which receives a coded signal from a radar site and sends back another coded signal which displays a positively identifiable blip on the radar screen.

Transponder code The sequence of numbers you set in the transponder to provide the desired radar-screen display. Most radar sets now display your code in digital form—when you're asked to change your code, don't do anything but change your code.

TWEB Transcribed WEather Broadcast—a continuous-loop recording of weather reports for significant locations in the broadcast area. Can be obtained from certain LF beacons and some VORs.

UHF Ultra-High Frequency—a radio spectrum used exclusively by the military.

Uncontrolled airspace That part of the sky for which ATC has no responsibility for traffic separation. Be it VFR or IFR, you're on your own.

V_{mc} Minimum control speed—with the critical engine windmilling and the remaining engine running at full power, this speed is required to maintain directional control. Anything less and the airplane will turn toward the failed engine, even with full control deflection against the turn.

V_{xse} Best angle-of-climb speed, single engine—this speed will produce the greatest altitude gain *per foot across the ground* during an engine-out situation.

V_{yse} Best rate-of-climb speed, single engine—this speed will produce the greatest altitude gain *per unit of time* (i.e., feet per minute) during an engine-out situation.

Variation The angular difference between true north and magnetic north. A true direction corrected for variation becomes a magnetic direction.

VASI Visual Approach Slope Indicator—two or three sets of lights which appear red or white or in combinations thereof as you approach a runway so equipped. Provides vertical guidance down a predetermined glide slope.

Vector A direction to fly based on a radar Controller's observation of your position. Vectors may aim you toward an airport or away from other traffic.

Vertical speed indicator An "altimeter with a leak," which indicates the rate at which you are changing altitude, in feet per minute.

Vertigo Complete incapacitation caused by conflicting visual and inner-ear senses. It will almost surely take over if you fly into a cloud and have no instrument training, or refuse to believe what the gauges are telling you.

VFR Visual Flight Rules—those parts of the regulations covering operation when weather conditions are at or above certain minimums. Also used to describe any type of visual flight operations.

VHF Very High Frequency—the radio spectrum used for most aerial communications and navigation.

Victor Airway   Electronic course defined by VOR stations.

VOR   Very-high-frequency Omnidirectional Radio range—"omni."

VORTAC   Combination of VOR and TACAN.

Vortex   The horizontal tornado that trails behind each wingtip of an airfoil when it's producing lift.

VOT   VOR Test facility—a VOR transmitter to be used only for checking the accuracy of omni receivers. It transmits only a 360° radial, and your receiver must line up within plus or minus 4 degrees to be considered accurate enough for IFR flight.

VTOL   Same as STOL, only more so—this is an aerial machine such as a helicopter which can take off and land vertically; no runway needed, thank you.

Warning Area   Although flight isn't disallowed in one of these, you should be super-cautious because there's something hazardous going on in there. Check NOTAMs before you take off, or call the nearest FSS if you doubt the propriety of charging through.

Waypoint   RNAV language for the location of an electronically displaced VORTAC. Some instrument charts have designated WPs, or you can make up your own.

Weather advisory   Either a SIGMET or an AIRMET.

Wilco   WILL COmply. Leave this one to the World War II film stars.

Zulu   Same as GMT.

Index